I hope you enjoy the story of Schwab. It would not have been possible without your trust in us for which I am grateful.

Charles R Schwab

"Like myself, Chuck is a dyslexic. He learned early on that he had his limits and—unlike most nondyslexics—discovered the power of delegation and that business is all about people who share your vision and values but bring their own passion and strengths to the tasks. He realized early on the world is full of people more capable than himself in 'a thousand different ways.' Most leaders and entrepreneurs never learn that simple lesson. *Invested* is a must-read for anyone interested in working in a business or becoming an entrepreneur. An extraordinary life and book."

—Sir Richard Branson, founder of the Virgin Group

"This is a fascinating story that teaches you about the never-ending evolution of an entrepreneurial company, but even more about personal learning from that experience. So read, learn how to learn from experience, and enjoy."

—George P. Shultz, former secretary of Labor, Treasury, and State

"Charles Schwab is a giant who transformed finance and investing for millions of Americans. His memoir is a textbook case on entrepreneurship and principled leadership."

—Hank Paulson, 74th Secretary of the Treasury

"Through Chuck's unique perspective, *Invested* details Schwab's history persevering through adversity while providing wisdom and encouragement along the way. I have admired and respected Chuck for many years. We share a passion for golf and how its challenges parallel those encountered in business."

—Phil Mickelson

"Chuck tells a story that very few can tell, a story of creativity, passion, and bravery trumping the odds. Chuck not only created the discount brokerage industry but grew a company in the face of a rapidly changing landscape and led the way in democratizing the market for the individual investor. I am proud to have been a partner with Chuck in the early days. I am especially proud to have him as a friend for the past fifty years."

—George R. Roberts, co-chairman and co-CEO of Kohlberg Kravis Roberts

"We learn best from the stories of others, and you'll be hard pressed to find one so interesting, inspiring, and educational as this one! An enriching read from a great and principled man."

—Steve Forbes, chairman and editor in chief, *Forbes*

INVESTED

How Charles Schwab & Company
Revolutionized Investing
with Innovation and
Customer Service

Charles Schwab

CURRENCY

NEW YORK

Copyright © 2019 by The Charles Schwab Corporation
Foreword copyright © 2022 by The Charles Schwab Corporation

All rights reserved.
Published in the United States by Currency, an imprint of Random House,
a division of Penguin Random House LLC, New York.
currencybooks.com

CURRENCY and its colophon are trademarks of Penguin Random House LLC.

Currency books are available at special discounts for bulk purchases for sales
promotions or corporate use. Special editions, including personalized covers,
excerpts of existing books, or books with corporate logos, can be created in large
quantities for special needs. For more information, contact Premium Sales at
(212) 572-2232 or email specialmarkets@penguinrandomhouse.com.

Library of Congress Cataloging-in-Publication Data
Names: Schwab, Charles, author.
Title: Invested: how Charles Schwab & Company revolutionized investing with
    innovation and customer service / by Charles Schwab.
Description: First edition. | New York: Currency, [2019] | Includes index.
Identifiers: LCCN 2018056049 | ISBN 9781984822543
Subjects: LCSH: Schwab, Charles. | Financial advisors—United
    States—Biography. | Financial services industry—United States. |
    Investments—United States.
Classification: LCC HG172.S39 A3 2019 | DDC 332.6092 [B]—dc23 LC record
    available at https://lccn.loc.gov/2018056049

ISBN 978-1-9848-2254-3
Ebook ISBN 978-1-9848-2255-0
Premium ISBN 978-0-593-72815-4

Printed in the United States of America

10 9 8 7 6 5 4 3 2 1

For Helen, my five children,

and my thirteen grandchildren,

you are my greatest blessings.

Contents

Part III: Boom and Bust

Part IV: Second Act

Part V: Time Tested

FOREWORD

A story like ours doesn't stop when you put down the pen and call a book done.

On October 1, 2019, just as this book landed in bookstores, a series of events changed the game. On that day Schwab eliminated stock trading commissions. Three weeks later we announced we were buying one of our oldest competitors, TD Ameritrade, owned by Toronto Dominion Bank, Canada's largest bank and the twentieth-largest bank in the United States, largely completing the consolidation of the discount brokerage industry fifty years after it began. And then in the early months of 2020, a new threat to the global economy—COVID-19—appeared, sending the financial markets into a dive.

Zero Commissions

In many ways going to zero commissions is the bookend to the beginning of my story building Schwab. I've been working to lower commissions since the day I started the company. It was the original big idea. In 1975, the Securities and Exchange Commission in the United States deregulated commissions and left it to brokerage firms to set a price for buying and selling securities. It was a historic step that cracked open the clubby world of stock trading to more Americans. Before discount brokerage, the commission on a hundred shares was $110. Thanks to the deregulation, we changed that. We dropped it immediately to just $70 per hundred shares. From there we went to $29.95 in 1999, to $12.95 ten years later, to $9.95 next, and to $4.95 in 2017. In one last step, on October 1, 2019, we went to $0.

It felt like a great victory to me. Back in the 1960s and 1970s, when I started in this business, a commission was an incentive to sell. Commissions were absurdly high and enriched the salesman. I always thought, "If I am being paid in commissions, my boss must want me to sell more, even if that's not the best answer for the client."

Selling stocks was all about creating exciting stories of future riches. The greater the risk to the buyer, the higher the commission to the broker. Investing in stock was relatively new for the average person, who was hesitant to take the risk with their savings. Many people simply relied on what they thought was unbiased advice they were getting from their broker. But advice and the sales commission were jumbled together in an unhealthy marriage. Transactional pay shaped the relationship between investor and broker and created a perverse incentive that favored the broker's interest, not the investor's. Over time it had a corrosive effect on people's trust in investing.

So when we started Schwab, we did something that rattled the foundations of traditional Wall Street. We eliminated the individual broker's incentive to sell. Our employees earned a salary and a bonus for good service, not a sales commission. We wanted customers to have the best answer without the influence of compensation. It created a different type of relationship with clients. Our brokers' job was simply to help the investor invest as efficiently and effectively as possible. Avoiding high-cost broker sales commissions, where 40–50 percent of the total commission went to the broker, in turn enabled us to cut the cost of investing significantly. As a firm, we still derived revenue from trades, but much less than the full-commission firms did.

The notion of eventually going to zero commissions was always lurking. We first discussed it in 2005, shortly after I returned as CEO of the company. And I remember in 2010 giving a talk to a group of marketing executives at other companies. One fellow stood up and asked me a question: What would I do differently if I was starting the company over? I said it's very easy to answer that question. I would do exactly what Google has done: Price your primary service at zero and develop other products and services that clients will value and which can provide revenue for the firm. A win-win. Because we started our business before the internet, that model, based on very high traffic, simply was not possible. The paperwork cost would've crushed any attempt at that!

Over time, as our company grew and created greater scale and efficiency, it was always a dogfight among the discounters over who was the lowest. At Schwab I never wanted to be absolutely the lowest because I always wanted to have the highest quality. This meant large investments in customer service. I wanted to develop the best and most reliable computer systems and the best people. I was in the business for the long haul. Sometimes we were the lowest; many times we were not the lowest. But I think we had the highest quality of service. What mattered to us was client success and satisfaction. Compensation for our employees reflected that. It was as revolutionary a change as lowering the cost of trading. A brokerage based on customer service? Unheard of on Wall Street at the time.

So how did we eventually do it? How did we make it possible to trade for zero commission?

Ultimately, we got there through a relentless focus on keeping operational costs low. Today, our operating expense per client dollar is about half that of our publicly traded brokerage competitors. We "pinch pennies" so we can charge our clients less.

Some people argue nothing is truly "free"; there must be a catch to zero commissions. As Milton Friedman famously said, there is no free lunch, and I agree. But there is no trick here, either. The business model is simple. Our job is to help people in the process of their saving, investing, and borrowing. To support that, we earn revenue in straightforward ways: through asset management fees from mutual funds, exchange-traded funds, and managed accounts, and through interest on cash balances, like all banks. We also earn some revenue from the businesses and exchanges we use to create speedy, liquid markets, having them compete for our business by matching buyers and sellers, narrowing the spreads between bids and asks, and ultimately improving the price of a trade for our clients.

And we do that at a very great value for the investor. For example, when it comes to services, Schwab clients spend on average about half of what they would spend per investment dollar held here than they would elsewhere. For that they get internet investing, phone service, branches, ETFs, mutual funds, bonds, managed accounts, trades, advice, banking, free ATM access, 24/7 access to people for help, financial planning—the list goes on. Today a Schwab client can open an account, pay no account or service fees, invest $1,000 in a series of Schwab ETFs, be fully diversified, pay in total roughly $2 a year, and access all our insights, our branches, our web and mobile experiences, 24/7 service, and more. That is innovation. And that is fantastic for our clients. A better value means investors can put more of their money to work building their own wealth, with less friction that might interfere with reaching their investing goals, and more confidence in getting there.

Without looking in the rearview mirror at history, it is hard to appreciate how much has changed for the better, all because of creative innovation and a focus on the client and what's best for them. For me, going to zero commissions represents a symbolic final step in a fifty-year process of eliminating bad incentives in the buying and selling of stock. The investing public is far more sophisticated today about investing and doesn't need to be "sold" on the benefits anymore. For me it's a dream realized.

It also set in motion a chain of events that brought us to where we are today: a much larger, stronger company that will endure in what is now a more mature and healthy industry.

Competition and Industry Evolution

The story of industry evolution starts much earlier, going back to the very early years of what came to be called discount brokerage. It was back then that I inadvertently helped create one of our biggest competitors.

The discount brokerage model we built was innovative and unique at first, but like all better mousetraps, it caught on quickly. I learned an important lesson along the way about competition and how easy it is to lose an edge if you drop your guard. My experience with one of our great competitors today, Fidelity Investments, is a good example of that. In the late 1970s, a few years into our launch of discount brokerage, I got a call from an executive at Fidelity asking if he could visit and talk about our new business model. Being the proud entrepreneur that I was at that time, I was happy to show the representative from Fidelity all the things we were doing and how we were doing them. I thought maybe Fidelity, being a leading player in the mutual fund business, would see some way that we could work together. To my surprise, just six months later, the older and wealthier Fidelity announced plans to offer their own discount brokerage capability. They thrived and became our largest competitor. My warning to all entrepreneurs is to be careful whom you speak to about your business. Don't spill all your beans!

Acquiring TD Ameritrade

I am sure Fidelity will always be there and we'll be fighting it out for clients every step of the way. They're a worthy competitor. Following our acquisition of TD Ameritrade, I believe we are an industry that has evolved to produce a healthy mix of strong competitors.

How did the acquisition come about? I first met Joe Ricketts, the entrepreneur founder and longtime chairman of Ameritrade, after his deal with Toronto Dominion Bank. TD Ameritrade was another tough competitor. Joe came to our office on Kearny Street for a visit. I enjoyed meeting him for the first time. He's an imposing and serious man of few laughs, and we shared a vision for our industry. We talked about the discount brokerage business in general and the importance of its role in the financial services industry.

In his original deal with TD Bank, Ricketts sold 45 percent of the company to the bank. It turned out to be a great deal for the Ricketts family: They continued to have significant control of the brokerage firm, but they also benefited from ownership of TD Bank shares and received dividends.

Within a few years of Ameritrade's acquisition by TD Bank, we began to get visits from investment bankers suggesting that we buy from the bank its 45 percent interest. It made no sense to us, as we needed to have a controlling interest. But by 2019, with the whole industry including Schwab and TD Ameritrade going to zero commissions, things began to change. I felt it was time for some industry consolidation. A bigger combined company would be a stronger competitor.

TD Bank, I am sure, had begun to think that maybe the economics within our industry would be substantially harmed by the trend toward zero commissions. Because Schwab was less dependent on trading revenue, we knew it would put us in a great position, and so we were able to make the move to zero commissions from a position of strength. Others needed that revenue to compete, but we didn't. TD Bank eventually decided that in order to compete they would need to make investments in TD Ameritrade, but they had other areas of their business they preferred to invest in. And we all knew that a combination of our two firms would be a force to reckon with, benefiting both of us.

We began our discussions, and voilà! A deal was done that creates what I consider a uniquely strong company.

We've built strength in other ways as well, adding the wealth management business of USAA, a company focused on those who served in the military, and then new fixed-income capabilities from a bond manager named Wasmer Schroeder. Because the future of investing is in greater customization of solutions, we also purchased a company called Motif, which allows us to create customized portfolios designed to match investments with individual needs and investing strategies.

COVID-19

Sometimes change is completely unexpected. The COVID pandemic is one of the most unusual events in U.S. history; the closest parallel is the Spanish influenza pandemic, which happened a hundred years ago, when the United States had a very different kind of economy. COVID pushed everyone back for a while and resulted in terrible suffering for millions, but it could have been so much worse, particularly for business. I believe what saved us from economic calamity is the internet—that revolutionary invention that is still just in its infancy. Without it, we would have had a quick slide back to the dark ages.

Yes, the markets dropped while trying to absorb the news of lockdowns, travel restrictions, and hospitalizations. But instead of a market disaster, we've had a boom. Businesses adjusted and found new ways to work. People have more time on their hands to explore investing. We've seen a huge influx of young people getting into investing—great news for the long-term health of our industry. At Schwab, before the pandemic our business was 50 percent internet-based, with the remainder over the phone or in branches; now we're at 90 percent internet-based. Roughly 85 percent of our workforce has been working from home; before COVID, that was close to zero. Zoom and Webex and countless other new capabilities enabled it. And there are significant implications for the future. Our workplaces will never go back to business as usual. Employees have new expectations about work, and we have new needs for training and communications. The crisis caused new investments in medical research that will have future impact, and governments are now alert to viruses in new ways.

Two short years and a world of change. The certainty and, I think, beauty of our system of free enterprise is that more change is certainly on its way. New companies and established ones alike are innovating every day. Bring on the change! The American investor is the ultimate winner.

Final Word

I've thought quite a lot about my legacy as the founder of Charles Schwab. As the founder and a significant shareholder, I've been able to influence the course of this company for nearly fifty years—and I know I can say with humility it has been for the better. Still, we all know a person doesn't last forever . . . but companies can. I want the passion and purpose of this company to endure. In a recent letter to my heirs and the leaders of our family foundations, I alluded to this. Here is some of what I said:

"When we created Charles Schwab, we changed the ways Wall Street helps individual investors. It was, and still is, all about how to make every individual a better, smarter, or more competent investor so they can participate in all that capitalism can provide. We helped make it possible for more people to participate in the great growth that the American system offers. It was also about building the backbone of capitalism and its best features, especially the way stock ownership can encourage new ideas, innovation, and growth. Capitalism is all about creativity!

Charles Schwab has been a leader in the democratization of the American individual ownership of stocks. No other company was established with this as a goal. We have been at it for nearly 50 years. I do not want the company to ever lose its purpose, or dedication! You, the descendants of Schwab, the owners of the Schwab stock, can make this happen.

I want our Foundations and our heirs of Schwab to never lose the passion and original purpose of the founders . . . hold on to every share of stock as long as possible. YES, enjoy the dividends and small sales to fulfill payout schedules and maintain a reasonable lifestyle, but holding on to your stock is very important to me! Through ownership, I believe every one of you will continue to have a very keen self-interest to see Charles Schwab grow . . . Our company will require a lively, flourishing capitalist system in America. And that means the engagement of shareholders like you.

I want my children, and their family tree of our descendants to follow, to maintain as much influence as possible with their stock ownership in the Charles Schwab company in perpetuity. And I hope they will always maintain the central purpose of Schwab as a service for individual investors, operating without conflicts of interest, devoid of commission driven investment bankers and insurance brokers. The company should represent the best principles of capitalism.

. . . And if you aggregate all the power of your holdings together, the descendants of Charles and Helen Schwab will have great influence in the direction of the Schwab Corporation into the future."

The history of so many companies has shown us that when the founder's influence fades with the passing of time, the original passion and purpose can easily slip away. I believe—and will do what I can to ensure—that won't be the case this time. If you are an employee, a client, or a stockholder in our company, I hope you'll join me in that cause.

Charles R. "Chuck" Schwab
August 2022

PREFACE

When I started Charles Schwab in the early 1970s, there were hundreds of brokerage firms in the United States.

But none were what I dreamed of building, a different kind of brokerage focused on independent-minded investors who wanted access to the markets without the middlemen and costly, often conflicted, "advice" that came with access back then.

Starting with an idea and little else, I spent the next 40 years with like-minded people building that different firm. As we did, the dream expanded in ways I never could have imagined and changed forever how Americans invest.

This is our story.

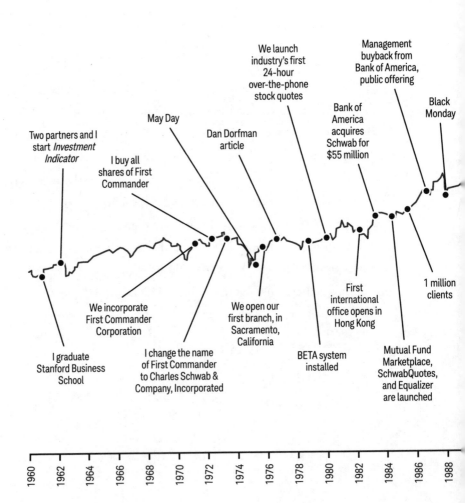

Charles Schwab Timeline

Two partners and I start *Investment Indicator*

I buy all shares of First Commander

May Day

Dan Dorfman article

We launch industry's first 24-hour over-the-phone stock quotes

Bank of America acquires Schwab for $55 million

Management buyback from Bank of America, public offering

Black Monday

We incorporate First Commander Corporation

We open our first branch, in Sacramento, California

First international office opens in Hong Kong

1 million clients

I graduate Stanford Business School

I change the name of First Commander to Charles Schwab & Company, Incorporated

BETA system installed

Mutual Fund Marketplace, SchwabQuotes, and Equalizer are launched

1960 1962 1964 1966 1968 1970 1972 1974 1976 1978 1980 1982 1984 1986 1988

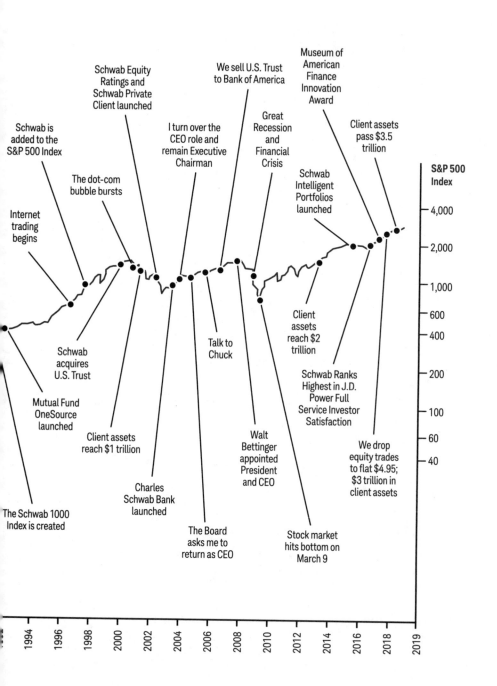

Schwab is added to the S&P 500 Index

The dot-com bubble bursts

Internet trading begins

Schwab Equity Ratings and Schwab Private Client launched

I turn over the CEO role and remain Executive Chairman

We sell U.S. Trust to Bank of America

Great Recession and Financial Crisis

Museum of American Finance Innovation Award

Client assets pass $3.5 trillion

Schwab Intelligent Portfolios launched

S&P 500 Index

Schwab acquires U.S. Trust

Talk to Chuck

Client assets reach $2 trillion

Mutual Fund OneSource launched

Client assets reach $1 trillion

Schwab Ranks Highest in J.D. Power Full Service Investor Satisfaction

The Schwab 1000 Index is created

Charles Schwab Bank launched

Walt Bettinger appointed President and CEO

We drop equity trades to flat $4.95; $3 trillion in client assets

The Board asks me to return as CEO

Stock market hits bottom on March 9

4,000

2,000

1,000

600

400

200

100

60

40

1994 1996 1998 2000 2002 2004 2006 2008 2010 2012 2014 2016 2018 2019

‖‖

PART I

Getting Started

Young people looking for career advice or insights into starting a business often ask me, "What's the key to success?"

What are you good at, what do you love doing, what can you talk about without even thinking about it and without tiring of it? I ask them. That's where you should put your energy. There is tremendous power in that because it drives you forward through the ups and downs—and there will always be plenty of both. That passion and knowledge also signal to others that you are genuine, with personal ambitions, true expertise, a direction in life—the real deal. People are attracted to that, and you will need the support of others.

The world of business, like the rest of life, is full of wonderful temptations, and making a choice about where you are going to devote your energy is often as much about dismissing things as it is about choosing something. A singular sense of purpose gives you focus and clarity.

Determine that direction but know that it is not the end; it can flower and branch out in many ways over time, some that you'd never guess when starting out.

In my case, I loved investing—everything about it: the idea that companies are meant to grow, that anyone can participate in that growth and build up their own financial independence over time. Feeling that passion and then learning that most people were missing out because the system wasn't designed to serve the average investor . . . well, that became an endless opportunity and a powerful cause that others would embrace with me!

1

—

MAY DAY

Wednesday, April 30, 1975. The day before what came to be known to people in financial services as May Day. I'm not sure if it was sunny or socked in with San Francisco fog. I had a lot on my mind. I do recall that investors had been in a good mood all spring. The Nixon impeachment nightmare was over, the Vietnam War was behind us, and the market was moving again; the Dow was up nearly 50% since late December. I'm sure I was as hopeful as anyone else. But I'd seen too much to believe the worst was over.

I was about to turn 38 in a couple of months. The Dow had been flirting with the magic 1,000 mark for the last 10 years, first breaking that milestone on November 14, 1972. At the moment it was hovering just above 800. So to say I was a tad skeptical of the rally's staying power would be an understatement. On the other hand, if you'd told me then that not until December 21, 1982, would the Dow finally break through 1,000 for good, I might have said to hell with it and found another line of work. In fact, I had been right on the precipice of that decision for some time. Who starts a brokerage firm in the middle of a two-decade stock market slump? This was my third go at starting a business since I had set out on my own, shortly after finishing Stanford Business School. Part of me wondered, *How many chances does one guy get in life?*

What's more, I was in a deep trough myself just then, carrying a six-figure debt. I owed money to Crocker Bank for a business loan I had used to buy out one of my partners. I also had a sheaf of personal loans that wound up in my pocket when I got divorced. I was now married again, but I had no assets to speak of. Helen and I were living with our baby, Katie, in a small apartment in Sausalito. Helen was selling real estate, while I was a year into launching my firm, an experiment in discounted stock trading made possible by the Securities and Exchange Commission's test of deregulated commissions. I was bound for parts unknown.

That Wednesday, I had one overriding question. The answer would make or break my plans, as deregulation was about to become the law of the land after a one-year test period. What would Merrill Lynch do? Founded in 1914 by the legendary Charles Merrill, with a vision to bring "Wall Street to Main Street," Merrill Lynch was the undisputed king of the retail brokerage market, and a billion-dollar-plus underwriter. It had branch offices from coast to coast, an army of thousands of highly motivated commissioned brokers, and a slogan known to everyone who watched TV or read the newspaper: "Merrill Lynch is bullish on America." Charles Merrill had built his firm on the idea of opening up the world of investing to the middle class. It was a goal I admired. He was the first to experiment with salaried brokers back in the 1940s, addressing the serious conflict of interest that I had disliked for years (they backtracked from that model in the early '70s under Don Regan's leadership to incentivize its large herd of brokers). And the firm was hugely successful. Everybody said to me, "Wait until Merrill Lynch decides to go into your business. You are going to be crushed."

I was worried, but Merrill was an entrenched member of the Wall Street establishment. It was still beholden to its many commissioned brokers, and its highly profitable investment banking and research businesses. It couldn't just chuck all that out the window. Still, the more I thought about it, the more I was certain that Merrill would have to lower its commissions at least a little in response to deregulation. In which case, I feared, I'd be dead in the water as soon as I launched my business. No way my little firm could compete with an industry giant like Merrill.

All that was on my mind when I arrived at 120 Montgomery Street that Wednesday morning, early as usual (I liked to be at my desk by 6:30 a.m. when the market opened in New York); I took the elevator up to the 24th floor and the small office the handful of us occupied. I picked up my copy of the *Wall Street Journal*, and there on the front page was the news: "Merrill Lynch will raise securities brokerage fees on most transactions under $5000." Was it true? ". . . will *raise* securities brokerage fees . . ."

Unbelievable. Here I'd been afraid that Merrill would lower its fees and meet my commission cuts and steal my opportunity. Instead, it had taken advantage of deregulation to raise its prices for the average guy and drop them for large institutions. Once I got over my shock, I was beaming. I saw an opportunity, and I meant to take full advantage of it. It had been a long road, with lots of bumps along the way. But on that day, Charles Schwab looked like it had a real chance in the marketplace. I remember saying to myself, *I've got a hell of a business.*

I HAVE LOVED THE idea of investing since I was a kid and my dad first showed me stock tables in the local paper. The idea that stocks captured a little bit of the magic in our economy and, if you worked at it, you could participate in that . . . well, that caught my imagination. That was exciting. Today, I remain more convinced than ever that investing is the individual's path to financial freedom. It is how people can participate in a growing economy, beyond just earning a paycheck. I'm an optimist. And investing has always seemed to me to be the ultimate act of optimism. You've got to have confidence that the money you invest today is going to grow; otherwise, you might as well stuff it under the mattress. You have to believe tomorrow will be better than today.

But back in the '70s when I was starting Schwab, I knew investing was deeply flawed. And I thought investors deserved better. Access to the markets came with outrageously high costs—average commissions and spreads could eat up nearly 10% of an investor's money! Mutual funds, which pooled investors' money together to be invested by a professional money manager, often carried 9% sales loads. That meant you needed to earn 9% on your investment before you'd break even. So much of those high costs were claimed to cover the "advice" that you were getting. But was it good advice, or just the price of entry? Wall Street had controlled commissions from its very first day under a buttonwood tree in 1792, where its founding members had established the New York Stock Exchange and agreed to do business only among themselves, and to never negotiate commissions.

So in a real way, Charles Schwab was born of my own frustration. I was an independent investor. I was passionate about the market. I did my own stock research. I believed in taking charge of my own financial destiny. I loved the thrill of the chase. The last thing I needed was some broker's questionable advice about what to buy, and when to buy or sell. And I resented paying for services I wasn't using. I was also deeply frustrated. For I had come to believe that the brokerage business had a nagging problem with conflicts of interests. I knew that the Wall Street big brokerage firms that were also investment banks—despite their so-called Chinese walls—couldn't easily put the interests of individual investors first. The same was true for commissioned salespeople, many of whom made their living by trading in and out of stocks—not by building up their clients' portfolios. Not their fault: it was just how the system worked.

But a new day had arrived. After years of mounting pressure for reform, the Securities and Exchange Commission (SEC) had begun a bold experiment aimed at dismantling the century-old Wall Street cartel. Under the old system, fixed brokerage commissions were held in place by a web of regulations that carried the full weight of law. If you made a trade, you paid a high price, and the price was fixed. Or maybe not, this being Wall Street. Small traders had zero leverage, but big traders were getting bigger and had plenty of leverage, and lately they'd begun to use it. They had worked out an elaborate system of special favors, hidden discounts, side deals, and mutual back-scratching—anything to lower the cost of trading. Take, for example, the four-way ticket, a crazy system that broke commissions up into pieces, with the proceeds spread around to provide some benefit to the large institutions making the trades. In a four-way ticket, an institutional investor such as a pension or a mutual fund, would buy 10,000 shares of a stock, for example, with a commission that might have been, let's say, $1 a share. One-fourth of that $10,000 commission would go to a research firm, who would provide proprietary research back to the investor; another quarter would go to reimbursing the investing institution for travel, under the auspices of "education"; another fourth went for entertainment such as a night out at a game or club, or a fancy dinner. And the last fourth would go to the brokerage. The same was true for a larger transaction of 100,000 shares. Only in that case there would be a $100,000 pie to be divided.

By the early 1970s, the system had become unwieldy. Something had to give. Institutions didn't like it, the SEC didn't like it, and Congress got involved. Bottom line: the power of the big traders was growing; the New York Stock Exchange was buckling under enormous pressure. Change was inevitable.

Which was all well and good for the big institutions. They would finally get some pricing power and force brokers to compete for their business. But what about the little guy? The person doing a 100-share trade, or an even smaller trade? I was starting Schwab hoping to take advantage of the significant changes that would come from the deregulation of the brokerage industry. But I was focused on that person, the individual investor. My first book, *How to Be Your Own Stockbroker*, said it all: "Today any investor can be truly independent—independent of unfair, bloated commissions and the . . . broker whose 'advice' is tainted. The sordid fact is that the riskier the investment that a broker 'advises,' the higher is his own take."

Many traditional brokerage houses were afraid of the consequences of deregulation. And with good reason: more than 30 NYSE member firms would close in 1975; more than 100 brokerages would fold or merge. But I was not afraid, because I had no stake in the system as it was. To me, here was an opportunity to advance the cause of reform, do right by the ordinary investor, expand ownership of equities to a bigger slice of the US population (which I've come to believe is essential to the preservation of democracy . . . call it skin in the game), and along the way build a substantial business. I thought if I could strip away all the fluff surrounding the purchase and sale of stocks—the tainted research, the bogus analysis, the flimsy recommendations, all the ways that Wall Street had historically justified high commissions—and sell just the plain-vanilla service of executing trades, I could slash overhead, focus on efficiency, cut prices dramatically—by as much as 75%—and still make a profit.

I knew exactly who my customers would be; I was one of them. If I hadn't started my own discount brokerage firm, I would have become some other discounter's happy customer. I had been waiting for something like this for a long time, and I was pretty sure I was not the only one. So when the SEC proclaimed the end of the experimental phase of deregulation and announced that as of May 1, 1975, selling stocks would be like selling anything else in America—with prices to be determined by no authority other than the marketplace—I was ready!

2

A SENSE OF INDEPENDENCE

On my list of good fortune, starting my company in the San Francisco Bay Area is high up there. It was a place where taking risks was part of the culture, and where "not invented here" didn't apply. Good ideas and creativity were welcome, no matter who they came from. There was less emphasis on who you knew, or where you were from, and more on what you could do. It was a place where amazing new technology blossomed right at the time I was starting out and I needed it to make my dream a reality, a place with a long tradition of big dreams. I don't know that I could have started Schwab anywhere else.

My family connection to the Bay Area goes back to the 1800s. My grandfather, Robert Henry Schwab, moved to San Francisco in 1905 from Long Island to practice law. He married my grandmother, Mary Gertrude Bray, in 1906. Mary was a native San Franciscan, born in 1885. On my mother's side, the California connection is just as deep. Her parents, J. Oxley Moore and Elizabeth Leona Hammond, were Californians born in the late 1800s—Oxley in Stockton and Elizabeth in Petaluma, the "egg basket of the world," as it was known for its chicken farming.

In 1917, my grandparents moved from San Francisco to Sacramento, where Grandpa joined a local private legal practice. Sacramento was the heart of the state's agricultural community—certainly not a finance-oriented place like New York, or even San Francisco, but growing, thriving.

Grandpa was stern, Germanic. He wasn't mean, just determined and disciplined and a bit formal, except when he was with his friends every Monday night at the German Club, where they got together to drink beer, play pinochle, and practice their German. Laughter would peal through the club; the jokes must have been good. I was too young to understand any of it, even when they joked in English, but I liked the sound. The laughter had that genuineness to it that you sense when good friends get together.

My dad, Robert H. Schwab, also became a lawyer. A graduate of the University of California and then Hastings College of Law in San Francisco, he, too, was a hard worker, passing the bar with the third-highest score in the state that year. He and my mother, Bettie Annabell Moore, married on August 29, 1936, and moved to Sacramento, where Dad joined his father's law practice. That arrangement wasn't going to work out for the long term. My sense is Dad and Granddad didn't get along too well in close quarters like that. My father wanted his independence and his own opportunities, and so in 1937 he accepted a position in the Yolo County District Attorney's Office in Woodland, California, about 20 miles northwest of Sacramento. Woodland was a small rural farming town of about 5,000 people and the county seat.

One of my early memories is of my father running for district attorney of Yolo County. He had printed up cards with his picture that he'd pass out all around town. "Bob Schwab for D.A." they said. I still have some saved. He was elected in 1942 and held the position for the next eight years while also keeping up his private practice.

———

I WAS BORN IN Sacramento, California, on July 29, 1937, just months before my parents packed us up and moved to Woodland. It was the tail end of the Depression and a Depression-era mind-set still permeated the economy. People wouldn't feel confident it was actually over and behind them until well into the 1940s, after World War II had ended. For many, the money scars never completely healed.

Don't get me wrong. It was a wonderful time and place to grow up. Summers in Woodland were sunny and warm. I hung out with my gang of friends and we had free range of the town. There was a lot to do for a young kid and plenty of freedom to do it . . . playing pickup baseball games on empty lots, swimming in the irrigation ditches that crisscrossed the local farmland, riding bikes, staying busy and mostly out of trouble with odd jobs like sacking the local English walnuts and picking tomatoes. But money was tight and you cherished what you had. When my father took me to buy my first bike, it wasn't at the local bike shop. He looked through the local *Woodland Democrat* in the "For Sale or Trade" section and found someone who wanted to sell a used bike, a Schwinn I think it was. I have no idea what he paid for it, but that bike was precious to me. I took it apart and put it back together over and over, keeping it in top shape. I rode it everywhere. I knew every street in town, every shortcut, every lot I could cut through.

During the war years when people were strapped for cash, my dad bartered his services. Once, a client paid him with a lamb; we ate some for Sunday dinner and froze the rest. We had a lot of lamb from the freezer that spring. Rationing was a way of life; so much of the country's supplies were going to the war effort.

Trying to build a life in the wake of the Depression had an enormous impact on my parents' attitudes toward money, saving, and risk that lasted their entire lives. No matter how comfortable they became, they always talked about the hard times when they were young. They'd seen people lose their homes and their independence, and they weren't ever going to let that happen to them. There was always that shadow that hung over their lives.

So much of a person's attitudes and habits toward money get formed while they are young. We see it with clients at Schwab every day.

> A person's approach to money, his or her saving and spending habits, and comfort or discomfort with risk are all deeply ingrained, and more emotional than rational.

My own attitudes about financial security and personal independence were a reaction against that Depression mentality.

I grew to hate the whole idea of limits and decided early on that I did not want to live like that, ever again. I wanted to be above such worries, to be truly financially independent. Consequently, I was always thinking about how I could make money, how I could save money, and later, how I could invest it.

IT ISN'T JUST ATTITUDES about money that form early in our lives. So much of who you are and how you act later in life is set into place early on, through parents, teachers, the way you fill your days. I learned about generosity watching my father. He was always the first guy to put a dollar bill in the basket coming around at church. He talked a lot about economic principles and about law, and he was pretty hard-nosed about ethics. He had strong opinions about good people versus bad people, and what made the difference. He expressed his principles and what he stood for as district attorney and as a lawyer. A law-and-order kind of guy.

Dad told us occasional stories about the cases he was working on.

Often it was the small-town stuff you'd expect for a rural area like Yolo County . . . fights, drunk and disorderly, the occasional marijuana arrest. I never wanted to be on his bad side—he was one hell of a disciplinarian. And like any kid, I managed to make enough mistakes to experience it firsthand. Once, some friends and I made a campfire that got out of control and burned some fencing and a chicken coop before it was put out. It didn't take our parents long to figure out who the culprits were. I got hell for that. I'm sure my dad was deeply embarrassed; he was the D.A. after all. To really make the point, my dad lit a match and held it to my hand.

My mom, on the other hand, was a fun-loving person with a great outgoing personality. She could charm anyone. I learned the importance of relationships from her early on, putting yourself out there, having an open attitude, listening to people. I was shy, but my confidence and curiosity had a way of beating the shyness. I'm sure one of the reasons for my success over the years has been that people generally like me—and the secret to that is just human nature: I pay attention to them. I listen to their stories and take a genuine interest. And it's made for a richer life. People are endlessly fascinating and their stories are motivating. I also think listening compensated for difficulties I had with reading. It was a great way for me to absorb new things. Overcoming shyness and mastering people skills has been one of the keys to success for me, and I owe a lot to my mom for reinforcing that when I was growing up. It's a perfect complement to the inner discipline my father encouraged.

I attended elementary school at the Holy Rosary Academy at 164 Market Street in Woodland. The nuns there were tough, but what they really taught was about making an effort and showing respect and developing beliefs. Lessons, again, that have stuck with me for life.

I didn't know it at the time—I only discovered it much later in life—but I have dyslexia. That made reading and studying incredibly hard. The nuns were very strict with me on preparation. They wanted me to learn. They had incredible dedication to what they were doing. Reading was a struggle. Until I memorized them, each new word was a jumble of letters that took time to decipher. As a consequence, I spent a lot of time at the blackboard after school, working on my writing and math. I can still remember the feeling of chalk dust building up on my hands as I wrote and rewrote words and calculations to help lock them into my memory. I'm sure it was obvious to my teachers that I had some kind of learning difficulty. It wasn't obvious to me. I just felt that school was a great struggle and didn't understand the reason until years later. But they worked with me to master the skills I needed. I think the nuns liked the fact that I worked so hard and was willing to put in the time it took to figure things out, even if I had to stay after school. I loved reading classic comics because it was an easier way to quickly get the content we were studying in school. And once I got it, however I managed to get there, my comprehension was great and I would do well on tests. Getting to that point, that was the challenge.

Many years after my school days, after I had some success with Schwab, I got a letter in the mail that included a copy of my six years of grades at the school. Those grades were not impressive. Along with it was a fund-raising plea for the school. Was it a veiled threat? *Help us out or we release the report card?* I don't know. But I was happy to send them a check.

MY GRANDDAD HAD A passion for horse races and took me with him sometimes to the Golden Gate Fields racetrack near Berkeley. I didn't have the money to gamble, but he'd give me a stake for the $2.00 window on occasion. We won a little once in a while, but I also learned that I could easily lose it all on the wrong bet.

It was my father who first introduced me to the stock market. I was about 13, and he pointed out the stock tables—the prices went up and down. And it intrigued the heck out of me.

I thought, *Well, if I could buy them low, and then sell them high, boy, wouldn't that be a great way to make money.* It was different from the horse races because there was some logic driving the market's ups and downs. It was still a thrill to be on the right side if you could, but it was also an interesting puzzle to try to figure out what drove one stock up and another down.

I also became increasingly interested in what makes one person succeed in life, and another languish. I read lots of biographies of people who had accomplished great things, people such as John D. Rockefeller, J. P. Morgan, Charles M. Schwab the steel magnate (no relation), and many others. I saw the importance of determination, of passion and fighting hard for what you believed in, and the importance of optimism and believing good things are possible. All the people I read about had a maniacal focus on growth, how step-by-step you could take an idea and expand it, reinvest in it, make it better, bigger. That had great appeal to me and it sparked my interest in business and finance.

IN 1950, WE MOVED to Santa Barbara and my father went into private practice. He handled real estate transactions, small claims, contracts of all kinds. As the years went by and his clients grew older, he came to specialize in trusts and estates. I attended La Cumbre Junior High School and graduated from Santa Barbara High School in 1955.

In Santa Barbara, I became "Chuck." As a kid growing up in Woodland, my nickname was Buddy. But I thought Buddy was too informal, too much of a kid's name. And when we moved to Santa Barbara, I wanted to drop it. A good friend of mine who I met in

Santa Barbara was named Chuck, Chuck Rudolf—he was a few years older than I was and I looked up to him. He treated me well. I thought, *Well, he's a really great guy* . . . so Chuck it was.

Moving to Santa Barbara was a turning point for me. I had come from a small farming town of about 5,000 to a city 10 times that size. I had a bigger stage, and the chance to try new things, to stretch myself and build my confidence—which I really needed given my struggles with school. I loved sports and got involved in many. I played every sport I could. But I had a great passion for basketball. I was fast and played well but finally had to face up to the fact that my height was going to hold me back. There was no way I'd move on to the varsity team at my height, so I gave it up.

> **I learned a good lesson: make a choice and don't regret it, don't look back.**

I finally settled on tennis and golf. I did well, and they were confidence boosters. Sports are powerful that way. You can excel based on your own strengths and effort. There's a sense of accomplishment in that. Golf in particular became a passion of mine for life. To this day I believe there are great parallels between golf and investing. Both require preparation, patience, practice, and a long-term commitment. Both require strategy. You need to think several steps ahead. What's the lay of the land? How do you control your emotions? Both are full of highs and lows.

Between my junior and senior years, Clarence Schutte, the high school football coach, started a golf team. I suspect he saw a good opportunity in a few of us, but especially my friend Allen Geiberger, who at the time had won two State Junior Championships. Al later became a pro and was the first golfer in history to shoot a 59 on an official course. He's been "Mr. 59" ever since. Al was newly arrived at our school from Sacramento—another valley boy like me—and we became great friends, double-dating and sharing our love of golf. Coach Schutte was able to get the team access to a wonderful course, the Valley Club in Montecito, as long as we teed off before 9 a.m. We got to be quite good, practicing on that difficult course, and went on to win at the California Inter-Scholastic Federation competing with a couple dozen teams from across the state. It was one of the only times I beat Al in competition, shooting the low score of 72 during one round. Golf was it for me.

I SUPPOSE I'VE ALWAYS been a relatively confident person. Or at least it is a quality I developed over time, without even realizing it was happening. A lot of it was just having the willingness to put myself out there and try things. Some people are born leaders, I guess, but for most of us the ability to lead comes from experience. The more you lead, the more it develops as a strength. I just dove in when I saw a void, putting myself in situations where I had to speak up. I joined the Key Club, for example, a youth organization sponsored by the Kiwanis organization that focused on civics and community service. When I was 17, I was elected president of the club at my school, which resulted in a whirlwind cross-country train trip with other California club presidents to the Key Club's annual convention in Philadelphia. It was a two-week economy trip: sleep in your seat, or if you were a bit shorter like me, climb up into the luggage rack for some rest. Those two weeks gave me exposure to parts of the country I wouldn't have experienced otherwise: segregation in the South, seeing Colored Only signs at restrooms and water fountains; Confederate flags still flying; poverty in the small-town train stops along the way; my first visit to the big cities of New York, Chicago, and Washington, the nation's capital. You can read about things all day, but that trip east made it real: the scale of our country, the differences from place to place, the accents that sounded completely foreign to my Californian ear. The opportunity was there to experience it all, and it only happened because I had put the effort into the Key Club. It hadn't been my goal—but a lucky aftereffect of stepping out and getting engaged in something.

I hit bumps, for sure, like the time I struggled to get through a speech in front of a high school assembly. I was running for school office and asking for my classmates' votes. I couldn't remember the words. I froze. I was completely aware everyone was looking at me, expectantly, watching me struggle. It felt like the moment would never end. My concentration left me, my heart pounded. I felt stuck. But the moment passed, and there were also plenty of successes, like speaking up at Key Club meetings, developing and presenting budgets as school treasurer, and getting recognized by the local Daughters of the American Revolution for service in school (I still have the medal; the little bit of gold leaf has worn off, but I still cherish it). With each, I learned and got stronger. To this day I encourage young executives to get training in public speaking. No matter how good they are, mastering those moments in front of an audience is crucial to leading others, and it rarely comes naturally.

3

I HAD A LOT OF JOBS

I had a lot of jobs growing up. And I learned something from every one. There were those walnuts and the tomatoes, and when I was little, I also plucked hunting birds for my dad. He'd go hunting and bring back a sack of ducks, 10 or 20. I'd get 50 cents a bird to pluck their feathers. For a while I was in the chicken business, raising hens and selling eggs and fertilizer. (My first vertically integrated business!) I mowed lawns and pushed an ice-cream cart around the streets of Woodland. I'd go to football games at the high school and rummage underneath the grandstands, collecting Coke bottles. Back then, you could get a nickel for the bottles, which they sanitized and reused. We'd gather up enough after a game to get a few bucks; maybe even $10 after a hot day.

Basically, if I wanted spending money, I had to earn it. I read a lot of comic books and I was a sucker for the ads in the back. Once, when I was 13, I ordered some kind of lotion that was supposed to make you look younger, cartons and cartons of the stuff. I was going to sell it to all the moms in the neighborhood. My dad was not happy; he made me send the lotion back. As soon as I was old enough, I started working as a caddy, giving me my first exposure to a game that became a lifelong passion, as well as a valuable introduction to the world of adults. Being around successful men and women, listening to what they talked about and how they interacted with one another, made a big impression on me. They became my role models, right up there with my golf heroes, Ben Hogan and Sam Snead.

From the time I turned 17, through college and business school, I was never without a summer job of some kind. As soon as school ended in the spring, I'd find someone who was looking for help. I worked as a roustabout in the oil fields one summer, moving pipes as the oil crews prepared to pump from the wells. I worked at the county fairground and local golf club washing dishes.

Sometimes the lesson I learned from these jobs was about what I *didn't* want my life to be. As my first real job, I drove a tractor on a sugar beet farm. The owner of the farm was a client of my grandfather's. He was from India originally, and a very successful farmer. He offered me a job cultivating the rows: six days a week, from six in the morning to six at night, a dollar an hour. It included a place to stay and meals for $2.00 a day. After starting up the Caterpillar with heavy turns on a hand crank, I had to line it up just right down the rows, or I'd swerve off and chew up a batch of beets. For that you'd get docked. One direction down the rows you breathed in the diesel fumes, the way back the dust was in your face. Sundays back at my grandparents' home in nearby Sacramento, I had to wash off the layers of soot and dust.

I was the only person working at the sugar beet farm who didn't have a Hispanic surname. I didn't speak Spanish and they didn't speak English, so we spent long days without a lot of conversation. But I loved earning some spending money. More important, it opened my eyes to how difficult the life of a farmer and a farmhand is.

My first summer after starting college at Stanford, I took a job as a life insurance salesman. To my credit, perhaps, I never sold a single policy. It was the worst insurance in the world: expensive whole-life policies that came with savings programs attached. They would try to indoctrinate you. I was supposed to call on all my family and friends. The more I read about it—and the better I understood exactly what it was I was selling—the more awful I was sure it was. To this day I am skeptical about insurance. There's a need for certain types, but honestly, I could see right through most of the stuff I was supposed to be selling. I couldn't do it.

I've never liked selling a bad product and I've never been any good at it.

After a while I just quit.

But now I didn't have a job. There were only two months left of summer before school started again and I still hadn't made any money. So I became a home insulation salesman for a little fly-by-night operation. They put me through a training program. I had to go door-to-door in San Jose to the new housing developments that were popping up. I started out around 11:00, knocking on doors, asking to see Mrs. Whoever-it-was, and trying to get an appointment to come back that night so I could talk to her and her husband about what a great deal we had on insulation for the house. I'd start off with a question that could only be answered with a yes, to get me in the door. Something like, "Are your electric bills too high?" or "Are you concerned about the safety of your children?" The insulation was just crumpled-up newspaper that had been treated with a chemical that was supposed to make it fire retardant. I had this kit I carried around, a little suitcase. I'd open it up in the living room and take out a Bunsen burner and perform a little test to prove that it didn't burn. It wasn't a very good product. Often it lit up. I did that for three or four weeks and failed to make a single sale. So I was fired. My salary was based on 100% commission, so, no, I didn't make any money that summer.

Another summer I was a switchman on the railroad in Chicago. That job gave me a lot of incentive to get through school. It was the summer of 1958, a year of recession in the US economy. In school at Stanford, a group of three friends and I had bought a boat together. It cost us $10 a month each to finance it. We went waterskiing near campus on weekends. But that summer we were all heading off in different directions, so we drew straws to see who got to keep the boat until fall. My friend Jay drew the long straw and since he was taking it to Chicago and I had no plans, I thought, *Hell, I'll go, too.*

My dad gave me $100 for the summer, but I spent it all by the time I reached Omaha, Nebraska. My car kept breaking down—the radiator and the fuel pump and God knows what else. By the time we reached Omaha, I'd lost first gear and was burning through my clutch, Jay had lost his starter motor, and we had to push his car to start it. We avoided stopping as much as we could and moved at a crawl through Omaha and then Iowa City, where the rivers were overflowing from late spring rains. When I finally got to Chicago, I had to borrow money from Jay's dad. I really needed a job. The first job I applied for was as a Yellow Cab driver. Luckily they didn't hire me.

I tried to get into the steel mill, but there were long lines that summer because of the recession. Finally, I tried the railroad. The Illinois Central and the Santa Fe were hiring, but they weren't steady jobs. I was on call and because I was a kid and a newcomer, I got all the shifts nobody else wanted—Friday, Saturday, and Sunday, working all night. I hated it, and not because the work was hard. In fact, I learned all about featherbedding that summer. We showed up at the job, more of us than were really needed to get it done, and finished our work in a couple of hours as switchmen, which entailed breaking down trains and then reassembling them to get them ready for their varied destinations. We'd then find a caboose with benches for the engineers to rest on during long runs, and we'd sleep for the next six hours. I found it depressing.

I did meet some terrific people, though, people who had lost their jobs because of the recession, and now were out there working on the railroad every day like I was. One was a school music teacher, about 35 years old, married, three or four kids. And he was getting paid the same amount as I was. He was very competent, but his situation made quite an impression on me. He made $19.95 a day in pay. I knew that was not where I wanted to be at his age.

4

ALWAYS A STRUGGLE

Seeing what was out there—how other people found themselves trapped by their jobs with little hope of escaping—helped me get through school. And frankly, I needed all the help I could get. School was never easy for me. I struggled with my dyslexia. I couldn't understand why learning was so much harder for me than it was for my friends. I was pretty good at math and science, but nothing ever came easy. English was by far my hardest subject. I have always been a slow reader. I couldn't write a composition to save my life. I would look at the blank page and my mind would start to race. I never knew how to begin. I decided I was just stupid, something I believed for almost 40 years. Then, in 1983, my son, Michael, started having the same kinds of problems in school.

At first his teachers recommended tutors. When that didn't work, they advised us to have him tested. And to my surprise, he was diagnosed with dyslexia. Dyslexia is a learning disability, neurological in origin. It mainly affects a person's ability to read and write. Dyslexics struggle with cracking the code of written language. Where others assemble letters into words that have meanings more or less effortlessly, dyslexics may see only a confusion of symbols. I like to compare it to what the image on a TV screen might look like if all we could see were thousands of individual pixels. Dyslexics have to spend so much time decoding those symbols that they can lose the meaning of the larger text.

For me, each letter first had to be converted to a sound, and then each sound collected into words, so that I could sound it out in my head. There was no instant recognition, "I pet the cat." Instead, there was a series of symbols to sounds to thoughts, "I . . . p . . . e . . . t . . . the . . . c . . . a . . . t." Sometimes I would come across a word I didn't know and try to figure it out by sounding it out. It really slowed me down and cramped my comprehension. I would be halfway into a paragraph and lose where I was. My comprehension was shot. I was dealing with word retrieval, not understanding.

Turning sounds and thoughts into written words is even harder, what the experts call "phonological processing." It is a huge handicap in school. My son's diagnosis was troubling, of course, but also, in a way, a kind of relief. For it showed us exactly what the problem was and how to address it. And it proved that whatever his challenges, he was not stupid. That's the big risk with dyslexics: undiagnosed, they may lose their self-esteem, lose their way in school, and end up in bad situations with the law, drug abuse, alcoholism, you name it. By some estimates, one in five kids suffers some degree of dyslexia. Most don't know it. Studies have found that roughly half of inmates in US prisons are dyslexics. It's a dangerous cycle: without the right support when they are young, dyslexics struggle with learning to read and write. So they search for other avenues, they veer off track, and many end up in trouble.

Once we understood my son's situation, I began to reevaluate my own. I learned that there is a genetic component to dyslexia. Clearly, I was dyslexic, too, and had been all my life. Unfortunately, when I was growing up in the 1940s and 1950s, nobody knew anything about dyslexia. If you had it, you were just considered "slow." I survived by developing close relationships with my teachers and learning some tricks to make studying easier.

I got extra points for effort, and that helped keep my grades up. But I absolutely could not write. And my SAT scores were not good. The only reason I got into Stanford, I'm convinced, is because I was a pretty good golfer. During my senior year at Santa Barbara High in 1955, Coach Schutte set up a match with our high school golf team and the Stanford freshman team on their course in Palo Alto, and we damn near beat them. I shot a 36 on the front nine even though it was my first time on the course. My back nine wasn't so great—I shot 77 or 78 for the round—but Bud Finger, the Stanford coach, decided I had potential. Shortly afterward, I got my acceptance letter.

Stanford was an eye-opener. It was full of smart people from across the country. I was competing with brilliant people from the best prep schools, and I continued struggling mightily with the challenges that came with my dyslexia.

My first quarter at Stanford, I almost crashed. I had all this amazing freedom. I was on the golf team. I had a '48 Plymouth. I had a fake ID, and I spent too much time using it at a place called Rossatti's in Portola Valley. I was embracing the college experience with a full hug. I assumed I could just breeze through my classes—study the night before, get by with smoke and mirrors, as I had in high school. Instead, I almost flunked out. They had a point system at Stanford to rank performance, and I was one point away from being sent home. If that had happened, I could have come back and tried again, but I would have had to stay out of school for a year. It wasn't an idle threat. I saw it happen to friends.

It was a huge wake-up call, and I quickly settled down and did what I had to do. "You're here to learn, not to play golf," my dad said when he saw my grades, and he told me to bring the grades up or he wasn't going to pay the $365 tuition any longer. I dropped out of golf to free up more time for studying. But it was still a struggle. I tried every trick I could think of. I had a roommate who took great notes in class, which I borrowed to study for exams; it ticked him off when

I got a better grade than he did! My own notes were practically inde-cipherable. There was nothing harder than keeping up with a lecture and taking good notes. If I worried about the notes, I'd miss hearing the lecture. If I listened carefully, the notes were a mess. It's hard enough just converting what I hear into words; then I have to write down the words, and that takes forever. A tape recorder would have helped, but people didn't have tape recorders back then. Besides, no one—least of all me—knew what my problem was.

On the other hand, because I felt so inferior, I may have overcom-pensated in a good way. I have always tried particularly hard to keep up, to tackle the things that were so hard for me but seemed so easy for everybody else. And that kind of approach is habit-forming—it sticks with you for life. The negative of having dyslexia in many ways turned into a positive. I believe I think more conceptually than others.

I think more conceptually than step-by-step. I get to the conclusion quicker. I don't get lost in details, and often get to the essence of something and see the bigger picture first, rather than focusing on the details.

And fortunately, I've gotten better at reading over time. Words that I once had to translate into sound, then into meaning, have now become automatically recognizable, and my speed has picked up. It has taken time, but I've gotten there.

The positive side of dyslexia, thinking differently, more conceptu-ally, helped me a lot in developing Schwab, where so much of what we were thinking about was creating a better end state for investors. Then we'd figure out how to make it happen. And I'm not the only person with dyslexia who struggled academically as a child but went on to succeed in business. John Chambers of Cisco; Craig McCaw, who pioneered wireless telephone services; John Reed of CitiBank; and Richard Branson of Virgin all had to face down their learning disability. The list goes on and on. It has to be more than just a coincidence.

FRESHMAN YEAR AT STANFORD I lived in the Soto dormitory in a double room: two beds, two desks, and two dressers. Sophomore year I moved into a fraternity house, Sigma Nu. Then in December of my senior year, 1958, I got married. Susan, also a Stanford student, was two years behind me, smart and Phi Beta Kappa; I was a struggling student who was barely getting by. I felt like I had a lot of work to do to pull myself up to her level. But I finally got my act together.

I had gotten good grades in economics the last two years, and my father-in-law, Ralph Cotter, introduced me to the dean of Stanford Business School, Ernie Arbuckle. Ralph and Ernie had been classmates and fraternity brothers in college. Fortunately, I had done well enough on my graduate admissions tests and I was convincing enough that I was willing to work really hard and that my grades were moving in the right direction, especially in economics. I told him, "I will do what it takes to succeed." And he believed me. Dean Arbuckle took a chance on me and I got accepted. Years later I was able to return the favor and gave the business school a new cafeteria in his name.

MY FIRST YEAR AT business school was unbelievably difficult, but I surprised myself. In one of my first classes I had to write a case study. Everybody got the same assignment. Some guys turned in 10 or 12 pages. Mine was two pages long. Two hard pages. About a week later, the professor left four or five papers on a table at the front of the classroom. He said they were the only ones that grasped the subject matter and analyzed it well. I went down to take a look and see what I could learn from them.

There were 200 people in the class and my paper was one of the five on the table. I was elated. I had sweated over that thing, but I really knew the case inside out. Getting that recognition gave me a huge sense of accomplishment. Nothing like that had ever happened to me before academically. I hadn't thought I was capable of that kind of work, and suddenly I realized that I was. I could see I had a knack for understanding what made businesses click.

The summer between my two years in business school I worked in the management training program at First Western Bank. It was my first experience with banking. Years later at Schwab we jokingly dubbed the banking business model the "3-6-3" approach. Bankers pay you 3% on your savings, lend it back to you at 6%, and are on the golf course by 3:00.

Carrie, our first child, was born in January 1960, during my last year at Stanford. I was up all night with Susan at the hospital, but as soon as I knew that my wife and newborn daughter were fine, I had to leave for school. I had three midterms that day. I got an "A" in the first two, statistics and mathematics, and an "F" in the third, employer relations, otherwise known as human resources. Already it was obvious that I had no talent for many tasks associated with running a business. If I was going to run an actual business myself, clearly I needed lots of help.

5

A PIECE OF THE ACTION

During my second year in business school, I needed work to cover our expenses. I happened upon an ad on the business school bulletin board that led me to a part-time job with a financial advisory firm in Menlo Park, not far from Stanford University, Foster Investment Services. I worked evenings and weekends while I was still in school, then joined the firm full-time after I graduated in June. Laverne Foster sold independent investment advice—we had a newsletter—and we managed money. I got paid $625 a month, plus half of an 8% commission if I helped bring in a new client willing to invest at least $25,000. Mainly, though, my job was analyzing companies and writing up reports for the newsletter. Foster was a brilliant guy in many ways, and intriguing to someone just getting started in the financial business. He had been an engineer at Ampex, and he had a great way of looking at growth companies. I learned a lot about how to analyze them and their potential. He was a colorful character as well. He drove me once in his '60s Jaguar coupe to San Francisco for a business lunch and then back to Menlo Park to finish the workday. At 24, I was pretty impressed with the car, the lunch, the whole adventure. Maybe mostly the car.

THE WRITING AT FOSTER INVESTMENTS was hard for me. Getting that first sentence down was almost impossible. I'd sit there looking at a blank page, my mind racing. Often I had a pretty good idea of where I wanted to end up but no idea how to get there, no notion of where to begin. But I learned a trick. I could dictate just fine—in other words, just say out loud what I was thinking—and I had a secretary who could take dictation. So I used her, and that helped me a lot. I'd talk, she'd put my thoughts down on paper, then I could go back and edit it.

We charged a lot for our services: 8% up front, 2% every year, plus normal brokerage commissions whenever we made a trade in a client's account. What you hoped for as a client was that we'd find enough gems to justify our fee. We were growth investors. Our targets were companies growing at least 30% a year, on the premise that 30% annual growth over 10 years, compounded, would deliver you over 10 times your original investment. That stuck with me, and I've always wanted my company to be a growth company as well. As it turns out, The Charles Schwab Corporation has been a great growth investment for its original stockholders. Since going public in 1987, with dividends reinvested we've had about a 19% average annual growth rate for our stock, twice the rate of growth for the S&P 500. As of today, original investors in Schwab who have hung on to their stock and reinvested their dividends have seen their original investment grow hundreds of times larger over our 31-year history as a publicly traded company, some 21,000%. I don't recommend investors put all their eggs in one basket—and there were years where our stock price suffered—but I regularly get letters from investors thanking us for the nest eggs they built with Schwab stock.

BECAUSE WE WERE INVESTED primarily in smaller growth companies, when the crash of 1962 came our clients took a huge hit. Everybody's portfolio went down 30%, 40%, including my personal account. We had a lot of unhappy customers. Among them, my own father. He had invested $25,000 and, like everybody else, he lost about 30%. We might have made it back for him one day, but he never gave us a chance; he closed his account. We never spoke of it directly, but I felt terrible.

I learned a valuable lesson about investing that I had known, but never really *known*.

With the stock market, there are no guarantees. You can guarantee service, costs, quality, and certainly integrity. But you can't guarantee performance. Risk is just part of the deal.

With investing, there are no guarantees, and the higher your aspiration for performance is, the higher the risk. Sometimes it takes a hands-on experience to make the abstract real.

Laverne Foster helped drive that lesson home—by firing me. With the market down, I was feeling bad that clients had paid us for our advice and now they were losing money. "We should refund our clients' fees," I said to him after a particularly tough stretch. "We should what?" he asked. I started to explain and when he could see I was serious, he barked at me, "Leave, you're fired." Fortunately, he took me back. But lesson learned.

That was my first experience with an investment bubble. I've seen several bubbles since: the dot-com bubble; the color television bubble; the photocopier bubble. My first, during that '62 crash, was known as the bowling bubble. In 1961 it was supposedly a well-known fact, heavily promoted by Wall Street, that soon every American would be spending an average of two hours a week bowling. So the bowling company stocks went bananas. As did the uniform companies, the bowling shoe companies, the beer companies, the chalk companies—all of them went up like crazy. Then they all crashed, big-time. In retrospect, the idea that everybody would take to bowling sounds ridiculous, but that's what the analysts claimed and the brokers were passing along. You take a claim like that and multiply it by the population of the United States and you come up with intoxicating numbers. The false dreams that Wall Street pumped out! The unrealistic expectations!

In my job, I had a lot of contact with Wall Street brokers and analysts. They'd call and regale me with stories about whatever stocks they were pushing that day. The stories were all basically the same. Revenues were rising, profits were growing, and, invariably, said in hushed tones, something was about to occur that made it imperative that I buy the stock today. Because I was conscientious, and it was hard for me to keep track of things, I kept a book on those calls. I listened carefully and took notes as best I could. And I studied the written materials they sent me. Afterward, I reexamined the claims to see how well they were holding up. More often than not—*much more often*—the claims proved false, or at least severely overstated.

At times I wondered how I could ever make a living in financial services. Here I was, an ambitious young guy, passionate about investing; I loved researching stocks and discovering winners ahead of everyone else. I believed in the power of equities to build wealth. But I was a terrible storyteller and an awful salesman. I knew I couldn't lie convincingly. Maybe it was my Catholic upbringing, or the nuns who taught me so well at Holy Rosary Academy, or growing up with a dad who drew strict lines on right and wrong. Or maybe it's my dyslexia. But I knew I'd have a hard time keeping my story straight if the story wasn't simple and true. I felt I had no choice but to speak from the heart. And that was no way to get ahead in an industry where you had to be good at storytelling.

So that first investing job was an eye-opener. I learned about risk;

about volatility; about markets, and how they can be influenced and manipulated. I learned about speculation and greed and fear. I learned about the stories they tell on Wall Street; the better the stories, the more stocks they'd sell. The riskier the product, the more they'd get paid. I found out who was too often the winner in the broker-client relationship—and it wasn't the client. I tested every part of the fire to see how hot it was, and I got all my fingers burned. And still I was not dissuaded. I loved what growing businesses offered. Through investing, you own a piece of that . . . *a piece of the action*. I hadn't exactly found my place in the finance world yet, but I knew I had discovered the work I was meant to do.

I HAD LEARNED A ton working for Foster and developed a passion for finding growth stocks. But I think I knew instinctively that real success meant owning the work I did, not just getting paid for it. Foster's Jaguar was a daily reminder of that.

I wanted to be out on my own, building something that was mine. This was the early 1960s. Most young men my age who were entering the workforce still believed that the surest path to success in life was latching on to a reputable firm and working their way up through the ranks. They expected to stay with one company their whole careers. With my interest in finance, I suppose I might have gone to work for Bank of America, or moved back east and found a job on Wall Street. On the other hand, that assumes that Bank of America or a company like Merrill Lynch would have wanted me. And I'm not sure that's true. Yes, I had two degrees from Stanford. But I was not a star. And there was that selling thing I wasn't good at. Lucky for me, I never wanted to be a cog in somebody else's organizational wheel. I had worked at a bank one summer while I was still in school and had met people who had worked there for 20 or 30 years, and I knew I wanted no part of that life. Insurance, same thing—not what I was after. The closest I came to anything like that was when I briefly considered becoming a CPA. I had the right academic background, and I even interviewed at a couple of firms. But I figured if I went that route, I'd be working for at least two years as a young accountant before I could take the CPA exam. Years would pass before becoming a partner. At that point in my life, that just seemed like a terrible waste of a life. Frankly, I couldn't afford to wait around for decades for a shot at a decent salary. My second daughter, Virginia, was born in 1962. My son, Sandy, was born in 1964. I needed to make something happen, fast. And I knew that my best shot at accumulating wealth—the kind of wealth that would ensure my independence—lay with starting my own company. Experiencing how powerful and motivating that sense of ownership is, I've always encouraged and helped my employees over the years to be owners in our company as well.

IN NOVEMBER 1962, John Morse and I left Foster Investment Services and started our own company. Morse was another young analyst working with Foster and he, too, was anxious to break out on his own. We convinced a guy named Desmond Mitchell to put up most of the money to start *Investment Indicators*, an investing newsletter to be owned by the three of us. Mitchell had made a lot of money in the mutual fund business in Canada. He was originally going to invest in Foster's company, but decided to back us instead. He liked our energy. Morse and I each owned 20%. Mitchell owned the other 60%. So here I was in my mid-20s, working for myself, launched on my entrepreneurial career.

We set up shop—Mitchell, Morse & Schwab—on the second floor of a walk-up in San Rafael at 1010 B Street. When we started, we weren't managing money. Instead, we published the biweekly newsletter, *Investment Indicators*, and let our clients choose the investments themselves. We offered a big-picture overview of the economy—"designed to assist investors in timing the stock market cycle" is how I described it to subscribers—as well as covering "a selection of growth stocks, with recommendations when and why to take action in these securities." We had several model portfolios—one for growth investors, one for conservative investors, one for traders, and so on. In the beginning we charged $60 for an annual subscription. Later we raised the price to $72; at the peak we had about 3,000 subscribers. We laid out our thoughts in a booklet called *Investment Insights.*

If you were a client of ours, and you wanted to actually buy or sell a stock, you had to go elsewhere. We were not a brokerage firm. We were proud of our research, we valued its independence, and we were bent on avoiding all conflicts of interest. The last thing we wanted was a traditional sales force out there telling stories and calling in to question our independence.

When I look back at that first issue of *Investment Indicators*—published in March 1963—two things stand out. One, the type of clients I was after, even then, were smart, curious, independent investors, people capable of making their own decisions. That's exactly the kind of investor who would later open accounts at Charles Schwab. And two, I see more evidence of my early interest in growth companies. While I was at Foster, we made a lot of money for our clients by investing in growth companies. Later, when the market crashed, we lost a lot of money for those same clients. But even after that painful, firsthand experience, I didn't lose faith. "We still hold to the fundamental belief (a fact of history) that the companies with expanding earnings will be the growth stocks and the more profitable investments over the long term," I wrote in our first issue. I've always believed in growth, both as an investor and as an entrepreneur. If I have to, I'll choose top-line growth over earnings. A colleague once asked me if I'd rather have a fast-growing company with modest earnings or a slow-growing company with higher earnings. I didn't hesitate: I'd much rather see fast growth. In my experience, earnings follow growth, and stock prices follow earnings. My philosophy is that with growth, everyone wins: clients get better service; investors get a better return; employees get jobs and rising pay; the community gets support; and, of course, the government gets taxes. As far as I'm concerned, growth is the key to creating wealth.

The Simple Truths I've Learned About Investing

Nobody can predict the movement of the stock market in the short term, but you can live with the short-term uncertainty if you believe, as I do, that:

- Companies are built to grow (that is management's mandate: perform or get replaced).
- The US and world economies will continue to grow . . . indefinitely, with hiccups along the way.
- The most important factors to put in your favor are diversification, time, and low costs.
  - Diversification lessens the risk that any one investment or asset class will harm you while capturing some of the growth of winning investments;
  - Time captures the economy's tendency to grow and helps you get past the downturns and recessions that occur regularly over time;
  - Low investment costs mean more of your money is working for you.
- Investing doesn't have to be complicated; index investing is among the simplest ways to invest, and today there are also low-cost managed accounts that take care of all the investment decisions for you.

During those early years, I really developed my skill at analyzing companies. I made a few picks that paid off spectacularly, and those made a big impression on me. One in particular I'll never forget.

Right after the Cuban missile crisis, stocks rallied, and I invested in a pharmaceutical company called Forest Laboratories; they're still around. Forest had just developed a new technology that allowed pills to enter the bloodstream gradually over many hours, in a "sustained release," as it was called. It was a huge advance, with applications for all kinds of diseases and medications. I invested about $5,000—a lot of money for me in 1962—and the stock went up 500% or 600% in a matter of months. It was an unbelievable home run. That's when I began to understand just how powerful the emotional factor can be when you're investing in the stock market.

Even when I wasn't hitting home runs, I found the work endlessly fascinating. I was beginning to get a feel for how to make money in business, how to add value to an enterprise, how to create market value. And I was learning that I had an ability to focus intensely, to put all my energy into my work. The downside was that I probably had an unbalanced life. I'd work all day, starting when the market opened at 6:30 a.m. on the East Coast, go home for dinner, then go back to work. We had a little house in Los Altos Hills, south of San Francisco. I converted the garage into an office. I'd head out there almost every evening, right after dinner, and often I'd be at my desk until midnight.

After a while, Morse went back to school and I bought his stake in the company for peanuts. Then Mitchell, who still owned 60%, began losing interest in the company. We clashed, as partners often do. We had different goals. He was in his late 40s and had already sold his first company, so he was more in the enjoyment stage of life. He had bought a nice ranch up in Sonoma and was raising horses. He loved to go to the track at Bay Meadows, and he wanted to use the profits from the company to buy more horses. I, on the other hand, wanted to plow the profits back into the business and keep it growing. Finally, in 1968, I told him, "Mitch, I want to buy enough of your stock to have a controlling interest. I want to grow this company." And he agreed to sell. He got a nice premium for it, but I didn't care. I finally had control of the company.

The elation switched pretty quickly to anxiety when the market turned sour; I had a very tough time for years. In retrospect, it's a wonder I stayed in business. The period from the late 1960s through the 1970s and on into the early 1980s was a long, hard slog for stock market investors. If you look at a chart of the Dow Jones Industrial Average over that span, you'll see that it reached 1,000 for the first time during its midsession on January 18, 1966, but then stumbled immediately. For nearly 17 years the Dow failed again and again to regain its footing, returning occasionally to the 1,000 mark but always falling below again. Not until December 1982 did the Dow finally leap past 1,000 for good. By then many small investors were so turned off by stocks that they missed the start of what turned out to be one of the great bull markets of the twentieth century.

6

—

ENTER UNCLE BILL

A pall had settled over the whole industry. That was the backdrop to my early years as a financial services entrepreneur. Plus I had serious debt problems. I had borrowed $100,000 from Crocker Bank to pay Mitchell; soon after the deal closed, the market slumped, the value of our company declined, and our income dried up. It took me years to pay off that loan. That's probably the reason I've been so wary of debt and leverage ever since. We face enough risk and uncertainty every day in our business, not just normal operating risk, like any other company, but also stock market risk. To compound that double uncertainty with a mountain of debt strikes me as unwise. Plus I spent too many years as a young man having to scratch and claw for money. If that means we keep more cash around than some analysts think is appropriate for maximizing shareholder value, so be it. But I was a long, long way from having too much cash around during those early years. I was carrying a mountain of debt, the stock market was flat or declining, and revenues were down.

Enter Uncle Bill.

Uncle Bill was William Schwab, my dad's youngest brother. After retiring from a stint in the navy, he built a successful wood products business in California, Lumber & Box Company, starting first in Corona in Ventura County and then moving up north to Red Bluff after a fire destroyed his operation in Corona. Originally, he made wooden boxes for the fruit growers in Southern California. Later, among other things, he made wooden crates in Texas for the military during the Vietnam War. I was his brother's oldest son. He had two daughters, and in many ways, I was like a son to him. For my tenth birthday, he gave me his navy hat. Of my dad's family, Uncle Bill was the businessman, and I watched and learned how he worked. In the late 1960s, for example, he wanted to buy some timberland in Northern California. I helped him find the funding. It is where I first met George Roberts, who would go on to found what became KKR: Kolberg Kravis Roberts & Co. At the time he was at Bear Stearns, but George and Bear Stearns did not end up doing the funding for Uncle Bill's venture. Prudential Insurance Company was interested in timber and they provided the long-term financing. But George and I became great friends over the years, and he played a pivotal role in Schwab's history some years later.

Uncle Bill was tough, even cantankerous, but we got along famously. He loved to gamble. Flying back from various meetings in the West, he'd often stop at Reno for a couple of hours at the casinos. He was a regular, with a line of credit that gave him room to lose more than $20,000, a pretty significant line of credit at the time.

With my business in dire need of an infusion of cash, I sat down with him and said, "Bill, I need $100,000 to resolve some debt and invest in this business to make it grow." And he said, "Fine." With Mitchell out of the picture, I found some new partners in April 1971, and with Uncle Bill's investment, I reorganized the business as First Commander, a subsidiary of his company Commander Industries. We joined the Philadelphia Stock Exchange and rented an office on the 24th floor of 120 Montgomery Street, my first office in San Francisco.

I was going through a lot of turmoil at the time, both professionally and in my personal life. Susan and I had been separated for a couple of years, and then divorced in early 1972, after 13 years of marriage. Maybe it's possible to be as focused as I was on building a business while still preserving a happy marriage and family life, but I know from my own experience that it is very hard to do. And especially during a particularly tough time in the investment business, as the market had been in a slump since 1966. I realize now that I was not what anyone today would describe as a great father. I missed a lot of family dinners, I wasn't helping with homework, I wasn't on the sidelines at my kids' sporting events. (Nor had my own father been, I should add, when I was growing up. I don't remember him ever taking me to a ball game, or showing up to watch me play. It's no excuse, but I probably repeated what I had learned growing up. It was a different time in our history, when men were expected first and foremost to be providers.)

I'm not proud of how I failed in that regard. But at the time, I really felt I had no choice. As a father, husband, and sole breadwinner, I felt tremendous pressure to provide for my family. I believed it was my most important role, and I took it seriously. It's what my dad had taught me. But I also think that Susan and I got married too young. I was 21, she was 19. We were still kids. But that's how it was for everybody in those days. We didn't wait around to get married and have kids. But as we grew older and matured, and muddled through the social upheaval of the '60s, we grew further and further apart. But more than anything, I think our marriage was a victim of my entrepreneurial drive and ambition. I loved working, and I'm sure I pushed everything else in my life to the back burner. Easy to see in hindsight, but not as clear to me at the time.

No question, if I wasn't working so hard all the time, and worrying so much about the future, I would have had more time and energy for my family. But I was struggling. I began to question whether I was really cut out after all to run my own business. Was I doing the right thing? As late as the early 1970s, I thought seriously about giving up and trying to find a job. By then I had the skills and the experience to work as a securities analyst, and probably for pretty good pay. But there weren't many jobs like that on the West Coast. I would have had to move to New York, and that just wasn't in the cards, with my kids living with Susan in California. I thought for a time about becoming a lawyer and went so far as to enroll in San Francisco Law School. My father had been a lawyer; he often told me a law degree was useful no matter what I decided to do in life. I finally decided to give it a try. I bought all the books and started attending class in the evenings in Haight Ashbury. That lasted one week, maybe two. I was a slow reader, for one thing. And I had no passion for the law. I couldn't imagine growing old in an office in a tall building somewhere, grinding out paper. I finally decided if I ever needed a good lawyer, it was best to hire one.

BY NOW I WAS in my mid-30s. I was still floundering and had no assets to speak of. All I had were debts. After my divorce, I had moved from Marin's Lucas Valley to the city, where I rented a one-bedroom apartment at a place called the Golden Gateway, not far from the new Transamerica Tower. It was on the top floor, not very expensive. I liked the building because it had a tennis court. At the time I was still commuting to the old First Commander office in San Rafael, but on nights and weekends I hung out a lot in the city with one of my oldest friends from high school, Hugo Quackenbush. Hugo had attended UC Berkeley while I was at Stanford. Afterward, he went to work for his father-in-law's firm in Los Angeles, which later merged with Scudder, Stevens & Clark, the investment management firm. But he had quit recently and returned to the Bay Area to start his own money management firm. I gave him a desk in my office. He had a house on Larkin Street, one of those classic Victorian town houses, and I was over there all the time. It was Hugo's girlfriend who introduced me to Helen O'Neill, who lived across the street.

Helen was a few years younger than I was and a widow; her husband had died in a plane crash. We met on a blind date and were married in 1972. Helen was a lot smarter than me. (Which by the way is my advice to my sons: marry someone who's smarter than you!) Her mother had died when she was young, but her father was still alive. Outgoing and ambitious, he was a great storyteller, as well as a savvy businessman—all qualities I admired. I really enjoyed being around him.

Helen and I got married just in time for the next bear market. The recession hit its depths in 1973 and 1974. Unfortunately, my investment company, First Commander, kept operating, but lost its focus.

I had plenty of friends in the brokerage industry who lost their jobs. It was a pretty desperate time for everybody, all the more so because we had all experienced some success in the not-too-distant past. At least I didn't feel like an outcast for not succeeding. Everybody was struggling.

It's hard to sell investment advice when you open up the newspaper every day and read about how the market went down again.

We were still publishing an investment newsletter and now had a mutual fund and a little venture capital arm, which led us in all kinds of crazy directions. I found myself grasping at straws. I did one underwriting for an air pollution control business. I flew to Cairo to investigate the possibility of building a hotel on an island in the middle of the Nile. Nothing ever came of that. I wish I could say the same about my brief foray into the music business. A promoter approached me with what sounded like a great idea for a big music show at the Cow Palace—Music Expo '72, something like that, a three-day musical extravaganza. We brought in busloads of schoolkids on Friday to hear the Roger Wagner Chorale. Saturday was rock-and-roll day, Sunday was country and western. We had all these acts, all kinds of musical and dance performances—Chuck Berry, Bo Diddley—plus a trade show where people could buy musical instruments. Sort of like the boat show they had every year in San Francisco. I have a weakness for big ideas and outlandish schemes, and this one won me over. I liked it so much I personally signed on as a limited partner, in addition to the firm's involvement as general partner. Well, it was a flop, an utter flop. I lost about $70,000.

With First Commander struggling, Uncle Bill had grown tired of his unsuccessful investment and told me he wanted out. He was preparing to sell his wood products business to a large lumber company and planned to start a money market fund, a new product that had just come onto the financial services scene as a way to earn a bit more on savings than you could get at the local bank. Money markets were investments, rather than federally insured bank accounts. They were designed to keep a stable value of $1.00 per share and throw off interest just like a bank savings account, but at a slightly higher rate. They offered a little more risk, a little more reward. Uncle Bill didn't want my small ragtag, relatively unsuccessful financial services subsidiary clouding up the deal. So he sold his entire interest in the company back to us in the form of 10-year notes, which my partners and I divvied up, with me responsible for the largest chunk. Dave Baldwin, Jack Hossfeld, Marge Wagner, and Joe Bowler, shareholders and my partners at the time, carved up the remainder. Later that year I bought them out as well. I couldn't afford to keep them as employees. Rather than giving them cash, which we didn't have, I agreed to assume all responsibility for the money we still owed Uncle Bill's company, about $100,000. The note, and the company, was now mine.

So now I was on my own, and carrying a good bit of debt. Since it was just me (and a handful of employees), in the spring of 1973 I reincorporated as Charles Schwab & Company, Incorporated. (The

California Department of Corporations objected to my using just my last name, because of the similarity to "Schwab's Pharmacy," the famous drugstore and soda fountain on Sunset Boulevard where aspiring stars went to be discovered.)

Little did I know that a revolution in the way people invested was about to take place, and Charles Schwab & Company would help lead the way.

7

THE TRANSACTION SPECIALIST

The reforms that took effect May 1, 1975, changed so much about how the brokerage business operates—and how America invests. It was a watershed day in Wall Street history, but the pressure to bust the Wall Street cartel had been building for a long time. Big institutional investors in particular, including the newly emerging powerhouse mutual funds, were fed up with having to pay high fixed commissions to execute routine trades. For years they had been looking for ways to jigger the system to their advantage.

By the time May Day rolled around, the SEC had been experimenting with negotiated commissions for more than a year. The prospect of deregulation stirred up a lot of excitement and concern on Wall Street. Many brokers were afraid. They thought it would so alter the economics of trading stocks that the traditional firms would be driven out of business. Those fears proved unfounded, although the economic pressure on many old-line firms was indeed severe, and not all of them survived. But that was none of my concern. I was never worried about preserving the status quo because I had no stake in it. To me, the prospect of change was frankly thrilling. Looking at what was happening, thinking about the implications, I saw an opportunity to relaunch Charles Schwab & Company as a new kind of brokerage firm, for a new breed of investor. And, of course, I desperately needed a new opportunity. If necessity is the mother of invention, there was a lot of necessity in my life.

Hugo Quackenbush knew about my plans. Because he shared office space with me, we often had lunch together at Sam's Grill over on Bush Street. Sam's is as old-school as it gets in San Francisco, and there had to have been thousands of new ideas cooked up there over lunch in the years before we came along. Hugo and I talked about the potential that could be unleashed under deregulation, and he encouraged me to refocus my business in that direction. We had seen the changes that occurred in other businesses when they were deregulated: the old blue laws in California that didn't allow stores to open on Sundays were scrapped and suddenly businesses could stay open seven days a week if they wanted to, or all night. New businesses were popping up all over. What would happen in finance? Hugo became so convinced of the opportunity that he gave up his fledgling investment management practice and joined me.

I was talking to a lot of other people as well. George Roberts and I had a regular Saturday morning tennis date at his house in Atherton. He was every bit as restless as I was, looking to make something big. While I was exploring the possibilities of a discount brokerage, he was preparing to leave Bear Stearns to start Kohlberg Kravis Roberts & Co., the leveraged buyout firm that has had a hand in so many big deals worth billions of dollars. After we'd finish our match, we'd sit around discussing the merits of each other's plans. George wasn't exactly skeptical of my idea, but he did have a lot of questions. He kept asking, "How do you ever create equity value out of that?" It was a good question, and it presaged all kinds of problems I had raising money in the years to come. Most brokerage firms in those days were partnerships; the only exceptions I knew of were Donaldson, Lufkin & Jenrette, which went public in 1969, and Merrill Lynch, in 1971. I had no immediate plans to take my company public, but as George anticipated, without a clear path to an IPO and few precedents for doing so, it was very hard to value such an enterprise. Still, George has always said that he would have liked to invest in my business, as I would have liked to invest in his. Unfortunately, neither of us had any extra money.

So how would my firm differ from the kinds of firms that had ruled Wall Street for so many years? For one thing, I meant to serve an entirely new client base, composed of what we now call independent investors: people who were passionate about the market; who wanted to control their own financial destiny; who did their own research and picked their own stocks; and who didn't need or want a broker's advice. In the early 1970s, I'm guessing that market was less than 10% of the investing public, although the truth is, I didn't really know. The only market research I was aware of at the time was an SRI report that projected an eventual 15% market share. Mostly, I was going on instinct.

However, I knew without any doubt—in my head and in my gut—that the numbers of such people were growing. Why? Because I was one of them. I loved to study stock charts. I loved researching companies. I loved making my own decisions. And I knew plenty of people who were like me; some of them had been subscribing to my newsletter for years. We didn't want advice from brokers, because we knew that advice was tainted. How could a broker truly have my best interests at heart when his livelihood depended on generating commissions? And we resented paying for services we had no use for.

Thirty years ago there was no CNBC, no Financial News Network, no Bloomberg, and no investing websites. Newspapers hadn't yet started covering the financial markets the way they covered sports. If you were an independent investor like I was, you read the *Wall Street Journal*, and maybe a newsletter or two. You subscribed to *Value Line*—I think it cost $60 a year—or else you read it for free at the local public library. Real-time market data of the kind we're inundated with these days simply wasn't available. As a matter of fact, after we launched the new Schwab and started opening branches with ticker tapes on display, we found there were lots of people who liked to come by our offices for no other reason than to keep an eye on the market.

Beyond the dearth of information, there was simply less personal wealth floating around in the US economy at that time than there is today. There was certainly a lot less discretionary wealth—the kind of money folks might feel comfortable investing. Few saw the need to invest in stocks. Older Americans who had lived through the Depression, like my parents, were afraid of the stock market; most preferred to keep their money in the bank. For the more adventurous, there were money market funds—still a novelty—offering safe returns in line with the high inflation of the era. Mutual funds had just begun and not yet started their meteoric growth. Younger Americans, meanwhile, weren't worrying about retirement the way we do now. A lot of them still had good old-fashioned pensions that guaranteed an income for life. And, of course, we all knew beyond a shadow of a doubt that when the time came, Social Security would take care of us. There just was not anything like the national conversation taking place these days around investing and financial planning. Most Americans weren't even thinking about that. Social Security was based on a median life expectancy of 65. Half the population was expected to die before age 65. Today, the median life expectancy is 80 years.

Those who did buy stocks or mutual funds were at the mercy of the stockbrokers, many of whom were out there pitching stories and selling their wares, same as always. As I saw it, it was a sales game, no different than selling insurance or flame-retardant insulation. Pitch a good story (the more exuberant, the better), earn a fat commission. Never a word about portfolio management, diversification or asset allocation, or addressing the total needs of the client. You can't even call that investing; it was speculating, hardly much different from playing the ponies or going to Las Vegas or playing the lottery. Now, admittedly, that's an oversimplification. Like any endeavor, there was a range of brokers—from good to bad. It's just that the compensation structure itself, driven by commissions, worked against the customer's interests.

On the other hand, if you take the brokers out of the equation—as I was proposing to do—how then do you sell stocks? Well, you don't *sell*. You market. I was never any good at selling anyway, but if I'd learned anything from all those years of publishing newsletters, it was how to do direct marketing. My big *aha!* was when I realized I didn't have to sell at all. All I had to do was market the discount brokerage service and then provide the best possible customer service. That simple realization was behind a thousand decisions I made in the years to come—decisions that helped me break out of the pack of newly established discount brokers, from putting my picture in newspaper ads to building a network of brick-and-mortar branches to opening call centers and taking orders toll-free, 24 hours a day. I knew that if I was going to succeed, it would be as a marketer, not a salesman. And I felt pretty sure I could pull that off, even if it had never been done that way before.

I think the coming changes were pretty clear to quite a few people at the time. But recognizing a business opportunity is only one part of succeeding as an entrepreneur. The key is acting on your business insight and following through. How many times have you slapped yourself on the forehead and asked, "Why didn't I think of that?" Successful entrepreneurs are idea people, to be sure, but more than that they are men and women who feel compelled to act. Otherwise, it's all talk. There were a few of us competing pretty aggressively: Quick & Reilly, Muriel Siebert, and Joe Ricketts, who eventually created Ameritrade. Even Carl Icahn was in the game. Friends today, I think Joe Ricketts and I agree that our fierce competitiveness 30 years ago is proof that market competition can be a source of miraculous innovation.

In April of '74, I re-formed Schwab as a "transaction specialist." The term "discount broker" came later and was largely an invention of the press. I'm not sure I really like the discount moniker—to me, it suggests a stripped-down operation, when in fact what I had in mind was a whole new business model. But it wasn't my call; the name stuck and I didn't fight it.

Helen's father, who was a successful oil and gas man in Texas, invested $25,000, along with Uncle Bill and a few others. I promised to pay half back in cash in two years, with half converted to shares in my company. I think one of the toughest things entrepreneurs have to do is go to friends and family, hat in hand, asking for money. It takes a lot of gumption. But, boy, are you ever motivated then to succeed. You'll work your butt off, if only to not let them down.

IN PREPARATION FOR May Day, 1975, I got out of all the other businesses I was in. No more investment banking; I saw the common practice of mixing investment banking with selling stocks to the public as the source of so many conflicts of interest in the industry, and I wanted no part of that. No more research. No more mutual funds or hedge funds. And no more newsletters. I sold everything I could, as fast as I could. I wanted to make this new venture extremely clean and streamlined. I wanted to cut out all the frivolous costs so that I could make the price to the investor substantially lower than had ever been seen before—as much as 75% lower than traditional firms were charging. It would be a fact that practically jumped off the page at independent investors when we began advertising months later. I wanted to eliminate anything that might distract me from what I saw as a major step forward in deregulation, a significant change in the markets, and a real opportunity for me. This was the brass ring, and I wasn't going to miss it.

PART II

Riding a Rocket

Before starting Schwab, I had studied businesses as an analyst. I knew the merits of long-term investing. It was all about growth.

Companies are built to grow. But it doesn't come easily. Some succeed, many fail. I believe it is incumbent on every leader of a company that the number one thing on their mind is growth. You don't prosper without it. You've got to inspire your organization to grow like a weed. And each year it has to be better than the last year by 10% to 15% minimum. It's not easy. Relax? You can't relax! Satisfied? You can never be satisfied!

Growth and opportunity are two sides of the same coin. If you are growing, there's a chance to grab new opportunities. If you're not always thinking about the next opportunity, the next great thing, your growth will stall, or worse, you'll be a sitting duck and someone will jump ahead of you with a better idea.

And opportunity is always shared: it provides the chance for employees to come up with new ideas and new products and services for your customers. It gives them the chance to do new and bigger things. It's personally fulfilling and leads to personal growth. Opportunity taps the best in us all.

A focus on growth doesn't mean being the most profitable company in your industry. I didn't want to be the most profitable. I wanted to be the one that was always thinking about growth and how we could find the resources to be innovative. I always believed that profits were something that come naturally at the end of the line, if you got the first part right—finding new ways to help the customer succeed.

8

A VAGUELY DISREPUTABLE THREAT

"Good morning, you've reached Charles Schwab."

"This is account number 12105002. Buy 2,000 shares of Motors, limit $57." *Click.*

That's it. Two thousand shares of General Motors at a price no higher than $57/share. Done. Most of our customers 30 years ago didn't even bother telling us their names. It was a radically new way of trading stocks, light-years removed from the old model. Charles Merrill, founder of Merrill Lynch, used to say, "Stocks aren't bought, they're sold." We came at it from exactly the opposite direction. In our case, the customer initiated the transaction, not the broker. We weren't out there buying lunches for clients or taking them golfing. We weren't calling anybody up with hot tips. In fact, I'd fire people if they gave stock advice. Nothing happened unless the customer asked first. Our only role was to carry out the customer's wishes. Period. I had put a couple of ads out to publicize ourselves, and people started coming in. I had a sense that people really liked what we were doing. It started slow, 20 or 30 trades a day, and then we got to 100, and on it went.

I could tell from day one that I was looking at a great business opportunity. That had become even more apparent that spring day when I opened the paper to see Merrill Lynch's fateful decision on pricing. But if someone had told me then that I'd be in the same business 40 years later, I would have been skeptical. The notion that I was on my way to becoming chairman of a publicly traded Fortune 500 company, with over $10 billion in annual revenue, I would have dismissed as fantasy.

I never gave much thought in those days to the financial value of what I was building. In fact, I didn't know what my company was worth until years later, when I tried to sell it. I was too immersed in the day-to-day demands of the business to spend a lot of time worrying about exit strategies. I loved doing what I was doing. I was passionate about my work. But I wasn't getting rich. My salary was $2,000 per month to start; after a year or so, I bumped myself up to $3,000. I was also making alimony and child-support payments, so I was tight with the purse strings. What little money we were making (and for the first couple of years, we weren't making any money at all) I plowed right back into the business. I was just trying to survive, and I knew that to survive we had to keep growing.

We were making progress. I could see that our revenues were growing fast and our losses were shrinking. I had a pretty detailed break-even analysis that I was always revising—that's how I was able to get people to invest in the company, though for years I relied entirely on friends, family, employees, and even customers for funds. Venture capitalists and private equity investors wanted nothing to do with me or my business. But I never said to myself, *This could become really big.* It just sort of unfolded, step-by-step. Back in those early years, I woke up every day grateful—and maybe a little surprised— that we were still in business.

We started with offices on the 24th floor at 120 Montgomery, known as the Equitable Building. When we ran out of room, we moved the margin staff who calculated and monitored the loans we could make to clients against the collateral of their stock (that was two people) down to the basement until space opened up on the

18th floor. That's where I eventually moved my office, together with the rest of the administrative staff. We had a little foyer out front, a couple of chairs, and a counter behind which sat a clerk who greeted walk-ins and opened new accounts. Most of our transactions were handled over the phone. But if a customer wanted to make a trade in person, then I or somebody else who had a broker's license walked out front and wrote up the order. At times it seemed like people just wandered in off the street, recognizing our name downstairs and deciding to come on up to make a trade. On the opposite side of the elevators were the cashiering department (responsible for delivery of cash and securities to clients), the margin department, dividends and reorg (they handled payments from stocks or changes in securities after a merger or acquisition), corporate accounting, HR, and the mailroom, all of which began as one-person operations. Some of the desks were actually pieces of plywood resting on sawhorses. The moment you entered our office, you knew you were in a discount store. I was chef, server, busboy, and chief bottle washer, working behind the counter, stuffing envelopes, licking stamps. When things got busy, it was all hands on deck.

From the outset, Wall Street pegged us as vaguely disreputable, and a threat to its livelihood. Whenever we tried to rent space in a building that had a Wall Street firm as a major tenant, the firm complained and the landlord caved. We were outcasts in the industry, pariahs. At one point we wanted to become a member of the Pacific Stock Exchange, but in their minds our business model was *unethical*—it was designed to undercut the power of the exchanges and the rest of the system—and so our membership was temporarily blocked. We beat that eventually, but you get the idea.

Deborah Hoke Smith, one of our earliest employees, might never have come to work for us if her widowed mother in Oklahoma hadn't seen one of our newspaper ads and asked her daughter in San Francisco to please go check out this Charles Schwab place and make sure it was a legit business; it was, and her mom opened an account. And Deborah was impressed enough to join us as an employee. Deborah lived in Marin County, as did many people who worked in financial services in the city. She'd be standing with the crowd on weekday mornings in front of the Golden Gate Transit terminal, waiting for the early bus, and somebody would pull up in a Porsche or a BMW and say, "Does anybody want a ride to the Financial District?" It happened every day. It was a casual carpool system that got the driver a quicker and toll-free trip across the bridge. She would slide into the backseat with a couple of others and off they'd go. After a while you were supposed to say where you worked so the driver would know where to drop you off. Deborah was deliberately vague. She only offered the cross streets. You never knew how people were going to react when they found out you worked at Schwab.

All the brokers we started with had at one time worked for old-school firms like Merrill or Dean Witter. They came to us for many reasons. Maybe they didn't like the pressure of working for commissions; or they were idealists, fed up with the whole undertaking and relieved not to be part of it any longer; or they just needed a job. One person I hired was employed at the time stringing tennis rackets. John had been a very successful stockbroker deep into commissioned selling when he ran into a wall with a drinking problem. He had lost his job, his marriage, and his money as a result, but now had turned himself around. I could see he knew the industry inside and out and I hired him, eventually giving him the job to open our first Chicago office. He was a great success and a great tennis player, always good for a game of tennis after work when I visited Chicago.

The people who came to work for Schwab probably could have made more money working just about anyplace else. I only paid my brokers about $18,000 to $20,000 a year; and it was salary and bonus only, of course, no commission. In fact, it's a little misleading to think of them as *brokers,* with all that term connotes; essentially they were taking client orders.

The brokers sat around the stem of a T-shaped table, five or six on each side, and took phone orders all day. The phones started ringing even before the market opened in New York at 6:30 a.m. Pacific time, and they rang continuously until the market closed at 1:00 p.m. Afterward, there was always a huge backlog of paperwork to complete before everybody could go home. We usually ordered up sandwiches and drinks and worked straight through lunch and into the evening.

A conveyor belt ran up and down the center of the T. That's how the brokers passed orders (blue paper for buys, red for sales) to the traders, who sat at the head of the table. So here comes that order for 2,000 General Motors, up the conveyor belt to the trading desk. It gets a time stamp and the trader checks to see whether it's an over-the-counter stock or a listed stock. If the trader has any questions, he returns the order form via the conveyor belt to the broker, who may have to call the customer back to fill in the missing information. But once the trader knows he's got a clear order, he passes it through a hole in the wall to a guy sitting at a big gray metal teletype machine, who sends a string of coded messages to the exchange. In this example, that message was "B 2,000 GM @ 57." Somebody rips the incoming order off a machine on the floor of the exchange, writes an exchange ticket, and hands it to a runner, who heads for the GM specialist's booth and completes the transaction. Finally, a message comes back over the wire to a person in our office whose job it was to call the customer back and say, "On your order to buy 2,000 General Motors we bought 1,000 at $57, leaves 1. Right?" There was nothing automated or computerized about it. But it was cutting edge at the time.

Orders for unlisted stocks went to a different trader who had a special phone with direct-line buttons to market makers around the country. He would punch the keypad, pick up the receiver, and say, "I've got 500 XYZ to buy at 53." He had a Quotron machine that showed him what the current bid and ask prices were from each of the competing market makers in that security. He might make a deal on the spot or look for a better price somewhere else. We were always very aggressive about best execution—getting the best possible price for our clients. The whole way we operated was designed not just to take what the market was offering but also to manage the order as best we could. That was the value we added. Remember, we weren't offering advice. Just quick, clean, efficient, accurate execution under the best possible terms.

> **I designed Schwab from day one to be the kind of firm I myself would want to do business with. If we let our customers down, I knew exactly how they felt.**

Or that was the goal. Sometimes we fell short. Part of the problem lay with staffing shortfalls. That's the nature of the brokerage business, tied as it is to the fortunes of the market. Rich Arnold, an Australian I met in 1975, and who joined us full-time in 1978 (after a stint as Jimmy Cliff's road manager), used to draw a two-line chart to illustrate how hard it is to strike the right balance with staff in our industry. One line is more or less straight, rising all the time: that's our cost structure. The other line is rising, too, but it zigzags sharply through peaks and valleys: that's trading volume, which is volatile and unpredictable. Sometimes the trading volume line falls below the cost structure line and we lose money due to excess capacity. Other times, when the stock market is taking off, trading volume soars and everything goes to hell.

That can happen literally overnight. You simply cannot plan seamlessly for every blip in the market. The art lies in managing your cost structure in such a way that you keep pace with demand without getting too far ahead of yourself. But it is definitely an art, not a science, and there were times (especially in the early days) when we miscalculated.

But when you go from averaging 300 trades a day (as we did in early 1977) to 800 trades a day (where we were six months later), you're going to have problems, there's no way around it. We disappointed many customers and lost some. Probably the main reason we stayed in business long enough to get our act together is that no matter how many left by the back door, that many more were arriving through the front door. I'm not proud of that. It was no way to run a business, and ultimately unsustainable. But I don't want to kid anybody, either. We had a lot to learn on the way to becoming a company that could be proud of its customer service, which was the goal, and it took us a long time to get there.

We were a start-up, a fast-growing start-up, with all that implies: inadequate, inexperienced staff (who worked long hours, didn't get enough sleep, and ate a lot of bad food); untested systems; just frequent problems of all kinds. To which you can add in our case the additional burden of operating in a highly regulated industry. If you asked Guy Bryant, who was our compliance officer for about 20 years starting in 1977, he'd tell you that his job back then was basically managing disasters—one disaster after another. It fell to Guy to make sure we had enough capital in the firm to meet the complex ratio requirements of the SEC; more than once, that meant asking me to take out another mortgage on my house. And it was Guy who had to clean up the mess if, say, a customer stiffed us for $20,000 on an options trade. (That happened. The firm made good, we had no choice. Paying the bill probably wiped out our profit for the whole month.)

The stress at times was almost unbearable, and Guy bore a good deal of the brunt of it. He lived in Petaluma, about a one-hour commute from the city. Every day he'd get off the bus at Sansome Street and walk one block over to Montgomery. What I never knew until years later was that he rarely made it that block without ducking into an alley and vomiting. The mere thought of what lay in store for him when he arrived at the office was enough to make him sick. Why does someone like that keep coming to work every day? Good question. I know Guy had a strong sense of mission; we all did. We were jazzed, we believed in what we were doing, and we could see how much was riding on our collective efforts. I made a conscious effort to hire people I thought would thrive in that environment— people who shared my passion and were willing to do whatever had to be done.

Schwab was an exciting place to work, but it was also incredibly demanding. People were always quitting. The turnover in the trenches put a lot of pressure on those of us who were in it for the long haul; it was not good for our sanity. But it created huge opportunities for people with ambition and imagination who might not have had those same opportunities elsewhere. Holly Kane, for example, employee number 19, started working for us before she even graduated from high school, in 1975, and never left until retiring in 2018. She eventually rose to become senior vice president in charge of our Central California branch network. I think it's fair to say that we always had more women on staff than our competitors did, and not just in support positions, but in management and on the trading desk. (Most Wall Street firms in those days had professional staffs that were overwhelmingly if not exclusively male and white.) Today, I am so proud when I travel across the country to visit offices and see the diversity of our employee base. I wish I could say that I deliberately set out to create a diverse workforce. I know I'm proud that it developed that way. But really, we were just trying to stay on top of demand with the best people we could find. We needed to be fair and not discriminate against anyone.

God knows there was a lot to do. I had a pretty clear vision from the start of the company's developing needs and the capabilities required to meet those needs. I also knew what I could not do, and consequently, where I needed help. I think that may be one of my strongest assets as an entrepreneur—the fact that I know my limits. I'm sure it's related to my dyslexia—to recognizing from an early age that the world is full of people more capable than I am, in a thousand different ways. Some entrepreneurs never learn that simple lesson and pay for their stubbornness with slower growth and a lower ceiling.

One key set of responsibilities I never had much patience for was operations. That's where I was lucky to have Bill Pearson. At the time I met Bill he was a bit of a rebel, not yet settled in life. Bill was from Texas, with that Texas drawl. He had been working for a small brokerage in Dallas when he got divorced, grew his hair long, left town in a Volkswagen, drove all over Mexico and up the California coast, and landed in San Francisco (following a girlfriend, as I recall) shortly after May Day. I hired him initially as a contractor to clean up some of the problems in our back office. Once I saw what he could do, I offered him $1,500 a month plus stock in the firm to join us full-time. He needed the money, I desperately needed his operational skills. It was a perfect match.

We were always playing catch-up with our records—in part because of the antiquated systems that prevailed in the industry at the time, but also because we were growing so fast. After the markets closed, we'd spend the rest of the afternoon trying to make sense of the trades we'd executed that morning. Some days it got so bad that after a while we just stopped answering the phones. I asked Bill to dive in and systematize our back office. He was very good—he saved us many times. But the challenges were enormous.

Late one night, for example, after most of us had left, the phone rang. This was in the fall of 1975, early in the history of the firm. David Taylor, who was my number two at the time, picked up. The voice at the other end said, "I'm with the SEC's regional office in Los Angeles and I understand that you have some problems in your bookkeeping." David's response was, "By what authority are you asking these questions?" Wrong answer! "Have Mr. Schwab in my office at 8:00 Monday morning," the SEC fellow said, and he hung up.

David called me, I called Bill, and together Bill and I hightailed it down to L.A. Bill wasn't exactly surprised by that phone call. A couple of weeks before, he'd made an emergency decision to freeze the firm's omnibus account, where all our trades settled. He felt he had no choice but to start fresh with a new account with the understanding that over time the problems with the old account would work themselves out. It was an unorthodox solution, to say the least, but under the circumstances, it was the best solution Bill could come up with. We would have two accounts for a while. That's not good, but at least with one of them, we'd know what was going on. That meant seeding the new account with something like a million dollars from the old account. The SEC heard about what we had done and concluded we were in trouble.

When we got to L.A., I let Bill do most of the talking. Operations was his job. My job was marketing. I focused on bringing new customers in the door. Folks like Bill and Guy were always begging me to slow down, but I refused, and consequently I leaned heavily on other people to satisfy the SEC, satisfy the customers we already had, and generally hold things together. So I let Bill explain our situation to the SEC that day. He was able to persuade them that we weren't criminals, that we knew what we were doing, and that it would all work out.

Which it did, of course. Somehow, it always worked out. In the years to come we would tumble into and climb back out of many more precarious situations. But with each one, we got stronger, and smarter.

9

NO SALESPERSON WILL CALL

"Chuck, I just talked to the treasurer of ABC Company. They're planning on doing some really exciting things that no one else yet knows about. I met the president yesterday and he confirmed it all to me. This stock is going to the moon."

That's not too far off from things I heard at Foster Investment Services when I got calls from brokers with their hot tips. I had no patience for the yarns that salespeople spin, and that became a pillar of Schwab's when we launched. No selling stocks in the guise of giving advice. When it comes to telling tall tales aimed at garnering sales—as I know from hard personal experience—brokers are the best. I suffered my share of bubbles as a young investor. Too often I fell for the seductive stories constructed by analysts and embellished by brokers, only to experience firsthand the pain and disappointment of unhappy endings. I think we are all suckers who give in to our greed. Some guy walks into a room, says, "I've got something you won't believe, it's going to make you rich," and we'll sit there with our mouths open, hanging on every word.

This quirk of human nature is especially bad when it's someone's financial security at risk.

We didn't tell stories. We didn't have to. We weren't in the invest-

|||||||||||||||||||||||||||||||||||||||||||||||||||||||||||||||||||||||||||||||||||||||||||||||||||||||

It's very hard to be skeptical and smart when there's money involved. Everybody wants to believe. But that's just it. Selling that way exploits human nature by telling people what they want to hear.

|||||||||||||||||||||||||||||||||||||||||||||||||||||||||||||||||||||||||||||||||||||||||||||||||||||||

ment banking business. Not that there is anything wrong with investment bankers. They help companies raise capital, they're vital to the smooth functioning of the capitalist system. But when you combine investment banking with a brokerage arm—which had been the standard setup on Wall Street—you created a conflict of interest that no Chinese wall could resolve. Better to stay out of investment banking altogether. That way you never accumulate inventories of stocks and bonds from offerings that then have to be offloaded onto your retail clients. Our model was fundamentally different, and a better deal for the investing public, I'm convinced.

Moreover, our employees weren't compensated in a way that encouraged them to persuade clients to do more trading. A traditional broker is trying to take your capital and turn it into his income as fast as possible. When I started in the business, the goal for brokers was to capture between 3% and 4% of their client's wealth each year in commissions. Our reps, on the other hand, had but one incentive, and it was perfectly aligned with the client's. The more the client made and the happier they were with the service they got, the more our employees made, period. We paid a salary and a bonus for client satisfaction—that was it. We didn't pressure anybody to make trades. We didn't recommend a stock or mutual fund just to make a sale. We didn't seduce our clients with questionable claims. We didn't tell stories. We don't today.

Then again, as I discovered very early on, being the company that does not tell sales stories can be the starting point for a terrific marketing story, a way of thinking about who we are and the services we provide that leaves no doubt in the minds of customers and employees alike about what sets us apart. How do you get that message across? Not the way brokers have traditionally gone after clients, by cold-calling. Maybe you can sell stocks to unsuspecting buyers over the phone, but you're not going to sell a stock-buying service that way. From the start, I had to depend on advertising, direct response marketing, and public relations. I'd been doing things that way my whole career, going back to my days as a newsletter publisher. I had a lot of experience tracking leads and measuring the costs of customer acquisition. Above all, I knew what themes resonated with my customers. They were the same themes that resonated with me.

For instance, I knew I was not the only person in the world who distrusted sales pitches. That's why in my very first ads I made sure to include the phrase, *No salesperson will call.* In my brochures, where I had a little more room to explain, I talked about the conflicts of interest inherent in the brokerage business and how, by eschewing commission-based pay and steering clear of investment banking, we were immune to those conflicts. I spent a lot of time repeating the message—giving speeches, meeting with clients, doing radio shows, and talking to reporters. Later, as we opened branches, we used the openings as excuses to garner coverage in the local newspaper. Reporters loved us. Ours was a classic David and Goliath story, not only because we were helping the little guy with lower costs and a square deal, but because I was a little guy myself, taking on the powerful barons of Wall Street from my perch in San Francisco.

The biggest obstacle we had to overcome was a perceived lack of credibility. Most of our customers knew us only as a telephone number. We didn't have fancy offices with wood-paneled walls and leather furniture. We didn't offer clients a one-on-one relationship with a particular broker who knew your name and gave you tickets to the ball game. Plus the descriptor "discount," while a draw to some clients, made others nervous. Our competitors did their best to exploit those misgivings by portraying us as unreliable, if not out-and-out disreputable. One way we fought that perception was the same way McDonald's did—by counting our customers and bragging constantly about our growing numbers: "16,000 investors can't be wrong," we said in one of our early newspaper ads. Then 19,000, 30,000, and so on. (We rode that campaign all the way up to 550,000 investors; we're at more than 10 million accounts now.) We wanted our customers to know that they were not alone, that plenty of other people were doing business with us every day, that we were growing, that history was on our side.

We got a big boost early on from a charismatic PR man from Boston, C. Paul Luongo. I hired C. Paul, as he liked to be called, because he said I didn't have to pay him unless he produced actual results, meaning published articles. The best thing he ever did was arrange a lunch with Dan Dorfman, a popular syndicated colum-nist, at the Four Seasons in New York. This was in 1977. C. Paul got us a corner table, and I proceeded to tell Dan all about how discount brokerage was going to change the world of investing forever. Dan thought it was the coolest thing he'd ever heard. He looked carefully at the rate card I handed him and smiled. "Let's call Merrill Lynch," he said, and he did, right then and there. The waiter brought a phone to our table with its cord snaked across the restaurant floor and Dan called in a trade. In the article that appeared shortly thereafter in hundreds of syndicated newspapers all over the country, "Shopping for Broker Commissions Is Good Strategy," he compared the cost of executing that trade with Merrill Lynch to the cost of executing the same trade with Charles Schwab. That one article was worth more to my growing business than a year's worth of paid advertising. It put us on the map. To this day I remind my marketing team that we built Schwab on public relations and third-party endorsements.

Of course, we were doing all this on a shoestring. Our entire advertising budget during our first year was about $3,000. When we inquired about placing an ad in the *Wall Street Journal*, and asked for help designing one, they sent us to a local firm, Albert Frank-

Nothing compares to the word of mouth that results from good PR. It was true then, and is truer today, with the explosion of social media.

Guenther Law, on Post Street. That was the beginning of a long relationship with Richard Kreuzer, who was our account executive there, and Dee White, a freelance art director. Later, when I created an in-house ad agency, both became Schwab employees.

Richard and Dee were the ones who floated the idea of using my picture as the centerpiece for all our print advertising. Dick said, "This gives this thing so much more animation than just a block of copy about how much you'll save. Let's try it." At first I wasn't sure what to make of it. I've never been comfortable drawing attention to myself. But I could see the concept made good marketing sense. We had to find a way to personalize our clients' relationships with the firm, or we were just a phone number and a mailing address. We had to show potential customers that there was a living, breathing Charles Schwab who stood behind the firm—someone who you could think of as your broker.

We had just been written up in a positive piece in the *San Francisco Examiner*. They took a picture of me with my arm draped over a file of daily trades; I looked happy, friendly, trustworthy. Hugo bought the rights to the photo for $1.50. When we came calling, people didn't see deep pockets. That simple illustrated advertisement became our trademark. It ran virtually unchanged in the *Journal* for years, originally in the Pacific edition, but eventually throughout the country—generally two days a week, Tuesdays and Thursdays. Most investors (myself included) paid scant attention to the *Journal* on Mondays and Fridays. And two days was all we could afford. Placement was always on the next-to-last page (the *Journal* was a one-section paper then), opposite the "Abreast of the Market" column—because that's where I always turned first. We included a toll-free telephone number. We wanted readers to call us, open an account, and start investing. The ad featured a photograph of me smiling, my hair neatly parted.

The photograph is what made the ad work. For one thing, it made us easy to spot; the *Journal* didn't print photographs with its news stories in those days, so the photo stood out. And my picture was a signal to the reader that we were a different kind of brokerage company. Others offered a personal relationship with a broker; we offered readers one with the CEO of the firm. Seeing my picture reassured investors who might have been uneasy about doing business with us. This was long before Lee Iacocca made himself the face of Chrysler, or Dave Thomas went on TV to sell Wendy's hamburgers. The idea of the boss putting himself out front like that was still a novelty in 1976.

That ad transformed me into a powerful marketing tool for the firm. Initially, that made me uncomfortable. I went home the evening Dick first proposed the idea and told Helen our plans. "Oh my god," she said. Friends in the industry thought I was some kind of egomaniac—at least I worried they would.

> You try a lot of things as an entrepreneur. You learn as you go. And sometimes you wind up with something that works that wasn't planned.

The results were immediate; I got over my discomfort pretty fast. Marketing was all-consuming and took many forms. As we began opening branches outside San Francisco, we found it helped build traffic to visit those places and personally introduce ourselves to the community. We would send out a mailing, rent a hotel conference room, and put on an investment seminar for 300 or 400 people. Most people at the time did not know what a discount brokerage was. We had to explain the concept, then convince them we were honest people who didn't bite.

For all that, it was hard for me. I was not a natural at talking to a large audience. I would stumble and look at my notes and lose my place. In 1984, when trying to film our first TV commercial, I stepped in front of the camera, the red light went on, I spoke a few lines, then nothing. I froze up. To this day I can't reliably memorize a script, and with my dyslexia, cue cards were not helpful. Finally, I just said, "I can't do this." We ended up hiring an actor for the commercial so that I could get some training in how to better present myself. I spent time with Bert Decker, a San Francisco public speaking consultant. One thing he told me that I never forgot: "Audiences don't remember information, they remember the man." And that no one knows the content or the order of your presentation, so don't worry about forgetting something. In the end, I learned to speak from notes, rather than a script. Once I was free to say what I wanted, in my own words, I could relax. I think people recognized my sincerity. I wasn't glib, and I obviously was not a salesman. And in the end, all that worked to our advantage.

I HAD ASSUMED FROM the start that most of our customers wanted to do business with us over the phone. That's why we never ran an ad that did not include our toll-free telephone number. I never gave an interview or did a press conference without reminding people how to get in touch with us. We were among the first in our industry to understand the power of the 800-number asset. In 1978, I extended our calling hours from 5:30 a.m. Pacific time, one hour before the markets opened, until 9:00 p.m., midnight on the East Coast. On November 4, 1980, the day Ronald Reagan was elected president, I opened our phone lines 24 hours a day. No one in our industry had ever done that. I felt that Reagan's policies would be kind to the markets and that trading volume would explode. I've been wrong about a lot of things, but I was right about that one. A colossal bull market—which wasn't interrupted until the crash of '87—was about to begin.

Early on we set up a telephone switching station in Reno, Nevada, to avoid a fundamental tariff problem in the US—the fact that it was cheaper to make long-distance calls between states than within states. Since most of our calls were coming from California, it made sense to route them through Reno, then back to San Francisco. Then Pete Moss came up with the brilliant idea of entering the call-center business. Pete Moss embodied the spirit of our young company. A Renaissance man, he was brilliant, creative, impulsive, and quite often a (wonderful) pain in the ass!

Pete was one of my first hires. He was an accountant at Ernst & Whinney, using Schwab as his brokerage firm, and he loved the fact that he was saving a ton of money. He came in one day in 1976 to complain about some of our paperwork, which was all manual, of course, and so things like filing and organizing were hugely important to get right. And, you know, in a friendly way I said, "If you're so smart about this, Peter, why don't you come on the other side of that desk and help us?" So he did, and he jumped right in with ideas. I was impressed. I hired him on the spot and he proceeded to make his mark.

Pete's Reno adventure began with the astute observation that while we handled a lot of calls during the day, after the markets closed, our lines were quiet. He thought, *Why not sell that excess capacity?* As it happened, there was a company in Reno, National Data Corporation, NDC, that was in the business of answering toll-free calls for other companies. After leasing our lines to NDC for a while, we ended up buying their call center. So now we owned a 100-seat call center in Reno. By day we handled stock trades. By night we answered pledge calls for KQED, provided dealer locator services for Ford, sold records, and even took orders for lingerie for Frederick's of Hollywood. It worked surprisingly well—until August 16, 1977, the day Elvis Presley died. Suddenly our lines were swamped day and night with orders for Elvis memorabilia and records. Some of our brokerage customers could not get through to make trades. I sent Rich Arnold to Reno to clean up the mess, and we wound up selling the call center back to NDC. That ended our brief foray into third-party transaction processing. Sometimes a bright idea with a bad outcome is the one that gets you back on track toward the right one.

10

UNCLE BILL GETS HIS BRANCH

Sometimes . . . often if you're lucky . . . a surprise comes along that fuels your growth in unexpected ways. Branches were one of those surprises for us. We opened our first branch office in September 1975. I'd been thinking about a branch strategy for a while, but I thought it was too early, and too expensive. We could already see there was a real attraction to actually coming in and seeing a place like ours in action. So many people came into the Schwab lobby in the early days to just watch the tape or get quotes and make trades and chat with other clients about their trades. Many of them spent time in the San Francisco Business Library, an annex of the main library downtown just down the street from us. They read the library's free copy of *Value Line*, where they researched specific stocks, and then came into our office with the photocopied page and made their trade. They were independent thinkers. They didn't want to pay a broker for advice. These were my kind of customers. They weren't interested, and didn't want, a commissioned broker and his stories.

Our whole business plan revolved around keeping costs low. No lavish expense accounts, no fancy digs, no high salaries or fat commissions for our brokers. Essentially no brick and mortar beyond what we needed for operations and administration. We preferred that our customers call, not visit.

So why open a new branch our first year in business? Uncle Bill forced my hand. I needed capital and Uncle Bill was willing to invest, but only if we opened an office near his home. That was the other problem. Uncle Bill lived in Sacramento. I knew where my best customers lived and worked and as fond as I was of my hometown, Sacramento was not on the list. Los Angeles made a lot more sense to me. In fact, I could think of a hundred cities I'd sooner start with than Sacramento. But what could I do? Uncle Bill wanted a branch and I needed Uncle Bill's investment. Sacramento it was.

Immediately after we opened on Cottage Way in Sacramento, we were flooded with new accounts. It turns out there is something about having a nearby physical presence that helps persuade people to do business with you. It gave me confidence that branches were critical for our future. I figured if we could do it in Sacramento, we could do it anywhere.

Our first branch outside of California was a similar success. A guy named Elliot Friedman contacted me out of the blue and said, "Hey, I'd like to open an office for you in Seattle." Similar to my uncle, Elliot was looking for something new. He had been in the money management business with an insurance company, All State I believe. He saw what Schwab was doing and thought it made sense for him. I replied, "That would be great, Elliot, but I have no money to do that. If you put some money in the company, we'll figure out a way to make it happen."

He pulled together some personal financing—about $50,000—and put it into the company, and we opened an office in Seattle. It was a bit like a franchise, but before franchising was a thing. Elliot was very successful. The branch model proved itself again even outside of our home base of California. I eventually bought back the rights to it with Schwab stock. Over the years it's been great to see Elliot show up at our annual stockholder meetings, a proud and happy stockholder. Then came Phoenix. Lou Hertzog and a couple of partners wanted to open a Schwab office there. And once again, I told them, "If you guys want to put some money in . . ." Which they did. After that, Schwab was in a better position in terms of cash flow and could finance our own expansion, which we've continued since.

To this day, while most clients interact with us through electronic channels, a significant share of our new accounts is opened in person, even by customers who subsequently conduct nearly all their business online.

All of which goes to show, once again, that there are limits to what an entrepreneur can plan for in the early stages of an enterprise. Sometimes the trick lies in making the most of necessity and not missing opportunities when they slap you in the face.

The branch offices turned out to be spectacular growth engines. We've always kept a close eye on our client demographics. I like to know exactly where our new accounts are coming from and how much we're paying to get them. And I can tell you that no marketing plan, no promotional push, nothing we ever tried in order to drum up new business has ever come close to the impact of simply opening a new branch in a new city. We opened somewhere and, boom, our business exploded there by a factor of 15. Here, I saw, was the key to growth on a grand scale—the kind of growth I had been seeking ever since I founded Schwab.

ALL I EVER SET out to do was build a firm that serves the customer the way I'd want to be served myself. And not just a local firm, a national firm. A company committed to growth. Once, when we were still small but growing very fast, Rich Arnold asked me if I thought The Charles Schwab Corporation might become too big for me to manage. That's a big issue for many entrepreneurs, so it was a good question. But I knew from the start that I was committed to growth—as much for me as for my company. "Being big is important," I said. "But not big for big's sake, but because it enables you to invest and improve the services you provide." Being big meant expanding revenue to reinvest and improve; that required growth.

Once we saw what the branches were doing for our growth, we threw everything we had into opening new ones. After Sacramento, we opened an L.A. office in Century City. (Cary Grant walked in one day and opened an account.) In 1977, we opened our first branch outside of California, in Seattle; in 1979, our first East Coast branch, in Fort Lauderdale, when we bought a small brokerage operation from a fellow named Joe Schaeffer. And in 1981, our first New York City branch, at 650 Fifth Avenue (in a building owned by the Shah of Iran, which turned out to be not such a great choice; too many bomb scares). By then we had about 30 branches coast to coast, on our way to hundreds today, including a franchise model we started in 2013.

My competitors weren't doing much of anything with branches. Les Quick, of Quick & Reilly, resisted the concept for years, and I know why. It took roughly four years on average for a branch to become profitable. Opening branches is expensive, it eats into profits. But not forever—that's the key. So while Les was building a $50 million company with 25% pretax profits and bragging rights to being the most profitable discount brokerage in America, I was content to be America's *largest* discount brokerage and *growing*. In the end, Les built a perfectly fine small company and made millions for himself when he sold it. Nothing wrong in that. But I built a company that size many times over, while building greater value for clients and shareholders along the way. The branches were a huge competitive advantage for Schwab when we were just starting out, and that advantage has stayed with us through the years. Our online competitors can never hope to match our size and capabilities until they can match our branch network, and frankly, that's a tough investment to make.

11

BETA

In the fall of 1979, Hugo Quackenbush and I were in the big room on the fifth floor of our newly renovated building at One Second Street, standing over Bill Pearson's desk, looking for answers. "Shouldn't we just stop this thing until we can get it fixed?"

Earlier that year we had signed a $500,000 contract for a cutting-edge computer software system. We were making the huge leap from paper-based operations to computer-based, something no one in the business had done. It was new territory, and we were doing it on a shoestring. We couldn't afford a new computer on our budget, so we had settled for a secondhand computer. Half a million dollars doesn't sound like a lot of money to me now for a completely digitized back-office system. Today, multiply it by a hundred and you're getting close. But at the time it was more than all the equity I held in Schwab. Which is to say (since I had few other assets), it was more than my personal net worth. I bet the company—not because I enjoy taking risks. That's a common misconception about entrepreneurs. We take risks, but we seek to control them as much as possible and look forward to the day when risk no longer dominates the equation.

|||||||||||||||||||||||||||||||||||||||||||||||||||||||||||||||||||||||||||||||||||||||||||||||||||||||||||||||||||

Gamblers like taking risks, not entrepreneurs. Entrepreneurs start with a vision and accept, reluctantly, that no vision was ever realized without risking something important. But a true entrepreneur seeks to control his risks as much as possible.

|||||||||||||||||||||||||||||||||||||||||||||||||||||||||||||||||||||||||||||||||||||||||||||||||||||||||||||||||||

Prior to 1979, we bought data-processing capabilities from a computer services bureau, a common arrangement in those days. Small companies like ours generally lacked the money, the expertise, even the physical space required to bring significant computing power in-house. When I told my friend Jeff Stein, the president of the computer services bureau we contracted with in San Francisco who did similar work for the Pacific Stock Exchange, what we were planning to do—that is, buy our own hardware and deploy custom software designed to automate our processes to an extent never before attempted in the brokerage industry—he tried hard to talk me out of it. "Look at the costs," he pleaded. "I've got programmers, I've got technicians. You guys are crazy." I listened to Jeff, I heard him, but in the end I went ahead. I felt we had no choice.

I'm not claiming it was a matter of survival, not yet anyway. I think we could have hung on for a while longer with paper and pencil and a teletype machine, plus the limited data services we were buying from outside bureaus like Jeff Stein's. But we looked at this thing very closely, we analyzed it carefully, and in the end we recognized a great opportunity—to expand our horizons, add new customers, and above all, provide a level of service that I myself would expect from a discount broker. To me, it was all about seizing that opportunity. It was about growing the company. Up until now, we were still hampered by paper processes. This was an opportunity to make a near complete transformation from paper to computer. That's really all I was thinking about. And that's the context within which I evaluated, and accepted, the risk. But I'm not stupid, and I'm not suicidal. Here we were three months into what was supposed to be a brave new era of automated simplicity—from the branches to the trading floor to the back office; instead, we were working twice as hard as we had before, for half the result.

In theory, the BETA (brokerage execution and transaction accounting) system worked like this: A customer called or came into one of our branches, a broker took his order, and the broker then entered the details into a networked computer that was wired directly to the exchange. That's old hat nowadays, but it was truly revolutionary at the time. At the exchange, a ticket printed automatically that was handled just as if it had been one of the old messages that arrived via Western Union. Once the trade was executed, we logged the details back into our system, then called the customer to confirm the trade, which triggered financial entries for our own books and the customer's account, as well as a printed confirmation that got mailed that same night to the customer.

As the stock exchanges developed their automated order systems (which began with the PACE system at Philadelphia, then SCOREX at the Pacific, and finally the DOT system at New York), we worked directly with them to connect our order systems to theirs. (Sounds simple but we had to contend with ancient regulatory structures that required human intervention. In the beginning, for instance, we had to route all trades through a single employee who sat at a terminal on the second floor, checking each trade as it flitted across his screen, saying "That one can go," "That one can go," and hitting a transmit button each time.) It was in the over-the-counter market that BETA really created a market advantage for us and value for our customers. Here we programmed BETA to gather competing bids from all the major market makers and help us pick the best terms. We also promised larger market makers in certain securities that they would get all our order flow if they promised to always match us with the best bid or ask price anywhere in the NASDAQ system. It was a huge step forward for individual investors, especially for small traders who before had had no choice but to accept unconscionable spreads that benefited the exchanges and brokers, rather than the customer.

But the BETA system was temperamental. The same trades we were accustomed to writing up on the spot were taking as long as eight minutes to work their way through the computer's primitive circuits. That would not have been so bad if our error rate had declined as expected. The problem was that the system kept shutting down for one reason or another. Whenever that happened, we had to go back to the old way of doing things by hand. Later, when the system came back online, we had to reconcile our records. This happened repeatedly, creating endless new opportunities for making mistakes. Our error rate, far from declining, shot up past 10%.

Until that moment when I met with Hugo and Bill—throughout the long months of planning and preparation and during the incredibly stressful implementation period—I had refused to ponder any alternative other than success. Even now, the implications of shutting the whole system down were too awful to contemplate. Yet I was ready to take that step, if that's what Bill advised. He was the technology expert. Hugo and I looked at Bill, waiting for his answer.

JOE AT MERRILL LYNCH has what, a couple of hundred clients? Even before computers, that was hardly an unmanageable number. Whenever one of them called (or more likely, Joe called the client), it was a relatively simple matter for Joe to check his files, confirm the status of his client's account, gauge his ability to pay, make sure the margin requirements were met, and so on. All prior to executing the trade.

Over at Charles Schwab, by the end of 1978 we had about 20,000 clients, any one of whom could call at any time and speak to whichever rep at our end happened to answer the phone. What's more, while most of the calls came into San Francisco headquarters, many were from customers who had opened accounts elsewhere in our ever-expanding branch network. We'd go to reconcile a trade, for instance, find no money in the account, and have to call the client back. If the stock price had fallen, the client might even deny having given us the order. We got stiffed sometimes, but amazingly, not often.

Our first stab at solving the problem involved setting up separate phone lines for quotes, trades, and customer service. You'd call one toll-free number, we'd ask you what you wanted to do, and we'd send you to the right place. Doesn't sound like much but it helped. It meant we could hire unlicensed reps whose only job was to give out quotes—people like my daughter Carrie, who started to work at Schwab when she turned 16, and then spent several summers at the quote desk. Next we built a primitive database—essentially a listing of all our clients with basic information about the status of their accounts. We updated the list every day, printed it out alphabetically on a fresh stack of computer paper, and left it where all the reps could get at it. The phone would ring, a rep would answer: "Hello, Mr. Babcock, one second please." Then, with Mr. Babcock on hold: "I need the Bs!" All helpful, I suppose, but far from a complete solution.

That's where things stood when we held one of our first management off-sites at Rickey's Hyatt House in Palo Alto in the fall of 1978. I believe that's where Rich Arnold trotted out his famous double-line growth chart for the first time, essentially confirming what we already knew: it was time to quit fooling around with halfway measures. We were growing like crazy, yet our customer service was still not where it needed to be, our record-keeping was full of holes, government regulators were bearing down on us, and our workload was insane. Enough already!

We knew what we were looking for; we just didn't know where to find it. I put Bill Pearson and Pete Moss and Guy Bryant on the task. They wrote a spec sheet that we sent out to everybody we knew who had any expertise in technology applications for the securities industry, including Quotron, Bunker Ramo, and ADP. Here's what was on our wish list: a single-view, centralized, real-time database of all our customers—regardless of which branch they opened their accounts in, or how they did business with us—that would empower the first person who answered the phone to handle any question and execute any request the customer had. Essentially what we were talking about was a *true relational database,* a term that was just then entering the tech lexicon. All the vendors said pretty much the same thing: "My god, you're right! Why hasn't somebody thought of this before? We'll put a team on it right away and you'll have it in three years." To which Bill Pearson replied: "You guys don't understand, we're going to be out of business if we don't have it in three months."

Our friends at ADP clearly thought we were out of our minds. They did up a little presentation hoping to persuade Bill to slow down and accept a more reasonable timetable. This was before PowerPoint, of course, so they used a flip chart and butcher paper. First they showed Bill a picture of a guy in a coonskin cap; his name was Pioneer. Then they turned the page. Pioneer, again, this time with an arrow in his back. Their message: don't try this at your company!

And then, by luck, Bill heard about a little trading outfit in Milwaukee, Blunt Ellis & Loewi, that was doing great things with technology. He flew out to have a look. The beauty of Blunt Ellis & Loewi was that these guys were brokers first and tech guys second. On their own, they had developed a program that was almost what we were looking for. Almost. It was a true relational database, it covered most of the data fields we were keen on; but in keeping with their specific needs, it was a back-office system. By that I mean it was spec'd, designed, and written around the requirements of the margin clerk, the dividend clerk, the reorg clerk, and the cashier, and was never intended to be deployed in a retail operation like ours. But Bill was impressed. He liked what they had done. He thought it could be adapted to our needs. So he made them an offer: "I'll write the specs for a front-office application, you guys write the code. We'll buy the code from you, we'll install it, we'll get it up and running, we'll scope out the bugs, and then you can have the code back to use for your own purposes." Oh, yes, and he asked for it by December 31 (already it was October), with a target date of June 30, 1979, for full implementation. The Blunt Ellis guys said they believed it could be done. We agreed to terms on the outlines of a deal and went to work. (But not before Blunt Ellis raised the price on us. Bill Pearson blamed me for doing an interview around that time that was quoted in the *Wall Street Journal*. He thinks that gave the folks at Blunt Ellis the mistaken impression that they were dealing with a big-shot firm. Pearson was furious. He made me stop talking to reporters until the contract was signed.)

Rich Arnold, meanwhile, was taking a hard look at our space needs. On the very day in late 1978 that we took over a new floor at 120 Montgomery Street, expanding our square footage by 50%, Rich walked into Bill Pearson's office, his face grim. "Look, I know you're busy working on the new computer system," he said, "but I just did some numbers, and I think you'd better sit down." Rich's conclusion, with a wisp of his Australian accent: "If you look forward nine months, we don't need another floor. We need a building. A whole bloody building."

So now we had two huge initiatives unfolding simultaneously: the sudden, total conversion of our databases and accounting systems (which Guy Bryant called the financial services equivalent of a "heart and brain transplant") and the sudden, total transfer of our executive and operational headquarters. Just to make it a little more interesting, Rich found a building he liked on Second Street, which (a) was south of Market Street, meaning beyond the frontier of the Financial District, where no broker had gone before (and we thought we were outsiders *before* the move); and (b), while spacious, was also very old, and so had to be gutted and retrofitted with a modern communication stack to carry all our wires. (The actual address was 39 Second Street, but we petitioned the city to change it to One Second Street, slightly more respectable.) Very stressful, very expensive. And have I mentioned that capital was scarce?

But these were all good problems to have! Here we were barely three years after our founding, and all our issues stemmed from the fact that we were growing so fast. By the end of 1978, we had 13 branch offices and 250 employees. Revenues climbed 110% from 1977 to $10 million, and net income approached $1 million. Discount brokerage as a whole still constituted a tiny sliver of the larger market—maybe about 5%—but our share was growing. If anyone had doubted there was a need for unbiased, low-price, high-value brokerage services, those doubts had been erased. What was most astonishing to me was that all our growth had occurred during a period of high inflation, double-digit interest rates, and lackluster stock market returns. Clearly, we were in the midst of what analysts call a secular, or long-term, shift in the way ordinary Americans thought about investing. When the market came back, and I knew it would, our growth would ratchet to a whole new level.

The pace, the demands, the market pressures—everything about the job was more brutal now than ever before. Four years was a long time to be operating in continuous start-up mode. When I think back, I don't know how we survived. There were a lot of ups and downs, and I know that cost us a lot of ticked-off clients. I do know that in this latest push, there was never any doubt in my mind that we had no choice but to proceed both with the new computer system and the move to larger quarters. It was what I wanted, it was what the customer demanded, and I had only to look at our astonishing growth to know that we were on the right track. The market was validating our approach; the possibilities for future growth were staggering. But we absolutely had to get our house in order, immediately. Under the circumstances, you do whatever it takes.

———

IN THE SPRING OF 1979, we took delivery on an IBM 360, Model 50. The 360/50 had been a landmark in the history of technology and a huge step forward in mainframe computing—in 1964. We bought ours secondhand (CBS had used it to predict elections, not always accurately), 15 years after it was introduced. Picture a massive control console studded with toggle switches, big black knobs, and flashing lights; glass-doored data storage boxes as big as refrigerators; tapes spinning like pinwheels on 15-inch reels; wires everywhere; everything perched on a platform in the center of the third floor of One Second Street.

We hadn't even finished installing the software before we hit a regulatory roadblock. The NYSE required all brokers to maintain a seven-year archive of order tickets. Fine, except that one of the key advantages to our new system was the ability—never before seen in our industry—to input orders directly without having to jot them down on paper first and pass the paper to the teletype operator. Happily, Bill Pearson was able to persuade the NYSE that since the regulations contained no explicit requirement to produce order tickets in the first place, we couldn't very well save what we had never possessed.

In the past, brokers had been wise to save their tickets to help settle disputes. There were dozens of reasons a trade might fall apart anywhere along the line, from order to execution to settlement, none of which a broker wanted to think about when he had a live client on the phone: just do the trade. That's how Wall Street did business, and that's how the industry came to accept normal error rates in the high single digits. We thought we could do better. Our goal was to reduce errors by editing orders up front, automatically. The system kept track of which securities you owned (and therefore which you could sell), it knew how much cash was in your account, it calculated your buying power, it measured your capacity to trade options—everything we needed to know before we pulled the trigger on your trade. Our error rate, called "cancel and rebill," prior to installing the new system was averaging 6%, very low for the industry. We were aiming for zero.

The weekend of the conversion we were all going flat out. The plan was to shutter both the office at 120 Montgomery as well as the additional space we'd taken on Sutter Street at close of market on Friday and open for business at One Second Street on Monday morning. That gave us two days to effect a total transformation of our business, from an old-style pen-and-paper brokerage to a modern electronic firm, with no downtime in between. I remember a last-minute meeting, 15 or 20 people in the room, Bill Pearson presiding. "If there's anyone here that doesn't think we can get this done," he said, looking fiercely around the room, "get the hell out of here right now because we don't need those vibes!"

The cabling company showed up on Thursday to run wires from the mainframe through the communication stack to every room in the building, plus the branch office on the first floor. When Bill Pearson and Rich Arnold arrived the next day to connect the desktop terminals (there were dozens) and test the system, they found that the plugs had not been labeled properly. It was impossible to know which screens connected to which ports in the mainframe. Pearson and Arnold were there all day and into the night on Friday, crawling under desks, tracing cables, relabeling plugs, sending test messages back and forth, making sure we were good to go. And that wasn't even the scariest part. To this day Rich Arnold swears that if he hadn't pulled the president of Western Union out of bed on Sunday night, we might not have been able to open on Monday morning. Under the old system, Western Union linked our trading desk not only to the exchange floors but to many of our market makers. BETA bypassed Western Union, but we wanted to run the old teletype system in parallel as backup for BETA if the computer broke down. We simply could not open for business without a live line from Western Union. We got it with scant hours to spare.

So we moved into the new building. We turned on the new machine. And immediately we had a whole new set of problems that plagued us for months. Blame the market, we were swamped with business. Blame the computer, it was big but it was slow and stupid. Even 25 years ago we recognized that. (For sheer computational firepower, you can do more these days with a smartphone.) And blame our inexperience. We were new to using computer systems, all of us learning as we went. Learning, for example, that when you automate some but not all the steps of a multistep process, you create pileups further down the line. Our new computer printed some really spiffy trade confirmations, but it was up to us to confirm the confirmations (not being sure at first if we trusted the computer) and stuff the envelopes. I did what I could, but frankly, there were times when I probably made things worse. Dividend reconciliation, for example—making sure the dividends from a stock are applied accurately to an account. It's a detail task, not my strength. Rich Arnold was our CFO by then. He'd see me coming down the hall and throw up his arms: "Chuck, will you get out of the bloody dividend department!"

Folks were working 80-hour weeks. On the day Guy Bryant's wife gave birth to their first child, he spent 25 hours with her in labor and delivery, then came straight back to the office to reconcile trades. What kept Guy awake at night (besides a crying baby) was the knowledge of how large our challenges really were.

That's when Hugo and I went to see Bill Pearson. I asked him, reluctantly, about the wisdom of maybe taking a breather. The problem with that—as Bill understood better than anyone else—was that there really was nothing to go back to. The old way of doing things was a swamp of uncertainty and errors. The BETA program, for all its faults, was a fresh start. It was our future. If we couldn't make BETA work, we couldn't survive. There was our answer. We weren't going to shut it down.

———

WE FINALLY GOT RID of the IBM 360 years later and offered it to the Glide Memorial Church here in San Francisco, where Jerry Chalmers, our data-processing guy, was on the board. They recycled it and got the gold out of it, apparently enough to make it worth the effort. We replaced it with a next-generation Model 370. That helped. So did the brief downturn in the market in early 1980, which cut down on the craziness. Finally, we were able to get control of our new systems, and after that, we never looked back. We paid a price early on by automating well ahead of our competitors, but the leverage we gained for later growth was enormous. Our execution error rate ultimately plummeted to less than 1%, by far the best in the industry. Our costs went way down. And what's key, we now had a technological framework in place that would allow us to keep growing.

|||||||||||||||||||||||||||||||||||||||||||||||||||||||||||||||||||||||||||||||||||||||||||||||||||||||||

That early experience gave us a comfort level with technology that hereafter set us apart. The lessons we learned positioned us ahead of the curve for decades to come and meant that when the internet exploded in the mid-1990s, we were ready.

|||||||||||||||||||||||||||||||||||||||||||||||||||||||||||||||||||||||||||||||||||||||||||||||||||||||||

Just how significant a leap BETA was, was underscored years later, in 1985. Rich Arnold and Woody Hobbs, our executive vice president for information systems, were working on one of our periodic attempts to reimagine how a modern branch office should function. Part of that involved a tour of IBM's facilities, which ended with a visit to New York City to meet IBM's securities industry team. We'd been an IBM customer for years, yet this was the first we'd heard of a research group devoted to our industry. Sounded promising.

So Rich and Bill paid a visit to the IBM office on Wall Street and sat for a presentation. The second slide that came up talked about IBM's plan to build a system that would allow brokers to sit at terminals and execute orders without generating paper tickets, someday.

This was 1985. This was IBM. Rich Arnold couldn't believe it. By that time we had pieced together with the help of dozens of vendors a nationwide fiber-optic network. Every workstation in every branch across the country tied into the network and had access to the same store of data. We had a centralized control room at 101 Montgomery managing the network. We'd even moved beyond worrying only about the efficiency of the machines into the second stage of technological innovation, which involved worrying about the efficiency of the humans who were operating the machines. "Hang on a second, guys," Rich Arnold, said, almost leaping out of his chair. "Stop this meeting. Don't you know what we've been doing out there in San Francisco?" They had no idea.

People often ask why Schwab got into technology so early and in such a big way to make it a defining part of who we are and how we operate to this day. In some ways, necessity is the mother of invention. We had to get more efficient or we were dead in the water. When I first started Schwab and slashed commissions by 75%, I had just a vague idea that I could make it work. I knew it would take volume. It was also a factor of where we were. San Francisco and neighboring Silicon Valley were all about technology. I was surrounded by people who thought adopting technology was as natural as childbirth. It was the air we breathed.

12

NEVER ENDING, ENDLESSLY FRUSTRATING

There is a story Larry Stupski used to tell about coming to work for me in February 1980; and if Larry said it was true, I won't disagree. I hired Larry ostensibly to run the San Francisco branch office, but I never meant that to be more than a temporary assignment. Really what I was looking for was a tough, smart COO: someone who knew the brokerage industry, had management skills that I did not, and could represent the firm in its dealings with other businesses. By 1980 we had 22 branches in 14 states, 90,000 customers, 130,000 accounts, and $60 million in customer assets—all by-products of an entrepreneurial culture at Schwab that was big on creativity and imagination and not so big on structures, details, and planning. But our little renegade firm was growing up fast; it was time for us to start acting our age. That is why I hired Larry Stupski. As a branch manager, he was pretty damn awful; but he was exactly the future chief operating officer I was looking for.

Larry was analytical to a fault, and anything but rash. He remembered asking me three pointed questions before he accepted my offer: "Do you have any operational problems?" He insisted I answered no. I'm sure I wasn't lying; probably I was being optimistic. Unfortunately, within 60 days we were scrutinized by the Philadelphia Stock

Exchange. "Are you profitable?" Apparently, my answer to that question was yes. Shortly afterward, however, we lost $300,000—10% of our capital base—in a single month, April 1980. All I can say is that I knew profitability was coming; I just couldn't say exactly when it would arrive. And finally, "Do you have plans to go public?" If I really said no to that, and he said I did, I'm sure I meant it in that moment. But when you are growing as fast as we were, plans change. Were those answers the reason Larry chose to work at Schwab? I don't know. I know I don't feel bad about it. He made the right choice and stayed with Schwab until retiring in 1997.

HOW I FOUND LARRY STUPSKI is another story, because it underscores how fortunate I have been at key points along the way. In those days I belonged to the Young Presidents Organization (YPO), a terrific group of entrepreneurs who met to socialize and learn from one another. I had gone to a dinner meeting at the time, where I had talked about the operational role I was hoping to fill at my company. Someone there recommended a local search firm. The next day, back at the office, I couldn't remember the firm's name, just that it sounded like two last names tacked together. On that basis my secretary searched the Yellow Pages and called Korn/Ferry—not the right firm I later learned, but no matter—which sent over a couple of recruiters, one of whom was Tom Seip. I told Tom (who later came to work for me) what I was looking for: a branch manager who had the chops to manage the whole organization one day; a strong administrator who had experience in the brokerage industry but wasn't bound by the traditional way of doing things; a savvy, no-nonsense leader capable of managing a disparate band of strong-minded executives, all of whom (myself included) were in one way or another corporate misfits. And since I could not afford to pay relocation costs, I wanted someone local.

Tom Seip was not optimistic. San Francisco, while still headquarters in those days to Dean Witter and several large banks—notably Bank of America—was a long way from Wall Street. Plus he knew it would be nearly impossible to find a stellar candidate willing to throw in his or her lot with a little-known firm operating in an obscure industry subset and tainted by an undeserved tawdry reputation. I was never surprised that Wall Street took every opportunity to demean our services and question our staying power. We were the common enemy of every big firm that had ever prospered under the old, protected system. Over time, as we became a more solid and respectable company, we were able to recruit more solid and respectable prospects. But for years, the kind of people we needed most were people who would never consider working for a company like ours. The only exception I can think of was in the late '70s, when I hired some well-trained margin clerks from Dean Witter. Dean Witter's office was right across the street from ours, and shortly afterward I got a call from their head of HR, Ben Eaton, who happened to be someone I knew; he was the brother of Helen's stepmother. He told me I had really upset the CEO and offered me this advice: "Do not take any more." Being a nice guy, and not wishing to piss off the giants that surrounded me any more than necessary, I took his advice.

A week or so went by when, as Tom tells it, he sat bolt upright in bed at 3:00 one morning and said aloud, "I know who the right person is but I can't remember his name." Tom lived way over beyond the Oakland hills in Walnut Creek, 25 miles east of San Francisco. Within an hour he was sitting cross-legged on the floor of his office in the otherwise dark Transamerica Building, riffling through résumés. (Tom was not so good with names but he never forgot a résumé.) The one he pulled belonged to Larry Stupski, a brilliant guy who had made his way through both Princeton undergraduate and Yale Law School on scholarships. A refugee from Wall Street (Larry had hated the long commute on the New Haven Railroad to Fairfield County), Larry was working, unhappily, for Western Bradford

Trust Company, a joint venture between Crocker National Bank and Bradford Computer Systems that was based in San Francisco.

Larry claimed he sent out 200 résumés when he moved to the West Coast and the only response he got, one year later, was from Tom Seip. The only way I can explain that is to point out that Larry was not such a good networker, probably for the same reasons he was not a good branch manager—he was impatient with people who weren't as smart as he was, he didn't smile very often, and he tended to make everyone around him nervous. But that was okay; he more than made up for his shortcomings as a front man with his outstanding skills as an operations manager. Within months of coming to work for us, Larry had deputized several underlings in the San Francisco branch office and was spending his afternoons in the executive suite. By September 1981, he was my president and COO. Finding him had been an accident and a series of improbable events. Larry often said I was lucky, and in this case he was certainly right.

IF I REALLY DID tell Larry in early 1980 that we had no plans to go public, it must have been because I was feeling especially hopeful that day about some other source of financing—likely a source that never materialized. The search for capital was never ending and endlessly frustrating. We had a very small capital base and we were up against an army of industry giants, any one of which could have crushed us in a moment had they cared to compete directly in our arena. Plus we were growing fast, and growth eats cash: cash for advertising and marketing to acquire new accounts; cash to support those new accounts once they come in; and cash to comply with the industry's strict capital ratio requirements—which are necessary, clearly, and protect investors, but which represented a daunting burden for us. You hope eventually to gather enough trading commissions to satisfy your thirst for cash, but new accounts are never profitable right away. Which means if you want to keep growing, you have to keep raising capital, pretty much nonstop. Today, with the growth of venture capital funds and other sources of private equity, I think it's a lot easier for young companies to raise the funds they need. Back then, Wall Street pretty much controlled the purse strings and since we were out to destroy Wall Street's monopoly, those guys were not exactly tripping over one another to help us.

I tried everything I could think of. I mortgaged my house, many times. I gave stock in the company to all my employees as part of their compensation, and I also encouraged them to buy even more stock if they could, for as little as 20 cents a share. I also offered shares to our clients, on the theory that anyone who used our services and believed in the firm would want to invest in us, too. And, of course, I was not above offering to open a nearby branch office if that's what it took to open someone's pockets.

But it was never enough. Rich Arnold, my first CFO, has described his job during the early days as an endless cycle of "do a debt round, do an equity round, do a debt round, do an equity round." None of those financings was routine. VCs spurned us, in part because many of them were advised by large brokerage firms who were always trying to squash us. Banks were suspicious—How long have you been in business? How many competitors do you have? What is a discount broker, exactly? And always, just ahead, was another crisis waiting in ambush. Such as the time we wrote a check to an elderly client for $90,000 that was supposed to be $9,000. She cashed it, we didn't discover the error until much later, and it took us forever to get the money back. That one incident all by itself was nearly enough to put us over the edge.

Finally, in early 1980, we decided to attempt a public offering. That's a hard step for many entrepreneurs. It opens the door to a level of scrutiny and accountability that can never be closed. But that prospect never bothered me. I saw no reason we should not be a glass house. In fact, I perceived financial transparency as a plus. If truly we were not like other brokers (and only a couple—Donaldson, Lufkin & Jenrette in 1969, and Merrill in 1971—had gone public); if we were really serious about eliminating conflicts of interest; if in fact our only aim was to serve the needs of independent investors, why should we be afraid of opening our books? We should have nothing to hide.

Moreover, I had some notions about ways to leverage the IPO as a marketing tool. I thought we could offer shares directly to our own customers, free of commission. I figured they would be my strongest advocates in the marketplace—my best salespeople, so to speak. I looked into the possibility of publishing the prospectus, in its entirety, in the *Wall Street Journal*, for all the world to see. And finally, in a move bound to raise eyebrows, I committed The Charles Schwab Corporation to underwriting the entire offering itself. That is, I was eliminating the traditional role played by investment banks in an IPO, that of buying the full allocation of shares up front and later selling them piecemeal to the investing public.

No one had ever done a big IPO that way, certainly not one involving a high-visibility financial services company. It meant bypassing the enormous fee-generating machine of the big investment banks. The idea of publishing the entire prospectus in the *Wall Street Journal* was totally unheard of. We had conducted the legal research, and though all our advisers were nervous, they agreed it could probably be done. We soon learned, however, that we could not cut the investment banks out of the process altogether. If you were going to act as your own underwriter, you still needed a third party—a National Association of Securities Dealers member firm—to put a price on the offering. We chose two small, local firms for the job, because I had no interest in involving the Wall Street establishment in my IPO. The feeling was mutual, I'm sure. By now the big brokers couldn't afford to ignore us anymore. Together the discounters—of which Schwab was by far the largest—controlled an estimated 8% of the retail market. But that just made the big boys more determined than ever to attack us. Which explains why I didn't join our industry's trade group—the Securities Industry Association—until the mid-1980s. Nothing against SIA. It's just that until we gained enough stature to make our presence felt in the industry, I felt the SIA did not represent our interests.

So we needed a couple of outside opinions on the value of our company. Of course, I had a pretty strong opinion myself. I believed we could sell 1.2 million shares at $4 a share and raise $4.8 million. All to fund expansion, by the way. I had no plans to convert any of my personal equity to cash. But I was in for a surprise. Simply put, it is one thing to take a philosophical stand in favor of full disclosure, quite another to experience firsthand the effects of that stand. Don't forget, all this was happening during the spring of 1980. We were still struggling to integrate our new BETA computer system. Our execution error rate had recently peaked at 10.5% of commission income, or a little over $1 million, which, of course, found its way into the prospectus. What I can accept now, with the benefit of hindsight, is that we simply were not ready for our close-up. Still, I was not willing to give up hope yet of garnering what I felt was a fair price for a firm whose future I believed in passionately.

Now comes what is known as the pricing meeting. The prep work is 99% done, the deal is about to go down. I'm sitting across the table from a bunch of lawyers and investment bankers. Finally, one of them slides a piece of paper toward me. The number. I looked at it. I didn't say anything, I just looked. Two dollars and seventy-five cents. Then I stood up and walked out of the room.

So ended my first attempt at taking The Charles Schwab Corporation public. Again, I am willing to admit that maybe it really was too early for us to invite the public to invest in us. We were still coping with operational problems. But in a way we were lucky the investigation occurred when it did. Six months earlier, whatever they found would have been worse. It's likely they would have forced me to raise more capital, immediately, or possibly even shut down the firm.

THE FAILED IPO WAS a tough break, and not just because we did not get the money we needed. The disclosures in the prospectus embarrassed me personally and confirmed some people's worst suspicions about discount brokers in general. The press was all over us. "What was billed as a triumphant coming of age for the mini-industry ended in embarrassment . . . ," *BusinessWeek* wrote in its August 18, 1980, issue. "Many observers think the swift turnaround has dealt a severe blow to the industry, postponing for a long time—and possibly canceling—any hope it had for becoming a credible part of the financial market mainstream."

Fortunately for us—not to mention small investors the world over—*BusinessWeek*'s dismal appraisal of our prospects proved to be way off the mark. I was not happy about that article when it came out, but even then I was a long way from despair. I had no doubt that our industry would survive, that discount brokers were the wave of the future. It had been quite clear to me for some time. By drastically lowering commissions, and by pointing out the conflicts of interest inherent in the traditional brokerage model, the discounters had revealed a whole new world to small investors; once glimpsed, there was no turning back. As for my own place in the industry, I knew that was safe. I had already lined up an alternate source of financing. My savior was Tony Frank, a close friend and fellow entrepreneur I'd met through YPO. Tony went on to become postmaster general under the first President Bush, but at the time he was a banker in San Francisco. He had recently sold his S&L, Citizens Savings and Loan, to National Steel in Pittsburgh, and had a seat on National Steel's board. I knew that National Steel was looking for investment opportunities. Once I saw what a lousy price we were getting on the IPO, I called Tony. "I'm really in need of capital," I said when we met. "We're growing like crazy."

"Tell me more about it," he said.

"I'd be willing to sell 20% of the company for $4 million," I said.

Tony did not blink. My recollection is that he said immediately, "You're on," although I'm sure it was more complicated than that. It just seemed like such a simple, straightforward transaction, especially after all the hassle associated with the IPO. Tony got right on it and was able to persuade National Steel to do the deal exactly as I had proposed.

That is how The Charles Schwab Corporation found the capital it needed to fight another day; and National Steel, as would quickly become obvious, made an extraordinarily high-return, short-term investment.

13

CAPITAL AND CREDIBILITY

Tony Frank's investment from National Steel helped tremendously, but the relief was short-lived; the pressure for cash continued to mount. It's an irony: growth is a sign of success and shows you're on to something that people want, but with a young company like ours the growth outpaces your sources of capital. You're reinvesting every penny of profit you can, and it's not enough.

So there I was, roughly five years into this new business, and our growth kept exceeding our ability to create enough capital on our own. That kind of success is a wonderful problem to have, but it was making me antsy as hell. We were searching for capital at all times in anticipation of future needs . . . which, being in California, naturally led us to Bank of America.

Founded in 1904 as the Bank of Italy by A. P. Giannini—BofA was by then the second-biggest bank in the country, a global financial powerhouse with $120 billion in assets and a ubiquitous retail presence in California. It competed ferociously with its neighbor down the street, Wells Fargo Bank, another San Francisco institution, and BofA was proud of its distinctive heritage as the bank for the little guy, an attitude I appreciated. Throughout the state, in nearly every town, the bank at the corner of First and Main was Bank of America.

Instrumental in building California's robust economy through most of the twentieth century, Bank of America financed the Golden Gate Bridge, built the tallest building in San Francisco for its headquarters, and dominated the Bay Area's civic life as much as its financial affairs.

Pete Moss had been in discussions with the bank to provide us a subordinated loan to augment one we already had with the Imperial Bank. These arrangements were very useful, as they provided an additional cushion against our capital computations. Landing a significant loan with BofA—we were talking with them about $7 million—would have been a major deal for us at the time.

In September 1981, Pete came to me with a surprise: Bank of America had changed their tune. The more they had looked at us, the more they liked. The bank was no longer interested in a loan; they were keen on *acquiring* Schwab.

To a little firm like ours, stuffed into an old building on the wrong side of Market Street, operating in an infant industry that still could have disappeared (and few would have noticed), it was hard to believe Bank of America had a notion to buy us. Until then my dealings with Bank of America had been only to request business loans, and we had always been turned down. In fact, we were turned down right and left. Most of the bank boards had connections to the full-service brokers. They didn't want to support the upstart competition.

I wasn't looking to sell Schwab. In fact, my independence meant everything to me. Still, I had to admit, the sudden unexpected prospect of selling my company to a highly respected organization like the Bank of America was intriguing, even pretty thrilling. Here, first of all, was the potential solution to all our capital problems. After the aborted IPO, we had been lucky to raise $4 million in the private placement through Tony Frank's connection to National Steel, but already we were scraping the bottom of that barrel. Our growth continued apace. Big customers who wanted to borrow on margin were forever taxing the limits of our ability to borrow to meet their needs.

And lately, as our industry slowly matured, we were finding ourselves on the buying end of deals for smaller competitors. The industry was consolidating; we knew there would be more opportunities to grow by acquisition. I wanted to be ready.

I also liked the message our courtship would send to the wider world of financial services and, most important, to consumers. We had taken a beating in the press after the failed IPO. There was a perception in the industry and among investors that we were not quite ready for prime time. But here was one of the biggest banks in the world coming after us.

The mere fact that BofA had pursued us would be seen as validation for me, my company, and the entire discount brokerage industry. It brought us instant credibility.

Bank of America's interest in Schwab came at a crucial time, I might add: for as fast as we had been growing until now, we were about to begin a period of truly explosive growth, marked by rapid expansion of our branch network. Of course, I had no crystal ball. I could not have known that the great bull market of the '80s was about to begin its historic run. But I will say this: I had been keeping a close eye on the presidential campaign. And I had a pretty good notion that if Ronald Reagan—with all his talk about deregulation and tax cuts—were elected president in November, the markets would applaud. The markets were closed on Election Day, 1980, but I decided to keep our phone lines open anyway, all day and all night, as I mentioned earlier. As it became clear that Reagan was winning, orders poured in. That experience convinced me that it was time we offered our customers the option to place orders for trades 24 hours a day, seven days a week, and in March 1982 we became the first in our industry to do so. Bottom line: a merger with Bank of

America could bring us two key ingredients for growth—*capital* and *credibility*—when we needed them most.

Finally, it was by no means lost on me that by exchanging my majority stake in The Charles Schwab Corporation for shares in Bank of America, I would suddenly become a very wealthy man. On paper only, granted, but at the time it was hard for me to imagine a more secure form of paper wealth than stock in one of the biggest, strongest, most admired banks in the world. To a young man who until recently had had no assets to speak of, and very little cash, that was heady stuff.

THE DEAL WOULD never have gotten rolling without a push from the other side, supplied in this case by a young Bank of America executive, Steve McLin. Steve, 34, was a mergers-and-acquisitions specialist newly arrived from First National Bank of Chicago. He had come to BofA at roughly the same time as Sam Armacost, 42 at the time, who succeeded the legendary Tom Clausen as CEO. Clausen left Bank of America in April 1981 to run the World Bank, but not before he had delivered 58 consecutive quarters of rising profits. Steve saw his mission as helping Armacost escape Clausen's shadow by ensuring a continuing steady stream of rising profits, and to put some big, visible wins on the board. To him that meant searching out takeover targets beyond the ordinary scope of banking.

Brokerage firms definitely qualified as beyond the scope. The Glass-Steagall Act of 1933, conceived in the depths of the Depression, built an impenetrable wall between commercial banks, which offer checking and savings accounts, and investment banks and their brokerage arms, which engage in the far more risky business of underwriting public offerings and selling stock to the public. Nearly 50 years later that wall was still standing, though both commercial and investment banks had begun probing its foundations, searching for cracks. In part because of the revolution started by the discount brokers, and the popularity of money market funds, which had broken the banks' exclusive hold on consumer savings, money was now moving more freely than ever between savings accounts and brokerage accounts; careful, middle-class savers were becoming aspiring, middle-class investors. Banks, brokerages, and even insurance companies were lusting for a piece of one another's business.

Glass-Steagall was ultimately doomed; we know that now. Memories of the Depression would fade, the pressure from consumers and service providers alike to combine a full range of financial offerings under one roof would grow, and in 1999 President Bill Clinton signed legislation formally repealing the law. For now, however, in 1981, when Bank of America came calling, the divisions remained absolute. If the deal were to work, we would be the first test case of a bank and brokerage marriage in half a century.

Steve McLin and Pete Moss had met and then suggested I sit down with Sam Armacost. Sam and I met in his private dining room on the 52nd floor of the Bank of America Building to discuss the possibilities. We were roughly the same age, both passionate golfers, both graduates of Stanford Business School, and both ambitious with lofty goals. Certainly I saw no reason not to proceed on personal grounds. Later Steve and Sam walked several blocks to One Second Street to tour our facility. I gather that was an eye-opener for both of them. Nobody anywhere in financial services—much less in the stodgy world of banking—could match our level of computerized automation; no one came closer to the ideal of a paperless office. Clearly, that was a big part of what made us so attractive to Bank of America: our technological edge. But it was not just our computers; it was our vitality, our spirit of innovation—in marketing as much as technology—that impressed Bank of America.

The core elements of the deal came together quickly: a stock-for-stock exchange, with Bank of America issuing us between 1.8 million and 2.2 million shares, the exact number to be settled at closing (which either way translated into a fast, 100%-plus return on National Steel's investment and a $20 million stake in BofA for me); a seat for me on the BofA board; and since both parties understood it was going to take months to finalize the agreement—we needed regulatory approval for what was shaping up as the first major challenge to Glass-Steagall—the bank offered an immediate capital infusion in the form of $7 million in subordinated debt. That was an extraordinary sum to us in those days, and a clear signal of the kind of support we could expect in the future from our new corporate parent.

The details took a little longer. For me the key issues in the contract all revolved around maintaining control of what was going to be my little corner of the BofA empire. We were to stay put in our own offices at One Second Street. I was to remain CEO and chairman of The Charles Schwab Corporation with two additional Schwab insider seats plus two BofA executives on our board. At my insistence, we were to keep our own corporate accountant (Dennis Wu at Deloitte & Touche, who had been our lead partner since launching in the mid-'70s), our own outside counsel (Larry Rabkin at Howard Rice), and our own internal auditor. These were highly unusual concessions. Generally, in a deal like ours, the big fish swallows the smaller fish whole. The fact that BofA was willing to grant us so much autonomy I chose to interpret as a measure of Steve McLin's and Sam Armacost's respect for us and willingness to give us the freedom to succeed. But I also know they understood that from my point of view, these issues were nonnegotiable; they were deal breakers. We had made it this far as heads-down, all-by-ourselves entrepreneurs—as creative outsiders—and I was determined that we not change now just because we happened to be owned by a bank. My greatest fear was that we'd be straitjacketed by the BofA bureaucracy and lose our souls. Rich Arnold, who negotiated the fine print along with our lawyer, Larry Rabkin, had an expression that covered that whole universe of concerns. He used to talk about "the couch department," as in he was going to make damn sure no bureaucrat from the BofA couch department ever tried to tell us how we could furnish our offices.

There was one other detail in the agreement I should mention. Years later it would make all the difference. It had to do with ownership of my name and likeness. By now we had been running the ad with my picture in the *Journal* for so many years that it was hard to pinpoint where my personal identity ended and the identity of the company began. For that reason Larry and Rich thought it reasonable to define exactly what Bank of America was acquiring, and to exclude my name and likeness from the bargain should Bank of America ever decide to sell Schwab. *Ownership would revert to me.* It was akin to a clause in a prenuptial agreement that protects certain assets in the event of a divorce. And as with any prenup, no one on either side of this deal seriously believed it would ever be relevant.

WE AGREED TO TERMS and announced the deal in late November 1981. Immediately we found ourselves party to a suit sponsored by the Securities Industry Association, challenging the merger under Glass-Steagall. No surprise there, we knew that was coming. And so both sides settled down and waited for the courts and the regulatory agencies to decide. The Federal Reserve had given their approving opinion in January when we closed the deal, but final approval, in the form of a Supreme Court decision upholding the Fed's opinion did not come until the summer of 1983.

A lot happened over the intervening 18 months to change the complexion of the deal—mostly bad for Bank of America, and mostly very good for Schwab. We had immediate access to the promised $7 million in subordinated debt, and that had a corresponding immediate positive impact on our operations. It allowed us to capitalize on the growth opportunities that developed once the markets got rolling again in the spring of '82. Although, truth be told, as Schwab thrived, we were increasingly able to meet our capital requirements through profits, and fund our own expansion. We never received another dollar from BofA and opened 16 new branches in 1982, including six in Texas, one each in Nashville, New Orleans, Oklahoma City, and Honolulu, and our first overseas branch in Hong Kong. Our customer base shot up 85% in 1982 to 374,000. Revenue climbed to over $100 million, and account assets more than doubled to more than $231 billion, as did profits, to $5.2 million.

Bank of America, meanwhile, took a sudden turn for the worse. Armacost's arrival coincided with the end of the bank's long string of quarterly profit growth. Not that I or anyone else yet suspected the depth of the developing crisis at Bank of America. All we knew was that the stock was falling—from $24 in November 1981, when we shook hands on the deal, to $20 in January 1983, when we closed. The original agreement allowed for some adjustment in the terms to account for changes in the value of BofA stock. The final terms— 2.6 million shares of stock, at the time worth $52 million—helped some, but not enough to recover all the lost value. Bottom line: Bank of America paid less than expected for a company that was worth more than expected.

Nobody on our side was happy about that. Least of all Pete Moss, who thought the math had changed enough that the deal was no longer right for us. In a fit of passion, he made the case in a memo to Schwab employees who were also shareholders taking sides against me. I couldn't abide by that and had to let Pete go. That was hard, but a deal is a deal.

I had made a commitment months before, knowing full well that markets are volatile and that a lot could change. They had my word and I had every intention of abiding by it.

And so began a new era in the life of my company, as a fully owned subsidiary of Bank of America. In retrospect, I can see the trouble ahead with the relationship. Had I anticipated it in advance, would I have stopped the deal? I don't know. It was painful, *and* there was a lot of good that came from the sale. It *did* legitimize Charles Schwab. It *did* legitimize the discount brokerage industry. It *did* give us credibility. It *did* give us access to capital, at least initially. But the extent of the troubles was just about to unfold.

14

THE NEW KID

My first Bank of America board meeting took place in a cavernous, two-story vault on the 51st floor, with floor-to-ceiling windows, and the city and the bay spread out below. At 46, I was the youngest director in the room. The 26-member Bank of America board was the most prestigious assemblage of business, academic, and political superstars on the West Coast, if not in the whole country. Among them were former Secretary of Defense Robert McNamara; Transamerica chairman John R. Beckett; Harvard economist (and future Federal Reserve vice chairman) Andrew Brimmer; Burt Gookin of Heinz; Walter Haas of Levi Strauss; Najeeb Halaby of Pan Am; Dick Cooley of Seafirst; Phil Hawley of Carter Hawley Hale; Franklin Murphy, former chancellor of UCLA and head of the executive committee at Times Mirror; and Peter O'Malley, president of the Los Angeles Dodgers. At each place was a leather-bound folder, embossed with the director's name. I was impressed. *My god, what have I achieved?* I asked myself.

But while I was the new kid in the room, I was also, amazingly, the bank's largest individual shareholder. The sale of my company to Bank of America for stock gave me a personal stake worth about $19 million. That was very hard for board member Claire Giannini

Hoffman to accept. Claire, the daughter of BofA founder A. P. Giannini, died in 1997 at the age of 92, but as long as she was alive she believed firmly that no one person should own more than 1% of her father's bank. In fact, I personally was under 1%, but Charles Schwab as a group came in just over the limit and that worried her. It worried me, too, but for the opposite reason. I believed in the power of equity. I still do today. I think having a substantial stake in the success or failure of the enterprise makes you a more involved director, a more effective manager, a more motivated employee. And it troubled me from day one, as I looked around the boardroom at my fellow directors, to know that my fate was linked with the bank's to a degree that theirs was not. I would have felt better if everybody there owned more stock, not less.

I had to work hard to persuade Claire of my good intentions. I had to promise her I would be a good corporate citizen, and I believe that I kept my promise. From the day I first walked into that boardroom until the day I resigned, three years later, I did my best to protect the interests of the shareholders of Bank of America. I just never imagined what a difficult job that would be, nor how many people I would tick off along the way.

SCHWAB MADE A LOT of progress as a wholly owned subsidiary of Bank of America, thanks in part to BofA capital and BofA credibility. But it was also the result of the times. The middle 1980s were good years for the brokerage side of the financial services industry. The Dow gained and finally held 1,000 in late 1982, ending nearly two decades of flat performance by US equities and unleashing a wild bull market that hardly paused to take another breath until the crash of '87. Also in 1982, Congress passed and President Reagan signed legislation simplifying the rules and expanding eligibility for Individual Retirement Accounts. Suddenly every American under age 70 who had a job could make a tax-deductible contribution to an IRA. IRA contributions took a huge leap forward from just under $5 billion in 1981 to more than $28 billion in 1982. With the bull raging, a lot of that money found its way into the stock market, sending prices higher still. It was the beginning of an important shift in the way Americans think about their money, with huge implications for the health of Schwab, and we took full advantage of it to strengthen our company.

Many of our signature products and services had their origins in those years. The enhanced Schwab One asset management account, for example, first offered in March 1983, was a key step in our transformation from a West Coast boutique tailored for active traders to a Main Street brokerage with a national footprint. Similar to an offering by Merrill Lynch, but with a lower account minimum—making it more accessible to small investors—Schwab One combined trading capability with a high-interest money market savings account and a debit card. Schwab One made us a viable alternative to Merrill Lynch for new investors, and it marked a turning point for us—away from a bare-bones service model aimed at a niche market and toward a full-service model aimed at the rising American investor class. We had about 500,000 accounts when we introduced the new Schwab One. In less than two and a half years we leapt past 1,000,000.

About this time a corner of the market was changing completely the landscape of investing for average Americans: the rise of mutual funds. At the time we weren't yet selling any funds of our own. We were brokers, not money managers. I still viewed our target market as people who wanted to pick their own stocks, not let a fund manager pick for them. But mutual funds were becoming too big to ignore. In 1980, fewer than 6% of US households owned mutual funds (compared to 13% who owned stocks). By 1988, nearly one in four did (and later, in 2000, nearly half). Leading the pack was Fidelity Investments. The privately held company of the Johnson family in Boston, they had quickly become the biggest player with a range of funds to choose from and high-profile fund managers like Peter Lynch, who had managed their flagship Magellan fund since the late '70s. As I saw it, they were clearly on their way to total domination of the mutual fund industry.

We noted the trend, while recognizing that picking funds, for some investors, was becoming every bit as involved as picking stocks. Investors were poring over the ratings in *Money* magazine or reading Morningstar reports and assembling portfolios of funds—and consequently drowning in paperwork. To sell shares in one fund and replace them with shares in a different fund from a different fund family was a convoluted, multistep process that ordinarily involved an investor's bank, too, and could drag on for weeks. Then came the avalanche at tax time. Fidelity made that easier for investors with their wide range of choices—you could easily use them as a one-stop way to shop and manage your funds.

I knew we needed a way into this market, but it wasn't going to be by competing head-to-head building and marketing our own funds. Instead, we figured, why not be a one-stop shopping place for other company's funds, with a focus on convenience. Schwab Mutual Fund Marketplace, announced in February 1984, was a first-of-its-kind service that allowed investors to buy and sell no-load mutual funds from different fund families and hold them all in a Schwab One account. Mutual Fund Marketplace simplified all the complexities of owning funds from multiple companies. One account at Schwab, one statement rather than many from all the funds you own.

It was a big step forward. But it was expensive—we were tacking commissions onto no-load mutual funds; it was the only way we could make it work. Not only was that counter to our profile in the marketplace, it was inherently inconsistent. For a while we were simultaneously the cheapest place to buy stocks and the most expensive place to buy no-load mutual funds. Consequently, we did little to promote Mutual Fund Marketplace. Few of our customers even knew it existed. Later, as the economics of fund distribution evolved, Mutual Fund Marketplace would be replaced by OneSource, which would operate on an altogether different business model, with the fund companies paying not only for access to our customers but also for the record-keeping and customer service we were providing for their shareholders. OneSource would become a revolutionary financial service, widely copied by our competitors, and it essentially opened up the market for smaller funds to compete with the Fidelity juggernaut. Mutual Fund Marketplace, while flawed, paved the way.

Finally, it was during the Bank of America period that we took the first steps toward online trading. Tentative steps, to be sure, but moving in the right direction. Now, I'm no technology expert, but I have always been willing to invest in technology, and not just because it lowers our costs and gives us a competitive advantage. The way I see it, every time we make another advance, we strip away one more layer of intermediation between the masses and the markets. That's always good. Anything that promotes stock trading and stock ownership, I'm all for it. I'm very proud of the role Schwab has played over the years to advance that cause.

||||||||||||||||||||||||||||||||||||||||||||||||||||||||||||||||||||||||||||||||||||||

When you buy stock, you don't just buy equity in that company; you buy a stake in the system. The more stock, the bigger the stake—and, as I have long argued, the more engaged the citizen.

||||||||||||||||||||||||||||||||||||||||||||||||||||||||||||||||||||||||||||||||||||||

EQUALIZER, LAUNCHED IN 1984, bypassed our people altogether. It let customers help themselves. With a personal computer, a modem, and Equalizer, a client could dial directly into our system via CompuServe, look up account information, obtain quotes, and place an order. This first form of online investing was roughly a decade before financial services began its mass migration onto the internet. It is nearly impossible for people who came of age after the 1990s to imagine the world before the internet. It's become such an integral part of life today, it is like the air we breathe. In the mid-'80s, only a small percentage of American households had personal computers, and only a fraction of those had modems for connecting to CompuServe, America Online, and other still-primitive online services. But among our target clients, we knew that the technology acceptance level was much higher. Equalizer gave us a big leg up in an emerging market. None of our competitors were offering anything like it.

On the downside, Equalizer was clunky and slow. Customers had to install it themselves from floppy disks. Every time we upgraded the software, we mailed a new batch of disks (not inexpensive), then braced for a flood of tech-support calls. Fortunately, I suppose, Equalizer was not a very popular product initially, although its popularity grew over the years as we made improvements. In fact, long after we migrated to the internet and could offer far more powerful online trading tools, we still had customers who insisted on using Equalizer. We didn't shut it down once and for all until 1998. In the beginning, though, Equalizer's biggest fans were Silicon Valley techies, many of whom at the time were starting their own companies. They were natural customers for us. Launching their own businesses, they understood stocks, they liked managing their own affairs, they weren't intimidated by technology, and they were beginning to build huge fortunes for themselves and their employees. Equalizer helped us penetrate that key market before anyone else did—an unintended benefit that paid huge dividends later on.

IT'S HARD TO SAY exactly when I began to worry about the health and strategic direction of Bank of America. I know it was early in the game, long before the purchase of Schwab was complete. I had agreed to an all-stock sale to BofA, and now many of my Schwab colleagues and early investors were seeing their net worth dwindle. For as long as I owned any BofA stock, the price was never again as high as it was on the day we announced the deal. I couldn't very well ignore that.

I was dismayed by the bank's failure to preserve its long unbroken string of quarterly profit growth. I worried about the Latin American loan portfolio, which was becoming an issue for many banks, not just BofA. There was a developing crisis with loans to Greek shipping interests, among others, as a combination of an OPEC-triggered energy crisis and an oversupply of ships was putting oil tankers out of commission and was starting to spread to dry cargo ships. And I wished the bank was doing more—faster and more aggressively—with technology. BofA's ATM network was not nearly as impressive as its branch network—a major reason BofA was losing market share. But all those, initially at least, were merely vague concerns.

Although I was initially awed by the board, I was beginning to have my doubts. It was too big. Part of me was thrilled to be a member of such an august assembly of managerial wisdom, but the entrepreneur in me recognized that there was a corresponding cost in efficiency and effectiveness. The size of a board matters, especially in times of crisis. As the bank's situation worsened, we had a duty as directors to act boldly and rapidly. Some of us tried; but as a whole, the BofA board was too cumbersome to lead. The bank had frightening holes in its loan portfolio, particularly in Latin America. We needed to recognize them, deal with them, and move on. The bank was inefficient, and expenses were too high. But a board that big wasn't going to dive into the details. All it could hope to do was work with existing management and avoid embarrassing the company along the way. Its members were probably incapable of digging down far enough on their own to solve fundamental organizational problems, even if they had thought that was their role, which most didn't.

I really wanted to believe that Sam Armacost and his team could pull us through—and I thought I could help them. I was no expert on loans to third-world countries, but I could read an income statement, I knew a thing or two about marketing, and I was a warrior for technology. I saw a role for myself in helping to plot the turnaround, and I assumed I'd be called upon to play it. I thought it no less than my duty as a director and a shareholder.

But before I lost my confidence that the bank could turn things around, I lost my innocent faith that the bank wanted input from its newest board member, Chuck Schwab.

15

A RAGING CASE OF THE YIPS

By late 1984, it was clear that Bank of America faced enormous problems. They weren't all Sam's fault. Those 58 consecutive quarters of rising profits that preceded him? Upon closer examination, they turned out to be at least partly a result of deferred decisions that would fall on Sam's shoulder's as CEO. For some time, Bank of America had been locked in an epic battle with Citibank. That meant intense pressure to keep the profit line rising—pressure that intensified with each passing quarter for as long as the streak was alive. But it meant deferring needed investments and postponing losses. Quarter by quarter, as reported earnings kept rising, Bank of America was falling further and further behind.

By the time the bills came due, Armacost, to his credit, took action, up to a point. Between January 1982 and December 1984, the bank closed 165 California branches. At the same time, it eliminated 11.5% of the payroll. (That was 9,000 jobs, or six times as many people as worked at all of Charles Schwab.) While Sam was cutting, he was also investing: more than $800 million in equipment upgrades alone. That was more in three years than in the previous eight years combined.

Sam also embarked on an ambitious corporate-wide restructuring led by Yugoslavian management guru Ichak Adizes. I knew and admired Adizes. He had spoken at some of our local chapter meetings of the Young Presidents Organization. Adizes could talk about the nature of entrepreneurialism and different styles of management, and really get down to some fundamental psychological truths about individuals and organizations. Fascinating stuff, definitely provocative, but maybe not the best basis on which to reorganize a $120 billion bank.

Meanwhile, the stock was still falling, market share was still slipping, and on July 17, 1985, Bank of America announced a second-quarter loss of $338 million. Not only was it the first quarterly loss in BofA's long history; it was the second-largest quarterly loss ever recorded by any US bank. Still, no one wanted to hear my concerns; or more important, my suggestions about how to pull the bank out of the monumental mess it was in. In my view, the bank was bloated. There were too many employees per revenue dollar. It was antiquated and living in an outdated reality, the "10–3" banking system, opening at 10 a.m., closing at 2:00, and on the golf course by 3:00. I made my case to Sam to be aggressive, to make significant cuts to staff, to get more efficient and increase our revenue per employee, and to be more competitive with other banks. By my calculations, revenue per employee at the bank was roughly $75,000 per year. Other banks were far higher. Early days at Schwab we were more than double that. We had to do better. But it seemed to me it fell on deaf ears. Sam insisted he didn't want to blow the whole thing up.

Old analyst that I am, I had for some time been digging through the bank's financials, searching for a true reading of the bank's health. You have to understand, Bank of America's reputation up to that point was unassailable. It represented the pinnacle of financial wherewithal, the pinnacle of ethics, the pinnacle of integrity in financial circles. But the deeper I looked, the more I was convinced that as bad as things were now, they were about to get much worse.

Obviously, I questioned my own thinking. That's when I called

Dennis Wu at Deloitte, Haskins & Sells, now known simply as Deloitte—he was Schwab's auditor for years—and asked him to look at the numbers. I did this quietly, there was no other way. Schwab was a subsidiary of the bank, and I was engaging Dennis in a matter relating to the parent. But the advice we got from my attorneys was that as a director, I was entitled to seek personal counsel, at my own expense, from whomever I chose. So I gave Dennis everything I had—all the public reports, including quarterly statements and annual reports going back five or six years. I told him I needed to know if I was right to be so worried or if I was just crazy, and I don't use that word lightly. My own analysis was so far removed from the consensus of my peers that I was beginning to question my sanity. I needed a reality check by having Deloitte reconcile my concerns.

From then on, with my lawyers' blessing, I shared all the financials with Dennis and his firm. Typically the directors received their packets of supporting materials the Friday before a Monday board meeting, and I then sent a copy to Dennis. Sometimes it was a stack of paper four inches thick. Dennis brought in other partners at his firm, including a banking specialist from Deloitte's Portland, Oregon, office, and together they'd crunch the numbers. Then we'd all get together at the Deloitte office on Sunday to try to make sense of what we'd learned.

Our focus quickly settled on nonperforming loans and the adequacy of the bank's reserves to support them. One day Dennis said, "Let's graph this thing." And there it was in black and white. The nonperforming loans line, steadily rising. The loan loss reserves line, flat. The gulf between the two, widening. Probably because of my dyslexia I've always been far more able to understand pictures than words. And that graph spoke volumes. It was a recipe for disaster, a clear indication that if present trends continued, the bank might soon find itself in deep trouble caused by bad loans. I was convinced the bank was simply overstating earned income while not reserving enough capital for potential loan losses.

That chart was among the materials I brought to an informal gathering of some of the bank's independent directors in the summer of 1985 at Bob McNamara's home in Washington, D.C. Dennis joined me, along with a couple of other partners from Deloitte's New York office. I had high hopes for that meeting. By then I'd come to expect skepticism from Sam and the board's internal directors. But on that Sunday afternoon in Washington, in the company of eminently reasonable outsiders like Bob McNamara and Andrew Brimmer, I let myself hope. I thought, *If I can only make them see what I see, they'll respond appropriately. Then I won't be the lone wolf howling in the woods. Together we can fix these problems before it's too late.*

I think it's fair to say that Bob and others appreciated my concern, and even shared it to some degree, but nobody shared my view that the bank was headed toward disaster. Have faith, that was the message I got from the independents. Management can handle this. No need to panic.

As I struggled with how best to proceed, one of the guys I talked to was Rich Arnold. Rich had been with me for almost a decade, going back to the days in the basement of 120 Montgomery. I'd always liked Rich, in part because he was loyal, and because he had skills I didn't, which is what matters most when you're putting together a team. An entrepreneur who is afraid to hire people who can do something better than he can is doomed. Rich was a fantastic salesman, for instance, and one of his most successful products was me. He could tell the loan officer at Security Pacific Bank, with conviction, "Chuck is a great guy, a brilliant entrepreneur, he'll make a lot of money for you," and the loan officer would believe him. Hell, I believed him. I couldn't sell myself as well as he could.

Rich was also a linear thinker—another skill that I admired. Within a year after we joined Bank of America, seeing how troubled I was by the bank's trajectory, Rich constructed a kind of road map that helped crystallize my thinking. He said, "Okay, let's look at this from the highest level. You are his subordinate, right? He's your boss.

He runs the bank. You run the subsidiary. First step: When you see your boss not performing, you try to get his attention. You go to him and you say, 'Hey boss, why did you do that? Why don't you do X? Why don't you try Y?'

"If that doesn't work, then you move to the level of being his peer. You meet on the golf course. You have a chat. 'Come on, Sam, you and I, let's work together and fix this problem.' If that doesn't work, then you have to take advantage of the fact that he's the president of the company and you're a director. He reports to you. So you speak to him as *your* subordinate and say, 'C'mon, Sam, I'm not happy. I'm a director of the company that you're running and you're not doing the job the way I think you ought to be doing it. Pull your socks up! Lift your game!'

"And if that doesn't work, you're going to have to become an activist director. You're going to have to talk to the other directors and say, 'Our boy's not doing his job. We've got to fix this.'"

By late summer 1985, I had passed through steps one, two, and three, with unsatisfactory results. I'd even gone so far as to approach what I had hoped would be a sympathetic subset of the board, again with unsatisfactory results. My next option was not one I was looking forward to, but I had no other choice. I had to break openly with Sam and state my case to the full board of directors. The next meeting was on August 5.

I DEVELOPED A SERIOUS case of the yips before that meeting. If you are a golfer, you know that's when your nerves affect your coordination. Your ability to concentrate evaporates, you shake, and suddenly you can't sink a two-foot putt. I had never had that before. And I've never had it since. Two years had passed since my first BofA board meeting, and I was still the youngest director in the room, still awed by my surroundings, still feeling a little bit like the imposter—the kid from Woodland, alone in a room with all those gray-hairs and blue bloods. Only this time, instead of just trying to fit in, I was here to challenge the leadership of the bank and carry a message to the board of directors I was sure no one wanted to hear: that in my humble opinion, Bank of America was a sinking ship and that all constituencies—management, employees, shareholders, and directors—had to pitch in to save it. I knew what the risks were: that I'd be maligned by these very powerful people as a rabble-rouser, a loose cannon, as someone who can't be trusted. It was the scariest thing I've ever done.

I walked into that meeting with no script, no handouts—just my handwritten notes and the big chart that Dennis Wu had drawn. I was one nervous puppy. I began by making the case for a huge dividend reduction. We had just reported our first quarterly loss ever, further losses loomed, and if Dennis's chart was to be believed we were in dire need of capital now to pump up our loan loss reserves. To me, it was lunacy not to eliminate the dividend altogether, at least for the balance of 1985 or until we stemmed our losses. I would have been a big loser. Stopping the dividend would cost me 70% of my personal income, but it was essential to turn the bank around.

Next, I recommended more layoffs. Even now, after three years of aggressive reductions, I saw room to eliminate another 4,000 jobs, saving the bank $200–$300 million. And for those who remained, pay cuts: 33% for the chairman and the president, 25% for the executive VPs, 20% for senior managers, and rescission of the recent increase in directors' pay. Finally, I called for a new quarterly bonus plan tied to earnings that would be more than enough to offset the salary reductions, provided we met our goals. That's how we had set up our compensation at Schwab. Performance-based rewards. Big when you succeeded, none when you didn't.

The bank had two or three big corporate jets. Unproductive assets.

I said sell them. I called for an independent review of the adequacy of our loan loss reserves. I talked fast, I tried to cover everything, but I ran out of time. I never did get into my senior management enhancement plan, which I had first raised at Bob McNamara's house, or my belief that we should terminate our relationship with Ernst & Whinney and appoint new auditors. My plan stopped short of calling for Sam Armacost's removal but did ask for a complete overhaul of his management team: new chief operating officer, new chief financial officer, new chief credit officer, and new chief marketing officer. Maybe it's better that I saved that part for later.

It all went over like a lead balloon. The reaction of most of the other board members was not just dismissive, it was angry. Maybe I was naive. Did I really expect them to welcome what I had to say? I wondered afterward, *Was my approach all wrong? Should I have written letters first? Tried to line up some allies? Should I have prepared Sam for what I was about to do?* Well, I had tried going to Sam, several times; he had made it clear he had no interest in my proposed reforms. At that point, I had to ask myself, *What is my responsibility as a director? As a shareholder?* I was still a huge shareholder, remember. Much larger than any of the other guys in that room.

I don't think I was looking for applause. Still, someone could have said, "This makes sense. Let's have a committee to review these things one by one." Or, "Maybe you and Sam could get together and come up with a focused plan." But no, nothing like that, not even close. I believe I had a few soft allies in the room, but no one willing to stand and be counted. I was on my own.

Later I had occasion to recall the last part of Rich Arnold's advice to me when I started down the path of trying to fix Bank of America—the part that comes after you go to the board and the board doesn't listen. "If that doesn't work," he had said, "what it means is that the directors aren't doing their job. And you're going to have to become an activist shareholder and say, 'We've got to fire this board and get a board that will do its bloody job.' And at that point it's going to become pretty public and pretty ugly."

Well, Rich was almost right. It did get public and it did get ugly. But somehow, before I came to the end of the script, I discovered a new ending.

16

OPEN REVOLT

At Schwab, just a few blocks from BofA, the bull market was raging. Average daily trading volume was soaring (about 8,000 in 1985, a fourfold increase since the beginning of the decade); total accounts and account assets were poised to pass important thresholds (one million accounts in August 1985, $10 billion in November 1986, respectively); and unlike our corporate parent, we were making money. We were not yet members of the financial establishment, but neither did we aspire to be. We were too busy fighting for the cause to bother a whole lot with appearances. We were too focused on getting things done to sit for hours in meetings. We still didn't have a formal executive committee, as did most companies our size; instead, we had the Popcorn Group, which met on Tuesday afternoons to eat popcorn and figure out what to do next. We didn't have an annual budget; instead, we had Barbara Ahmajan (after she married she became Barbara Wolfe), who scrutinized everyone's expense reports and chaired the Monthly Nut Meeting, as we called it, where the department heads defended what they'd spent last month and tried to predict what they were going to spend next month. We didn't have a personnel grading system like the civil service (or Bank of America, for that matter); instead, I paid people what I thought they were worth, regardless of seniority, and I used perks and bonuses to reward my stars. My top managers all drove cars the company paid for, nice ones, basically whatever they wanted. "Just keep it sane," Barbara advised, before sending them off to the dealerships.

Sometime around then, Herb Caen mentioned in his San Francisco *Chronicle* column that a handful of top BofA executives were driving company Chevies while the Schwab guys were driving Porsches, BMWs, and Datsun 240Zs. It may have been true. I didn't know, and I didn't care, though it caused a big stir at the time. If buying people nice cars made them happy and got them to work on time and helped them focus on their jobs, I bought them nice cars. For some of them it was the first car they had ever owned. We ended up having to reverse all that later, at Barbara's urging. It was an administrative nightmare with all the tax issues and whatnot, and it was taking time away from important stuff. No big deal. We got rid of the fancy perks, systematized our comp practices, and went on with it. All part of the firm's passage from adolescence to adulthood.

David Pottruck was one part of that passage. David's arrival in March 1984 to lead our marketing and advertising was a watershed for Schwab. David had spent the last two and a half years as senior vice president of consumer marketing at Shearson/American Express. Before that he spent six years at Citibank as a division controller. We had never hired anyone like David before. It wasn't simply that we did not recruit on Wall Street; in fact, we viewed having worked on Wall Street as a blot on your résumé. The feeling was mutual—Wall Street firms were not exactly raiding our executive team—although as with most rivalries the passion was a lot more intense on the part of the underdog. I think David's colleagues back east were mainly puzzled by his abrupt career move. Why would a rising star leave the center of the financial universe for a tiny discount firm out west? In their minds, ironically, the only thing we had going for us was what I had come to believe was the only thing holding us back: our connection to Bank of America.

I am sure David thought joining Schwab was about leaving the dark side and coming into the light. He made it plain that he had as strong a distaste for the full-commission brokerage business as I did. Here he was the marketing guy for a big Wall Street firm and he knew in his heart that the branded investments he was touting—stocks, mutual funds, limited partnerships—were ones he would not choose for himself. The way he tells it, the people he worked with used to sit around laughing about the products they were pushing. It was always, How much money is in it for the broker? How much is in it for the firm? And, Will the client make money or not make money? That was almost incidental.

David was thrilled to join a firm defined by what he recognized as a missionary zeal. He didn't mind our ragged appearance: the fact that the couch on the executive floor of One Second Street where he sat waiting for his job interview was Naugahyde instead of leather, that the stuffing was spilling out of one arm, that the springs were shot. He was even okay with moving from an office on the 106th floor of the World Trade Center to an office on the 6th floor of One Second Street, where on rainy days we put out garbage cans to catch the drips from the leaky roof. The fact is, by the time Dave arrived, we had already come a long way. The days of working at plywood-and-sawhorse desks, of monthly capital shortfalls, were over.

I hired David mainly because I wanted his marketing expertise, but I also wanted his Wall Street experience, his East Coast sensibility, and even to a certain extent his drive that could manifest itself as gruffness. Dave had been a wrestler and football player at the University of Pennsylvania and behaved like it sometimes. He scared people. About a month after Dave arrived, Larry Stupski stepped into his office in an effort to soften him up a bit and said, "Dave, you need to change your approach. You can't schedule two-hour meetings that start at 5:00 in the afternoon." Dave was baffled. Where he came from, 5:00 was the middle of the day. Everybody stayed late whether they had to or not; it was *expected*. Well, our people worked long hours, too—when necessary. Otherwise, they went home (or out on the town). Larry's message: scheduling regular meetings for the end of the workday was some kind of corporate macho thing that Dave picked up in New York. Not our style.

> **I needed someone who would push the team out of its comfort zone with fresh perspectives and energy. That was important if we were to keep on growing. Dave was that guy.**

ANY CULTURE SKIRMISHES WITHIN Schwab, while spirited, were family issues, all part of growing up; they were nothing compared to the ever-escalating *war* between us and Bank of America. To a certain extent, I had anticipated such problems. We were a mouse moving in with an elephant, we had to protect ourselves. That's why I'd insisted on all those "couch department" clauses we wrote into the contract, ensuring that we could keep our own auditor, our own legal counsel, and so forth. It was in their best interest as much as ours that we be left alone.

I had also sold Schwab to Bank of America because of the potential synergies between us; I had visions of two powerful institutions combining to offer our customers more than either of us was capable of providing alone. In almost every case the results were disappointing. We thought we could take advantage of some of that prime BofA real estate to reach new customers. So we put Schwab kiosks in bank branches. Yes, we got some new accounts. Not many, though, and they were generally small and not very active. Bank lobbies, it turns out, are not great places to find brokerage customers.

We also had high expectations for a combined Bank of America/Charles Schwab IRA. In the mid-1980s, everyone in the financial services industry—every bank, brokerage firm, and insurance company—was keen on capturing IRA money. We were all trying out new tactics; nobody knew what was going to work best, but everyone rightly saw a huge opportunity for gathering long-term assets. As the only big bank with a brokerage arm, we thought we had something unique to offer our customers: a single account where you could keep some of your money in an FDIC-insured savings account and the rest in a brokerage account. It was a good idea, and Sam Armacost liked it as much as I did. But coming up with an actual product that passed regulatory muster was no small task. We worked at it for months and finally gave up. In the end, the best we could do were two separate accounts on a single application—one of those multisheet forms where if you pressed down really hard with a ballpoint pen you only had to write your name and address once. BofA got the top sheet, we got the bottom sheet. Not exactly what I had in mind.

Meanwhile, with Bank of America now deep in retrenchment mode, cutting costs to improve their numbers, we suddenly needed permission for every capital investment, every business expense, pretty much every move we made. Under orders from on high, we began churning out detailed management plans with 12-month revenue and expense projections. Then word would come back: "We're asking all departments to cut costs by X%, please resubmit." We would try to explain why we couldn't really do that, not at the rate we were growing; that if we spent less money, we'd make less money and no one would be happy. And they would say, "Yeah, well we can't give any waivers. Everyone has to cut X%." What could we do? We promised them whatever they asked for, then proceeded as normal—and, by the way, always beat the plan. Other kinds of foolishness I refused to tolerate. For example, when they tried to tell me I had to move our corporate headquarters into a vacant, windowless building the bank owned. There was no way.

All those qualified as hassles. Of far more consequence were the roadblocks to growth our marriage to a bank had created. We had won regulatory approval to combine with Bank of America on the slimmest of terms, in accordance with the Glass-Steagall Act of 1933, which, as I mentioned, had separated banking and brokerage following the Great Depression. Under existing regulatory constraints of the Office of the Comptroller of the Currency (OCC), one of the country's federal banking regulators, and Glass-Steagall, a bank could garner no more than 5% of its revenue from sources other than banking. Our brokerage services fit that bill.

Glass-Steagall was ultimately doomed. Over the next decade or so it gradually became less of a limitation on banks that wanted to expand into the investing business and was finally repealed entirely in 1999. But at the time of the merger we clearly understood that we were not to stray from the narrow path of discount brokerage. Fine. We had no intention of straying—no interest in underwriting stock offerings, no plans to hire a commissioned sales force, no desire to start roping in customers with tall tales about getting rich quickly.

On the other hand, we felt we were indeed on a path, not in a box, and the path was leading us to new and interesting places, and we wanted to explore them. After we started our Mutual Fund Marketplace, for example, we wanted to offer our customers fund-performance numbers to help them make smart choices. No advice, mind you, just numbers: *information*. This was hardly a new concept for us. I've always believed that when it comes to investing, the more information, the better. But anything that so much as hinted of "advice" was seen by the regulatory overlords—initially, at least—as beyond the mandate of discount brokerage and therefore not okay.

Same thing with our Schwab One account. We had a lot of great ideas about how to make that better—credit cards, credit lines—but we couldn't do anything without prior OCC approval. It felt to me as if we'd been frozen in time, forever restricted to whatever functions, services, and offerings were deemed kosher in 1981. I was forced to sell the insurance brokerage company I had launched,

SelectQuote. Banks couldn't be in the insurance business. I wanted to have money market funds and portfolio management products, but there was no mechanism for easy, fluid responses to forces in the marketplace—we couldn't match what our competitors were doing, much less break new ground—and it was costing us business.

As hard as it was from day one living with regulatory roadblocks, it kept getting harder. The more precarious the bank's condition, the tighter the regulatory clamp. It was frustrating the heck out of me. At the August 1985 board meeting, I had made plain my alarm at the state of the bank's finances and the failure of the bank's management team to face facts. I offered a drastic plan to cut expenses and restore the bank's capital base. And unfortunately, in the months that followed, BofA's financial health went from being the subject of an internal dispute between me and the rest of the board to an agenda item for the US government. That summer, the Office of the Comptroller of the Currency (OCC) ordered Bank of America to write off more than a billion dollars in bad loans, and in late 1985 made each director pledge in writing to achieve a 6% capital ratio (a measurement of a bank's capital versus its riskier holdings that's used to measure a bank's health) by the end of 1986.

That was a very big deal—horrible news not only for the bank but for the directors themselves. It reflected the now widely recognized disarray in BofA's multibillion-dollar loan portfolio. The problem loans were by no means limited to Latin America. Domestic real estate, oil and gas, even the Greek shipping portfolio, were hemorrhaging cash. You know what happens when you loan a shipbuilder $70 million on a $100 million vessel and the technology changes and suddenly the ship has no value? One day the owner shows up in your London office and drops the keys on your desk and says, "She's parked in the Mediterranean." Then it's up to you to hire a crew, sail it to Saipan, take it apart with blowtorches, and sell it for scrap to the Koreans so they can build another new ship that will put another one of your old ships out of business. That sort of thing was happening across the bank's entire loan portfolio.

Despite frenetic efforts to sell assets, including the iconic headquarters building itself to Shorenstein partners for over $600 million, losses piled on losses—$178 million in the fourth quarter of 1985, followed by a small profit in the first quarter of '86, followed by a devastating $640 million loss in the second quarter. And the sharks were circling. First Interstate was making a case to the bank that a merger of the two, with First Interstate to take the management lead, was the ultimate solution and would put to rest BofA's problems. Then in March, Sandy Weill, former chairman of Shearson, which he had sold to American Express, presented himself to Armacost and the board as a solution, with aggressive ideas for turning the bank around that were focused on cutting costs and selling off some parts of the bank, and he presented a letter of commitment for $1 billion in fresh capital from his friends at Lehman Brothers. I thought it was an offer worth considering.

Sandy's proposal did not come as a surprise to me. He had come earlier to see me in San Francisco after we spoke briefly on the phone. We met in my office at 101 Montgomery (our new Schwab headquarters). Sandy was just a few years older than me, energetic, full of good ideas for the bank, and had a great reputation for turning businesses around. He was an analytic thinker and persuasive. By then it was well known that I was unhappy. Sandy had two things on his mind: one, would I support his offer?; and two, if he succeeded in buying Bank of America, would I stick around and continue running Charles Schwab? The first question was easy: I had no doubt that Sandy's capital and management expertise would be of great help to Bank of America, and I told him I could support his plan. The second question was even easier. I had no interest in giving up on Schwab, but I wanted our freedom. I told him I could not guarantee how long I would remain with Bank of America. At this point I had no interest in becoming part of another banking or financial services behemoth. One way or another—either by buying back Schwab or by leaving to start another business—I was determined to go back to doing my own thing. I said to him, "Sandy, you have great ideas for the bank that I could support. My only condition is that you spin us off."

But a faction of the board had no interest in talking to Sandy Weill. They were firmly behind Sam Armacost and they weren't looking to make a change. This was Bank of America, after all, the most prestigious financial institution west of the Hudson River. Maybe some of that was their distaste for the New York rough-and-tumble that Sandy represented, I don't know. But I've often wondered what might have been if Sandy had succeeded with his plan. Later he took Citigroup, of course, and built an international banking and finance juggernaut, largely through acquisitions. BofA's fate, meanwhile, was to become the incredible shrinking bank and ultimately sell to NationsBank of North Carolina. Today, the Bank of America name survives, but that's about the extent of the original San Francisco company. Maybe having Sandy in charge wouldn't have made much difference in terms of my wanting out from under the BofA umbrella. We needed our freedom if we were ever to realize our own ambitions. But I do wonder what Sandy might have accomplished at the helm of Bank of America. We'll never know. The BofA board rebuffed his overture and sent him on his way.

By now my own posture was angling toward open revolt. Sam was floundering, the board was in denial, and the regulators were bearing down. Every original plus of being associated with Bank of America was now a minus: instead of providing us with capital, BofA was telling us we had to cut our budgets; instead of giving us a platform to enter new markets and offer new products, it was blocking our every move; instead of buffing our reputation, it was tainting it. My discomfort with the bank was now very public. The *Wall Street Journal* even reported rumors that I favored Sam's removal as head of BofA. I was running out of options.

By early summer 1985, I was openly divesting myself of BofA stock, hoping to salvage some portion of my net worth before it was too late (and to make it available to help buy Schwab back should that be possible). The stock had started at $24; by the end it was $11. The thought of all that wealth evaporating—not just mine but that of all the employees who had helped build Schwab—was making me sick. I felt responsible for all the people I'd brought in as new BofA shareholders, I couldn't just abandon them. Of course, no one stood to lose more money than I did, but that was never my main concern. Maybe if I had inherited my money I'd feel differently about the possibility of losing it all.

I'd just always assumed that even in a worst-case scenario, if I had to start all over again at zero, I'd be okay. I would land on my feet again.

I was confident I'd be okay in the long run. What I wasn't sure about was if I could ever build anything like Charles Schwab again. I was proud of the company, proud of what it represented. I believed it would be my legacy. I wanted it to last. Driving me forward now was a sense of responsibility to my customers, to my employees, and to the company we had built together over the past decade—a company that was just now hitting its stride. At stake was nothing less than Schwab's shot at fulfilling its destiny. The original problems with our industry that we had set out to address—high costs, conflicts of interest—they were still there. It was an industry that still held out huge opportunity for someone who wanted to do things in a different way. All of which meant the consequences of failing to extricate myself from the quagmire at the bank were pretty damn severe.

ON AUGUST 13, 1986, I resigned from the board of Bank of America. Sam Armacost took it as a personal insult, but that's not at all what I intended. I just had to get out of there—mainly because I had begun plotting how to get my company back and was worried about conflicts of interest; I couldn't very well negotiate with myself. But also because I was completely frustrated, tense, and unhappy. It was weighing on me. The board's response surprised me. As obstinate a colleague as I had become, when it came right down to it, no one actually wanted me to quit. Lee Prussia, the chairman, tried to talk me out of it. He was worried how my departure would play at a time when the board was fielding lawsuits from angry shareholders (I wasn't alone anymore) and denying rumors that the bank was on the verge of collapse. He asked me to think it over. I did, but only for a couple of days. Instead, I honored their request to delay the resignation until month's end to give them some time to prepare. Few choices I have made in my life have been more agonizing, yet none felt more right in the end. I left town shortly afterward for a week of R&R in Hawaii, and I remember distinctly what a revelation it was—that sense of having escaped from under an immense burden. I felt free like I hadn't felt free in years.

Immediately after I resigned from the BofA board, the directors took away my seat on The Charles Schwab Corporation board, along with the seats of the other two insiders, Larry Stupski and Barbara Wolfe. Just a little reminder that as employees of a wholly owned subsidiary, we served at the mercy of our BofA overlords. I was still CEO of my own company, but who knew for how much longer? It did not sit well with me. Still, it was useful information. It wiped away the last of my illusions. I understood now that to win what I wanted more than anything in the world, I had to fight like I'd never fought before.

———

I STARTED GETTING UNSOLICITED calls from investment bankers who wanted to help me structure a deal. Among them, DLJ and Stephens Inc. down in Little Rock. Jack Stephens himself sent a plane out to San Francisco to fetch me. I flew to Arkansas for the day and met with his people. Jack had an idea for a leveraged buyout (LBO). I was open to considering an LBO, but the deal he offered wasn't attractive. Stephens wanted to own 80% and give us 20%. I thought we could do better than that, so I turned him down. Ultimately I came to the conclusion that if I could do the LBO myself it would be a much better deal for me, my management team, and our employees. Better for our clients, too, I thought, because I'd have control over how we shaped the company going forward. The larger question was whether the bank would entertain an offer from me. The fact that I had been kicked off my own board immediately after resigning from theirs was not a good sign.

On October 7, 1986, less than two months after my resignation, the board fired Sam Armacost. I was totally surprised. I suppose I felt vindicated. Finally, my former colleagues had recognized what I'd been saying for so long: that Bank of America was broken and Armacost was not the man to fix it. Then all hell broke loose. For a while it looked as if the end were near. Joseph Pinola, a onetime rival of Sam's for the top job at Bank of America, made a hostile bid to absorb BofA into his much smaller First Interstate Bancorp of Los Angeles.

At which point who should come back but Sam's predecessor, Tom Clausen. Put back in charge by the board of directors, Tom made it clear from the start that he was not interested in selling out to Joe Pinola or anybody else. He was here to save Bank of America. To that end he began the most aggressive effort yet to raise capital, cut expenses, and restore the bank to its former glory.

My interest in all the corporate drama at the bank began and ended with whether it affected my prospects for regaining control of Charles Schwab and getting on with what we had begun in 1975. Here the news was mixed. I met Tom Clausen for lunch on Halloween day, 1986, having no idea what to expect, and was gratified to learn that Schwab was indeed on his list of disposable assets. No one at the bank had ever said that to me before. In fact, Tom felt he had to sell Schwab. It was a quick way to raise a chunk of capital. I'm convinced he thought selling to me was the easiest and most logical thing to do. He offered me a window of time to put together an offer to purchase Schwab. I was thrilled, and to this day thank Tom for opening that possibility.

The first time I had approached Sam Armacost about buying my company back, in the late fall of 1985, he shot me down. I wasn't surprised. He had every reason to keep us then and no reason to let us go. Nearly a year later, the best of Sam's reasons for not selling still applied—we were among the crown jewels in the otherwise crumbling Bank of America empire. On the other hand, Bank of America now had a compelling, nearly desperate reason to sell. It was under orders from the OCC to raise capital. Already it had sold Finance America as well as Banca d'Italia, both part of a grand divestiture that ultimately brought in over a billion dollars. And the greatest reason of all, Tom's ace in the hole: by selling Schwab, BofA virtually guaranteed that First Interstate would back away. A big part of First Interstate's interest in BofA was Schwab and the potential that the bank and brokerage model presented. Nothing was sacred anymore, not even the crown jewels. That gave me hope.

FIVE DAYS AFTER MY meeting with Tom, hope was replaced by anxiety when BofA announced publicly its intention to sell Schwab *at auction to the highest bidder*. Now I had a new threat to worry about—the awful possibility of exchanging one corporate master for another.

My parents, Bettie and Bob Schwab, in Woodland, California, the late 1930s. *Photo courtesy of the author.*

Happily working my chicken business with friends and my grandad, Santa Barbara, early 1950s. *Photo courtesy of the author.*

Practicing my golf swing in Santa Barbara, early 1950s. *Photo courtesy of the author.*

Uncle Bill: business mentor, early investor in Schwab, and operator of our first branch (in Sacramento, California, 1975). *Photo courtesy of the author.*

U.S. | the Federal Reserve Board and its | ... are
duct | critics, the measure apparently
with | pleases neither.
:om- | (Story on Page 6)
the | F
pre- | cans
T

Merrill Lynch will raise securities brokerage fees an average 3% on most standard transactions under $5,000 when the industry adopts competitive rates tomorrow.
(Story on Page 5)

Eastman Kodak unveiled its plain-paper copier at its annual

May Day, 1975. To my great relief, Merrill Lynch raises prices on the little guy. *Photo courtesy of The Charles Schwab Corporation.*

The simple advertisements that created a new category, Discount Brokerage. *Photo courtesy of The Charles Schwab Corporation.*

Technology becomes the lynchpin that makes rapid growth possible.
Photo courtesy of The Charles Schwab Corporation.

Our data command center in the early 1980s. *Photo courtesy of The Charles Schwab Corporation.*

Milton Friedman (with John Coghlan and me) is a featured guest speaker at a Schwab client event celebrating new technology capabilities. *Photo courtesy of The Charles Schwab Corporation.*

BankAmerica Corporation CEO Sam Armacost and me in 1983. *Photo courtesy of The Charles Schwab Corporation.*

Standing in front of our new branch in the Bank of America lobby, circa 1986. *Photo courtesy of The Charles Schwab Corporation.*

Signing papers for our management-led buyback, 1987. With me and other members of the team are Chris Dodds (with mustache) and Dennis Wu (far right). *Photo courtesy of The Charles Schwab Corporation.*

Larry Stupski, me, David Pottruck, Barbara Wolfe, Bob Fivas, and Woody Hobbs in the late 1980s. Holding the place up, or knocking down walls? . . . I can't recall. *Photo courtesy of The Charles Schwab Corporation.*

Clients crowd the branch in San Francisco on October 17, 1987, "Black Monday," to watch the ticker as the market drops 22.6 percent, the biggest one-day percentage loss in U.S. stock-market history. *Photo courtesy of The Charles Schwab Corporation.*

"Wall \$treet Week with Louis Rukeyser," summer 1989, with Perrin Long, Sandy Weill, and Louis. Publicity helped drive our business from day one. *Photo courtesy of The Charles Schwab Corporation.*

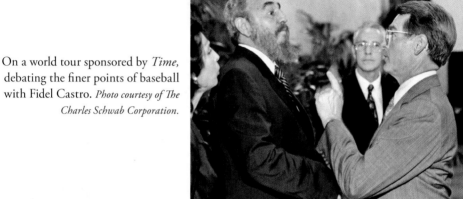

Prepping for filming in the early 1990s with colleagues Beth Sawi and Jim Losi. *Photo courtesy of The Charles Schwab Corporation.*

On a world tour sponsored by *Time,* debating the finer points of baseball with Fidel Castro. *Photo courtesy of The Charles Schwab Corporation.*

Fortune features a young me on their dyslexia cover story in May 2002. *From FORTUNE, May 13 © 2002 Time Inc. All rights reserved. Used by permission and protected by Copyright Laws of the United States. The printing, copying, redistribution, or retransmission of this Content without express written permission is prohibited.*

In the summer of 2002 during the peak of the Wall Street research scandal, we launched a new stock-rating system and wealth-management service that turned the traditional approaches on their heads, landing us on the cover of *BusinessWeek.* *Used with permission of Bloomberg L.P. Copyright © 2017. All rights reserved.*

Visiting our annual meeting for independent investment advisers in 2007. IMPACT is the biggest event of its kind, attracting thousands of advisers from across the country. Andrew Schofield and Michelle Draper describe the latest Schwab technologies. *Photo courtesy of The Charles Schwab Corporation.*

In January 2008, President George W. Bush named me chairman of the newly created President's Advisory Council on Financial Literacy, an initiative to promote financial literacy. My daughter Carrie Schwab-Pomerantz participated as well. To my left are John Hope Bryant, Jack Kosakowski, David Mancl, Carrie Schwab-Pomerantz, and Ignacio Salazar. To my right are Dan Iannicola and Ted Daniels. *Photo courtesy of The Charles Schwab Corporation.*

CEO Walt Bettinger and I preparing to address the senior management team during the depths of the financial crisis in January 2009. Three months later, the market hit bottom and began its nine-year climb upward. *Photo courtesy of The Charles Schwab Corporation.*

Each year thousands of Schwab employees blitz the country with volunteer activities. In May 2011, I joined a team putting together New Mom Kits for local hospitals in the San Francisco Bay Area. *Photo courtesy of The Charles Schwab Corporation.*

At the Museum of American Finance in January 2016 with family to receive the Lifetime Achievement Award for Innovation. Helen surprised me with a table full of my family supporters: Kids and spouses Courtney, Virginia, Mike, Carrie, Gary, Matt, and Katie were there to cheer me on. *Photo by Elsa Ruiz, courtesy of the Museum of American Finance.*

Spring 2016, Bob Fisher and I help open the new SFMOMA with museum director Neal Benezra and others. One push of the button and the confetti flew! *Photo by Drew Altizer, courtesy of SFMOMA.*

Below: One of my favorite activities, visiting our many regional offices and the dedicated teams that make it all work. Here, in Westlake, Texas, 2018, for a group selfie. *Photo courtesy of The Charles Schwab Corporation.*

I had other ideas. After resigning from the board in midsummer 1986, I had lined up a team of three lawyers, each with their unique role, starting with Larry Rabkin, who helped me think through my options. I had known Larry since 1980 when he represented one of the underwriters involved in our aborted IPO. Larry learned a lot about us during that whole fiasco and convinced me that he had a deep understanding of the brokerage industry. After we put the IPO to rest, I started calling on him to represent us. He served as the firm's primary outside counsel for years after. Larry is eminently reasonable, a consummate problem solver, the kind of lawyer I knew was well matched against the best that Bank of America could throw at us.

Larry was my corporate lawyer to help guide a transaction. Sandy Tatum from Cooley, Godward, Castro, Huddleson & Tatum was my peacemaker lawyer. Sandy had just finished a term as head of the USGA, golf's national governing body. He had impeccable establishment credentials, a gentleman's way about him, and knew George Coombe, BofA's general counsel through golf circles. I wasn't sure yet where all these preparations were taking me, but I knew that whatever happened, I could count on Sandy to keep things civil.

Finally, Bart Jackson was my bulldog. Bart had earned a reputation in town as a really tough litigator with Jackson Tufts Cole & Black. (Years later, in 1993, when a rail car filled with sulfuric acid blew up in the East Bay, Bart would represent General Chemical against 100,000 claimants in the kind of nasty case where there are no winners, just enormous legal challenges.) Bart was a fighter. I figured I could use him to balance Sandy if things got ugly down the road.

I asked Sandy and Bart for their advice on a possible dramatic course of action I'd been quietly pondering for months: Did I have a case for rescission—for an annulment—against Bank of America? My first experience with a rescission suit had been on the receiving end, back in the days of Mitchell, Morse & Schwab. In 1970, the

SEC had cited us on a technicality related to the marketing of one of our mutual funds. After the fund lost value, a Texas investor used the SEC citation as the basis for a rescission claim. A rescission meant he went back to square one and any losses in value became ours, not his. So I knew firsthand how powerful the threat of rescission could be. I also knew that the threshold for succeeding with such a claim was very high. Still, I wondered: Had Bank of America so misrepresented its true financial condition when it issued stock to buy The Charles Schwab Corporation in 1983 that I and everyone else who took part in the deal—all my employees, all my shareholders—were now entitled to be made whole? Was it possible that Bank of America could be ordered to give me back my company at the cost they originally paid, plus damages?

Sandy looked at the documents—the original agreement, plus reams of forensic accounting I'd been collecting from Dennis Wu and his team at Deloitte—and concluded, no, he didn't think I had a case. But Bart Jackson thought otherwise. He came back from vacation in the woods of northern Wisconsin having studied the documents, all fired up to go to war. It would be a monumental fight, he warned. I would be attacking the credibility of a revered institution at its roots. There could be severe personal and professional repercussions. And yet, Bart clearly wanted to give it a shot. He really thought we could win. I told him I needed some time to think it over. I went home and talked to Helen, and the next time I met with Bart, Helen came with me. I wanted her to hear firsthand what we were getting ourselves into: a potentially ugly fight with some of the most well-known names in San Francisco. After that second meeting, I still wasn't ready to drop the bomb, but I knew I wanted it in my arsenal. "Fine," I said to Bart, with Helen's blessing, "draft a complaint."

17

FREE AT LAST

By the fall of 1986, we had outgrown our building at One Second Street and were in new headquarters at 101 Montgomery Street. That was a big step up for us. We had 28 floors now, including a big, bright, high-tech branch office at street level, in the heart of the Financial District. My own office was with the rest of the senior managers upstairs on the 28th floor. Marketing and advertising—including our in-house ad agency, CRS Advertising—was one floor below on 27. Close but not as close as I wanted. Before we moved in, I had the contractors cut a hole in the floor of 28 and build a staircase for me connecting the two floors. My passion lay with marketing and advertising. That's where I wanted to stay connected.

> There are some areas where I always trust my own knowledge and instincts, and never completely relinquish control; there are others where I'm eager to have help.

Keeping tight, personal control on marketing was one thing, but Charles Schwab was about to go on the auction block. I knew that if I was to have any hope of preventing the sale of my company to a third party, I could not do it by myself.

One of the first people I called on was Rich Arnold, who had been so pivotal at other points in the past. Rich had left Schwab in the summer of 1985 to lead Bank of America's proposed expansion into retail banking in his native Australia. When he got there, he saw that for various regulatory reasons peculiar to Australia, BofA's plan was not going to fly; eventually he called the whole thing off (preventing BofA from making a $100 million mistake). At the moment he wasn't doing much of anything. When he volunteered his willingness to return to San Francisco, I asked him if he wanted to be my field general in the coming battle. He must have bought a ticket on the next plane because he arrived the very next day.

I knew what Rich could do for me in this situation and I needed his skills. I also knew that while it was critical we not lose Schwab to another buyer, it was just as important not to allow the whole organization to be drawn into the fight. I needed David Pottruck and the others to stay focused on their duties. So to assist Rich I chose Chris Dodds, a recent young hire who later became my CFO and among my most trusted advisers. Chris had played basketball at Clemson University—he hit a jump shot over Isiah Thomas at the buzzer to beat Indiana in 1980, the season Indiana won the national championship. Obviously, he wasn't one to buckle under pressure. He was also an expert in the mysteries of finance theory, discounted cash flow, discount rates—all the financial minutiae that went into valuing companies. Chris would help Rich run the numbers.

I already had all the lawyers I needed: Larry, Sandy, and Bart. Finally, I turned—as before at critical junctures in the company's history—to my old friend George Roberts. George's involvement began inconspicuously enough, as an informal adviser. Bank of America had retained Salomon Brothers as the agent for the seller, so I asked George to recommend a good investment banker for my side of the table. George came up with several names and sat with Rich and me through the vetting process. George said from the start that I should look for a firm that was willing to step up and help finance the deal. Everybody wanted to advise us—and collect a big fee—but nobody wanted to commit to providing the capital we needed to make the deal work.

Part of the problem was the same issue George had warned me about on the tennis court all those years ago, when I was just starting to think about the discount brokerage business. Namely, how do you put a value on such an enterprise? Wall Street still wasn't sure. In the end, I realized that the best advice I could hope to get I was getting already from the guys sitting next to me. Maybe I didn't need a big investment banking firm after all. Maybe all I needed were my lawyers, my accountants, and George. "Well, okay," George said, when I asked him to join my team as chief strategist. "If you want me to, I'll help you."

Salomon Brothers, meanwhile, had come up with a valuation of $250–$350 million. I didn't want to pay that much for a company I'd sold only a few years before for $52 million. On the other hand, I was determined not to let this opportunity slip away. So I approached Tom Clausen and Frank Newman, the bank's CFO, and asked for a two-week window of exclusivity in which to present an offer. Clausen agreed, though he wasn't quite ready to give up on the idea of an auction. On the other hand, he was on a mission to shed assets, raise capital, and stave off bankruptcy at Bank of America. The sale of Charles Schwab to its current management helped accomplish all that, plus it had the virtue of simplicity. Clausen recognized as much, and as I tell him now whenever I see him, he's been my hero ever since.

TWO WEEKS IS NOT a lot of time. We were not even sure yet what our strategy should be. The big unknown was the rescission lawsuit. I thought it was potentially a very powerful weapon and Bart Jackson agreed. Bart really wanted to try the case. He was practically drooling at the thought of putting me in front of a jury. He believed that for many of the same reasons I was a credible, effective advocate for my company in our advertisements, I also would make a credible, sympathetic witness on the stand. I agreed, and I was ready to give him the go-ahead, whatever the consequences.

A suit would be messy. Bart had warned Helen and me about the risks of taking on one of the most powerful institutions in the city. He was not exaggerating. Already I was hearing from people saying, "This is a small community, you don't need this kind of trouble." But that hardly scared me; all I was thinking about was, how can I right this wrong? I felt deeply responsible for the early investors in The Charles Schwab Corporation, a group that included most of my employees. They had followed me into the arms of Bank of America, only to wind up paying a huge price for their loyalty when their converted stock tanked. I paid a price, too, but I had cashed out early. I still had about $10 million in my war chest, and I was prepared to blow it all if necessary to correct what I perceived as a grave injustice.

Maybe I was letting my passion for the cause get the best of me. Luckily I had George Roberts. George didn't like the rescission suit at all. He argued that to win, we needed to establish fraud, and as George put it, "There's a big difference between stupidity and fraud." In other words, yes, Bank of America had misrepresented its financial health when it bought us with inflated stock in 1982; that much we knew and could probably prove. But could we prove it had done so intentionally? Much more difficult. And if we failed, we'd certainly have created deep resentment. It would be that much harder to come back and bargain with the enemy. Better to at least begin negotiations on civil terms, that was George's advice. And after hearing him out, I agreed.

Besides, even just the *threat* of such a lawsuit, coming from a former director, was huge leverage all by itself. Already Bank of America was the subject of several third-party suits brought by angry investors who, like me, had been harmed by the bank's failure to make adequate financial disclosures. As a former director, I was a named defendant in those suits. Imagine if I were suddenly to file my own claim sympathetic to the plaintiffs' claims, and by the way bring to light all the communications and internal documents I'd analyzed during the course of my research. That was a potential bombshell the bank wanted no part of. Moreover, the bank was clearly desperate to rebuild its reserves and get the regulators off its back. Selling Schwab was not a choice, it was an absolute necessity. But a sale to anyone other than me would be all but impossible under the cloud of a major lawsuit. Whoever bought us would be buying the suit, too. No one wanted to inherit that mess.

So yes, I believed I had significant leverage. But only if BofA and its lawyers believed I really was capable of taking drastic legal action. Since Bart Jackson had already drafted the complaint, I gave him permission to share it with George Coombe, the bank's general counsel. I wanted Coombe to see exactly what I was holding in reserve. The complaint referred to $5.5 billion in assets that "should have been classified as substandard or doubtful" in 1982, a sum exceeding the bank's total shareholders' equity at the time of $4.6 billion. It demanded rescission plus damages "in an amount which cannot be presently ascertained but which exceeds $200,000,000." I can only imagine the expression on George's face as he read it.

Meanwhile, Larry Rabkin, who unlike Bart was seen by his adversaries as reasonable and temperate, went through back channels to convey to his friends inside Bank of America that I was dead serious (and maybe a little crazy); that I had suffered a severe erosion of my net worth with the collapse of BofA's stock and was willing to examine any and all remedies to make myself whole, including rescission. That spooked them. It also made them furious. There was a definite component of blind rage in this affair, coming mainly from George Coombe and directed at me. And no wonder. My finger was resting on what Rich Arnold liked to call the "red button." If I pressed the button, Rich used to say, I could break the bank.

WITH BART JACKSON PRESSING hard for all-out war and Larry Rabkin doing his best to persuade Bank of America that it was all he could do to keep me contained and reasonable, it fell to Sandy Tatum to convey some very bad news to the bank. Sandy had a long and illustrious career at the San Francisco bar. Still, if you asked him years later about his most satisfying professional experiences, I'm pretty sure he would have included the memo he wrote to BofA's general counsel in the fall of 1986, alerting him to an almost forgotten clause in the original sale agreement.

In retrospect, the fact that we were careful to exclude my name and likeness from the sale to Bank of America made us look like geniuses. Not that anyone could have foreseen the critical role that clause one day played. But thank goodness Larry Rabkin had made sure to include it. Essentially it confirmed that when I sold my company to Bank of America, I would only be *licensing* the rights to my name and likeness; in the unlikely event Schwab were ever shuttered or sold, such rights reverted to me. Nothing in the agreement prevented Bank of America from one day selling to a third party, as they now threatened to do. But in that case I would be free to cross the street and open Charles Schwab the sequel. The bank could sell my business; it could not sell me or my management team.

That simple fact, conveyed by Sandy to George Coombe, utterly transformed the environment in which the transaction took place. While the threat of rescission was real, it was just that, a threat. Reasonable legal minds could differ on what the outcome might be if such a suit ever went to trial. All anyone could know was that it would take years to resolve, would be wildly contentious, and could very well destroy all prospects for my company at a critical stage in its development. I didn't want that any more than Bank of America did. The ownership rights to my name and likeness, on the other hand, were plainly, indisputably mine. The implications of that fact proved devastating to Bank of America's negotiating stance.

WITH OUR TWO-WEEK WINDOW of exclusivity about to close, we presented Bank of America with an offer. Not our final offer, of course. Our strategy was to first make an offer so outrageous that if there were 11 people in the room on their side of the table, 10 of them would get up and walk out. When we offered $190 million, that's pretty much what happened. Steve McLin was the only one who, figuratively speaking, stayed behind. He looked at the terms, thought about what the bank's alternatives were at that point, and essentially said to his colleagues, "Hang on a second, guys, I think we have to listen to these folks."

In the end, I agreed to pay $280 million, plus a stake in future profits ("sucker insurance," George Roberts called it) that was ultimately worth an additional $50 million when we bought Schwab back at full value. Not a bad return on an asset for which Bank of America had paid $52 million four years earlier. In fact, before I agreed to go through with it, George needed to convince me I wasn't being fleeced. Truth is, the deal was terrifically advantageous to me, and fully reflective of the powerful leverage I brought to the negotiating table. Yes, BofA was making six times their initial investment, but I like to remind people that we sold to them at three times revenue and we were buying it back at that same ratio, essentially the same deal in reverse, and largely on borrowed capital.

The key lay in the innovative structure of what amounted to one of the first leveraged buyouts ever involving a service company. LBOs themselves were nothing new. But until now few had ever attempted one unless the company to be acquired had actual hard assets—

factories, equipment, inventories—that could be priced and sold if necessary to service the massive debt that went along with such buy-outs. Ours was a cash-flow LBO. Schwab had very little in the way of hard assets. We had a few computers, of course, and lots of office furniture. But our only substantial assets were our customers, for the trading income they represented. In other words, the value of Schwab was imbedded in our clients. Recognizing that fact—and more important, persuading our lenders to recognize it—unlocked the value of Charles Schwab and allowed the deal to go forward.

We borrowed a lot of money, starting with $150 million of senior debt from Security Pacific Bank. Senior debt meant if we ever went bankrupt, Security Pacific was first in line to get paid. Lined up behind that was $50 million in senior subordinated debt and $55 million in junior subordinated debt, both from Bank of America. All told we borrowed $255 million, or a little more than 90% of the purchase price. The remaining $25 million came from just a few sources: Security Pacific Bank, which provided $6 million of preferred stock; and $19 million of equity, half from me and the rest from senior managers of Schwab. We used all the resources we could muster, including proceeds from my sale of BofA stock and the employee stock option plan funds we had built up handily while part of BofA. That was all the equity in the deal.

In recognition of the assets we acquired, we created a $137 million depreciable asset for tax purposes—our customer list. That was something never before seen in the brokerage industry. It took some wrangling with the IRS, but in the end we obtained a ruling that allowed us to write off, year after year, a portion of the value of our customers at the time of the buyback. On the one hand, that meant we reported lower profits, which became a problem after we went public. I'm sure our stock suffered as a result. On the other hand, having that write-off significantly reduced our tax burden, thereby freeing up cash, cash that reassured our lenders and proved vital in eventually paying down our enormous debt.

Finally, I made sure anyone who had stuck by me benefited. I offered George Roberts and his partners at KKR a 15% stake in the new Charles Schwab, which cost them less than $3 million. Most of what George invested ended up in his foundation and has since funded his charitable endeavors. Later, pulling from my 50% ownership, we granted stock warrants, which are similar to stock options, to Schwab employees and friends and family of mine who had supported us along the way. The warrants we granted were equal to about 15% of our shares. To receive the warrants, employees had to submit claims detailing how much money they had lost by virtue of owning BofA stock during the period of time that BofA owned Schwab. In effect, we were granting to one and all the retroactive benefits of rescission I had sought when I first contemplated suing Bank of America. Those warrants became the foundations of huge fortunes for many longtime employees, but more important, they gave everyone incentive to make Schwab a great company and go after its mission with zeal. I was told at the time that this approach of giving so much to employees and clients was unheard of and unnecessary. Not in my mind. It was the right thing to do for all those who had loyally stuck with us.

Yes, it was a terrifically advantageous deal, but also terrifically risky given the historic volatility of the brokerage industry. When we agreed to terms in January 1987, the stock market was five years into a raging bull market, with no end to prosperity in sight.

If I had learned anything after years in the business, it was how little I could ever know about what the market would do tomorrow.

But one thing was clear: We had very little margin for error. Should the market turn suddenly and Schwab's recent profits flip to losses, I could quickly lose my company to its lenders.

THERE WERE SO MANY pieces and so many players that it's hard to know who or what was really responsible for making the deal happen. Looking back, I can say that yes, absolutely, the licensing agreement was key. But so was the threat of rescission. So was the foresight that went into protecting my right to retain my own lawyers and accountants even after I sold out to Bank of America. So was George Roberts, for his creativity and expertise, and the respect he commanded on both sides of the table. So was Rich Arnold, who had a knack for getting things done and could often present my case better than I could present it myself. And so was my entire senior management team, which made it clear at a critical point in negotiations that if Bank of America sold to a third party, it was sticking with me.

A lot of factors went our way. But letting go of Schwab was hard for Bank of America. We were one of the few remaining jewels in a badly tarnished crown. We were profitable, we were growing, and we were the bank's only foothold in the public markets at a time when middle-class savers were increasingly becoming middle-class investors. Essentially all the same factors that had made us so attractive to Bank of America four years earlier still applied.

So why sell? Because now there were new factors that trumped the old. Bank of America needed cash. Charles Schwab was a valuable asset. Therefore selling it made perfect sense. And Steve McLin, who was leading the bank's aggressive divestiture efforts, recognized, like Clausen, that selling to me rather than to a third-party bidder carried a decisive advantage. It was a clean deal. Even if my best offer was disappointingly low, it wasn't likely anyone would offer more. Not with rescission and the prospect of never-ending litigation, not with management departures, or the loss of our name hanging over them.

THE BUYBACK OF CHARLES Schwab, completed just a few months before my fiftieth birthday, was tremendously gratifying. It underscored for me at an important time in my life that hard work pays off. And that good things follow from doing what you know is right, but only if you're willing to fight for what you believe in. It marked how far we had come as a company in a very short time: from upstart to pariah to up-and-comer (though still dependent on richer, more established patrons like Bank of America) to our present position as an industry force in our own right. We sat poised as never before to prosper and grow and spread more widely and more deeply than ever before the ethos of investing and stock ownership.

Of course, I shared in the elation. But already I was looking ahead, and I was concerned. Even as we gathered in Larry Rabkin's office at the Embarcadero building to sign the closing papers and pose for celebratory snapshots, I was thinking about ways to reduce our leverage. Never comfortable with debt, I now found myself more deeply in the hole than I had ever thought possible. That was fine as long as our cash flow held up. But cash flow was dependent on trading volume, and trading volume depended on the market, and the health of the market was beyond my control. I remember chatting at the closing with Dennis Wu, my longtime accountant, who reminded me of a basic, hard truth: rising interest rates are the stock market's enemy.

When the stock market falls, it's usually because interest rates are rising.

For brokers, especially highly leveraged brokers, rising rates translate into a deadly combination of falling revenues and rising expenses. The market had been hot for some time. It looked to me like we were in a peak period. Down was a logical next direction.

Later that afternoon I addressed more than 1,500 of my employees in the big ballroom of the St. Francis Hotel. There I formally announced the creation of the new Charles Schwab Corporation. We all wore buttons with *Free at Last* boldly printed in blue. It was the happiest moment of one of the happiest days of my life. Crossing the stage to the podium, I felt like I was floating. But already I was also thinking about my next move. Before I left the law firm's offices on the morning of the closing, I had grabbed Larry Rabkin's arm and pulled him out into the hallway for privacy. "Please," I said quietly, "start working on the IPO."

18

DON'T PUSH YOUR LUCK

Seven years after my first attempt at going public and just days since our leveraged buyout from the Bank of America, I was all set to give an initial public offering of Schwab stock another shot. Back in 1980 I had hoped to raise north of $4 million, money I badly needed to keep Schwab growing. When the investment bankers priced the shares at $2.75, which would have brought less than $3 million, I had pulled out. Happily, that's when Tony Frank had stepped in on behalf of First Nationwide Savings and National Steel and offered to buy a 20% stake at a price that made much more sense to me. Cash in hand, I had put my IPO dreams on hold and gotten back down to business.

In retrospect, it's obvious why the first IPO did not succeed. As far as most observers were concerned, our nascent industry had not yet built a track record that inspired enough confidence in our future prospects. Of course, *I* saw a brilliant future—for discount brokerage in general and Schwab in particular. But I can see now why others did not share my vision. It had been too early.

But a lot had changed during the past seven years since that first attempt. Discount brokerage had grown up, shedding its rough-at-the-edges image and steadily stealing market share from traditional brokers. The union with Bank of America had helped considerably with that. More than ever, Schwab was the undisputed category leader. Our revenues had risen 50% in 1986 to more than $300 million while our net income had nearly tripled to more than $30 million. And, after years of aggressive advertising, I think it's safe to say that investors everywhere finally had a good idea who we were and what we were about. Schwab was now a recognized feature on the financial services landscape, and to my surprise, I had become a household name. Last but not least, the mood on Wall Street heading into the summer of 1987 was nothing short of euphoric. The bull market that began in August 1982 was nearly five years old and showed no signs of weakening. With the Dow surging toward 2,500 and beyond, many companies were taking advantage of high valuations and going public in record numbers; and few were as reputable, profitable, and fast growing as we were. All that combined to exert a powerful force pulling me toward an IPO.

Internal factors, meanwhile, were pushing me hard in the same direction. Though our debt was set up advantageously in layers of senior and subordinated debt, it was still enormous. Now that I had my freedom from BofA, I was determined to pay down those loans as quickly as possible. I hated owing so much money. It felt like I was wearing a financial straitjacket. Big bank loans come with all kinds of restrictive covenants: you can only devote this much to capital expenditures; your profits must be such and such; if you want this or that you need to ask us first. I've never liked managing my business in the face of such constraints. The marriage to BofA proved that. I need freedom to act quickly, to invest in new products and new markets even if it means sacrificing short-term profits. That makes for a better business in the long term, and it certainly made for a better experience for our clients along the way. There were so many great opportunities ahead that I wanted to go after. And we had strong cash flow to help us be aggressive. The sooner I could pay down the debt and get out from under those covenants, the better.

Certainly there are other ways to pay down debt than with an IPO. I could have sold another piece of Schwab to private investors, and in that way sidestepped the public scrutiny and regulatory oversight that goes with listing stock on the exchanges. The fact is, going public to reduce debt often amounts to trading one set of operating restrictions—bank covenants—for another that may turn out to be even more onerous: namely, the markets' insistence on steady, predictable profits, even at the expense of growth. I learned early in my career as an analyst, and it has been confirmed to me many times since in my role as head of a public company and as a director on many boards, that investors won't long tolerate interruptions in the flow of earnings. For that reason alone, many successful private companies (Fidelity Investments is the best example in the investing services industry) choose never to go public. The Johnson family at Fidelity has always had more freedom to make big investments in their business. Part of me is envious of that.

Competition and market forces urge you to do more, be better, find new ways to attract customers, innovate, use your capital efficiently, hire more people . . . *grow*.

But I believed that transparency with respect to our clients as well as investors, while occasionally burdensome, was ultimately going to be a good thing for Schwab. Going public, I believed, would confirm our commitment to our existing customers while reinforcing our marketing message. Our story, remember, was that we didn't tell stories. We let the client decide how he or she wanted to invest, and then we executed the transaction as cleanly, efficiently, and inexpensively as possible. So why not open our books and let our clients see for themselves? And if some of those clients should decide to become investors in The Charles Schwab Corporation, so much the better. Already I was committed to giving as many of them as possible that opportunity. I also believed the discipline of being a public company is one of the great strengths of free-market capitalism.

I wanted us to be part of that vibrant system.

Of course, we know now, with the benefit of hindsight, that there was one more excellent reason to proceed without delay with an IPO—Black Monday. The market was about to crash and with it our potential sources of capital would dry up for some time.

AN IPO IS A daunting task under the best of circumstances, and this one was all the more so coming on the heels of a monumental leveraged buyout from Bank of America. Breaking free of BofA had been incredibly draining and thoroughly distracting for everyone involved. Pat McManus, our CFO, had left prior to the LBO; and no sooner was the IPO accomplished than we lost our head of back-office operations, Bob Fivis, as well. A certain amount of turnover was to be expected. When you're going from a subsidiary of a bank, to an independent private company, to a company on the verge of an IPO, all in a matter of months, you are going to lose people.

On the other hand, you can't very well take a company public without a CFO. Someone had to step up. Larry Stupski agreed to serve in that role until we could find a permanent replacement. But poor Larry was already functioning as president and COO, the last thing he needed was more responsibilities. I'm sure he preferred that we take a breather from the hard work of recapitalizing Schwab and refocus for a while on the brokerage business. But as always with Larry, he stepped up to do what was needed.

He wasn't the only one who felt overwhelmed. I remember tapping Rich Arnold on the shoulder soon after the buyback closed and calling him into my office. He stood there looking at me with a smile like he thought I was going to shake his hand and give him a gold watch for the great job he'd done. Instead, I asked him to get going right away on the IPO. "Chuck," he said, almost pleadingly, "you've got to be crazy." Rich's best argument for standing pat was that with our healthy cash flow, the leverage wasn't really a big deal. He figured that the way we were going, we could pay down the debt in two and a half years. But Rich's scenario assumed the bull would keep running, and I wasn't prepared to bet on that assumption. It felt to me like wishful thinking. This was no time to stand pat, no matter how well we were doing at the moment, and how thrilled we all were to have freed ourselves from Bank of America's control.

Compared to the first go-round, this IPO was more conventional. For one thing we never had any illusions about underwriting it ourselves. Instead, we engaged Morgan Stanley and First Boston, two prominent Wall Street firms whose willingness to participate I viewed as yet another sign of how far we had progressed as a company and an industry during the 1980s. That said, I introduced a couple of elements that added to the complexity of the deal and ultimately forced us to delay the offering until September of '87.

One, I set aside a big chunk of stock for our own customers—50% of the shares. The investment bankers fought me, I expect because it left them with fewer shares for *their* customers. This is unheard of, they said. And it probably was. But I was sure this was going to be a successful IPO and I was determined to give Schwab account holders a piece of the action. And as committed investors, they were also committed to Schwab.

Two, we went into this IPO knowing that many of our employees were holding warrants I'd apportioned during the buyback from BofA. Those warrants were designed to make my people whole after the BofA debacle when the shares they received then shriveled up. We had received $22 per share in BofA stock at the close of the deal in 1982, and by 1985 the value was down to $18, heading to $9 by 1987. My employees had seen a lot of their personal wealth evaporate. As part of the buyback, we gave warrants to purchase future shares in Schwab to employees. They were given out proportionally to the losses they had incurred in BofA stock. To me, it was a matter of integrity. I had led them into the acquisition and I wanted to be sure they had the chance to make up for the financial losses of that decision. So I wanted them calculated into the mix for this IPO. As it happened, the warrants did much more than make people whole. They would form the foundation of large personal fortunes for many longtime Schwab employees.

In August I left the country for a long overdue vacation, a three-week photo safari in Africa with my family. It was not the most relaxing vacation I have ever had. Now that the decision to go for the IPO had been made, the risks of something getting in the way loomed in my mind. Those ominous rumblings in the market had gotten worse.

||||||||||||||||||||||||||||||||||||||||||||||||||||||||||||||||||||||||||||||||||||||||||||||||||||||||||||

You control your decisions and you control how well you execute them; you don't control the environment.

||||||||||||||||||||||||||||||||||||||||||||||||||||||||||||||||||||||||||||||||||||||||||||||||||||||||||||

I was calling San Francisco and New York every chance I got. Let's go, let's go, I encouraged. After a sharp run-up in July, the market had leveled off in August. We know now that August 25, when the Dow closed at 2,722, was the peak of the bull market. No one knew that at the time, of course. Most saw it merely as the pause that precedes the next advance. Still, I worried. The sense of urgency I had felt in the spring was greater now. We kicked into high gear.

We did the road show in early September. Larry, Rich, and I spent a week making presentations to institutional investors in major cities all over the country, followed by a flight to Paris on the Concorde and quick visits to London and Frankfurt. Heady stuff, and I enjoyed it, even on those days when I found myself making the same pitch three times a day to different groups in different cities. One of the most memorable stops we made was in Boston, where we met with Fidelity. The room was packed with more than two dozen analysts. Fidelity carried a lot of weight on Wall Street—it was critical to the success of our offering. But Fidelity was also a direct competitor, and therefore intensely curious about our operations. They grilled us for two hours. We had answers for everything they threw at us. We got nothing but good reactions. We were ready!

ON SEPTEMBER 22, 1987, 15 years since I bought out my partners in First Commander and launched my fledgling company on a wing and a prayer, and just six months since buying Schwab back from Bank of America, trading in The Charles Schwab Corporation commenced on the New York Stock Exchange under the symbol SCH.

We went off at $16.50 per share, well above the $12–$14 range we had anticipated when we first contemplated going public. The total value of the eight-million-share offering was $132 million (we closed at $16.625). Within 24 hours we wired $87 million to Security Pacific Bank, not the whole nut but enough to lessen our debt burden and still leave us with a comfortable cash cushion and ensure smooth operations even in a choppy market. A huge chunk of my discomfort with our debt had disappeared. At the same time, my net worth took another huge leap forward. My personal stake in Schwab was now worth $100 million. I was by any measure a rich man, wealthier than I had ever imagined. It was less than 100 miles away, but Woodland, California, and all my parents' worries about money seemed a universe away.

WAS I LUCKY? WELL, SURE. I have been lucky many times in my career: lucky I learned young that what drove me was a desire for independence; lucky to have Uncle Bill to invest in my company at times of need; lucky to be in the brokerage business at precisely the time in our history when middle-class Americans had the wherewithal to participate in the stock market, and when deregulation opened completely new ways of thinking about investing; lucky to be surrounded by people whose skills complemented my own; lucky to complete our IPO less than a month before the 1987 market crash left most investors for months to come with no appetite for IPOs.

Luck is almost never *only* luck, especially in anything having to do with the stock market or in building a business.

But luck is never enough alone. Insight, reasonable expectations, and experience all contribute and turn luck into opportunity. And most important, being prepared to take advantage of luck when it comes your way; making your own luck whenever you can.

Just because I had no way of knowing that on October 19, 1987, the Dow would plummet 508 points, nearly 23%, does not mean I had no notion of what *could* happen, sooner or later, given the dramatic run-up in recent years and the market's recent wobbliness. I knew I needed to be prepared for something like that, and sitting on a mountain of debt was not a good way to do it. I remember talking to my friend George Roberts soon after the LBO, at a time when, by all rights, I should have been refocusing on our products and services and marketing, not worrying about rebuilding the financial framework of my company. George as much as anyone understood my discomfort with debt and my impatience to pay it down. "When you can raise some capital, go do it," was his plain advice. Go pay it down. "Don't mess around and try to time the market." My feelings exactly. Don't push your luck.

And, of course, it wasn't lost on us that I was now in a position to answer the question he asked me so long ago after our weekend tennis matches when Schwab was just an idea, *How do you create equity value out of it?* Here was my chance.

19

TSUNAMI

Here, along the West Coast of the United States, you'll see tsunami warning signs that alert you when you're in the potential path of one of these rare but devastating waves. A tsunami needs certain elements all in combination. If the right kind of earthquake happens deep down under the Pacific Ocean—a sudden crack and shift along a fault on the ocean floor—a surge of water moves up toward the surface and then rushes outward from the quake. As it approaches the coast, it compresses into a giant wave and the tsunami becomes a wrecking ball of water.

Schwab experienced its own tsunami in 1987. The right combination of factors that set us back on our heels for a moment—a management-led buyout from BofA and the debt that came with it, then going public and the scrutiny that creates, the market crash on October 19 that unleashed a sudden surge of client calls and trades, and our discovery that client margin debt was a bigger risk than we ever anticipated and certainly hadn't planned for. It all happened fast, forever changing our perspective about risk and how we have managed it since.

In the midst of it all, it's terrifying; all you can do is concentrate on getting through it. With luck you have a little warning and the wherewithal to protect yourself. Everything you know is being tested! But get through it: learn from it, that's the thing.

THE DAYS AND WEEKS following our IPO on September 22, 1987, were pure elation. There's no other way to describe the feeling. We were independent. Schwab was growing . . . fast. Average Americans were discovering the benefits of investing and believing the system actually could work for them. More and more people counted themselves as investors. We were on our way to adding over 400,000 customer accounts at Schwab, crossing the 2 million mark at the year's end, and revenues climbed over 50% compared to 1986. Our earnings had nearly tripled in the first nine months of 1987 to $38.4 million, giving us the fuel to add new services and grow just as I had said we would when we announced our buyback from BofA.

We were investing in new computer systems and increasing our marketing. Our management systems were mature. We had solid risk controls in place that met industry standards and regulatory requirements. We weren't the upstart of 1975 where every decision was a new one. In every way we were on a roll. Trading and the revenue it earned was growing at a rate of nearly 50% over the previous year. At an average trade commission of $72 and the business on track to do over 4 million trades, the future was bright. With so much going well, it was probably a good time to be on our guard.

The market had been zigzagging on record volume since August. Up 50 points, down 50 points. The economy was cooling down from the strong recovery it had made after the recession in the early 1980s and that was bearing down on investor sentiment. Interest rates were rising across the world, and we anticipated it was just a matter of time before that was true in the US. And higher rates are usually a drag on the stock market.

We know now in retrospect some of the volatility that summer was the result of "program trading"—new computerized strategies involving options, derivatives, and other sophisticated financial instruments, as well as something called portfolio insurance, in which large institutions manage their risk of losses by hedging those holdings in the futures markets. The purpose of these relatively new tools for institutional investors was to reduce potential losses and also to make a buck on the market's occasional inefficiency. Traders could pick off small spreads between what people were willing to pay for these new strategies versus what people were willing to sell them for. In theory it would smooth out the whole price discovery process, improving the match between what an investor was willing to sell a stock for and what another would pay for it. The irony is that ultimately the tools had the opposite effect, freezing markets, eliminating liquidity, and fueling a crash. All summer long, the wagon was rocking us hard. Fear was building.

||||||||||||||||||||||||||||||||||||||||||||||||||||||||||||||||||||||||||||||||||||||||||||||

I've gotten comfortable with the roller-coaster ride that comes with a market correction and the resolve it takes to ride through it successfully. It's not easy and I don't believe it comes naturally.

||||||||||||||||||||||||||||||||||||||||||||||||||||||||||||||||||||||||||||||||||||||||||||||

Today, having experienced many market corrections, crashes, and long bear markets in my career, I can roll with them. But big or small, they still focus my attention in a big way. And as it happened, this one in 1987 would turn out to be one for the record books.

NO ONE ACTUALLY *saw* the crash coming until we all woke up to it. Not to say there weren't warnings. Markets are inherently risky. They generate fresh warnings every day. But only in retrospect do the warnings build unmistakably to a climax. I didn't have a crystal ball to see the crash coming, but the rumblings were ominous. Yet as anxious as I was, I certainly didn't expect it would arrive as soon as and with the force it did.

The week of October 12 was tough, starting with a 3.8% drop on the Dow on Wednesday the 14th, then another 2.4% on Thursday triggered by a negative report out of the Commerce Department about trade deficits and rumors that a House committee had filed legislation to eliminate tax benefits associated with financing mergers. Then on Friday, October 16, the Dow plunged 108 points, or almost 5%, on the New York Stock Exchange volume of 343 million shares, twice the usual volume and the first time there had been a drop of 100 points in one day. The markets didn't seem able to handle the heavy program trading that was happening.

Trade volume at Schwab, already high, picked up each day, and by the time the market closed on Friday we had broken records. We averaged 19,000 trades per day for the week, nearly 60% higher than typical of the year before. In many ways, that was great news. Trades meant more revenue and the business was humming. But my emotions were mixed. The large number of people stopping by at branches to watch the tickers—and often simply selling when they saw what was happening—was a sign to me customers were in uncomfortable territory. People just aren't wired to take big stock market swings in stride.

The tension at the office was also high with the extra-long hours and extra paperwork at the end of each day that week. Today, there is a clear picture in real time about what's going on in investors' accounts. Thirty years ago, with computer technology in its infancy, it was a different story. Long after the market closed on Friday, we were still gathering data from our worldwide network of branch offices and evaluating the results. The same thing was under way in every brokerage business across the country. For them the calculus was compounded by the fact that many were involved in so-called principal transactions, buying and selling for their own investment accounts, or by exposure through stock underwriting in their invest-ment banking arms. The specialists on the NYSE and market makers on the Over the Counter Market felt it the worst. Their function was to ensure there was an orderly market for stocks (a buyer matched to every seller), and that often meant putting up their own capital to buy shares in companies when investors were urgently selling and a buyer couldn't be found. Not only were their clients seeing the pain of declining stock value, so were those industry players as they lapped up stock from panicked sellers only to watch the value drop as they were left holding the bag.

One thing was clear heading into Monday: trading volume was likely to be extremely heavy. Keeping up with it was our major con-cern. We'd managed through the past week, but what if volume went higher? Could we handle it? There were two issues we faced: maintaining client service and getting through the system-wide is-sues that were jamming up the markets. We would do all we could to manage the first; the second was out of our control and we would have to ride it out. So we made sure we had enough staff lined up in advance to man the branches and answer the phones. We canceled vacations and called in temps. We employed about 2,500 people at the time, many of them certified to handle brokerage transactions. Regardless of their current duties, all would be expected to help take orders on Monday if needed.

ONE IMPORTANT RISK EVERY brokerage was watching intensely was margin balances. Borrowing on margin is a tool used by sophisti-cated investors to increase their buying power by borrowing against the market value of their investments to buy additional stock. When stock prices fall, the borrower may be forced to deposit more money or face a margin call, which is an order to sell shares to boost collat-eral against the rest of your margined holdings. An isolated margin call is one thing, bad for that single client. But when falling prices trigger widespread margin calls, and those in turn trigger more selling, that can lead to a run on the market. It was one of the big threats we saw developing across the industry.

Tom Seip, then in charge of our international branches, was sufficiently concerned after conversations with his team that he came into the office that weekend to catch up on the latest news from our far-flung outposts and make sure we had done all we could to prepare for the coming week. Others were checking the databases to look for any accounts that might pose a risk.

That was when Tom first learned about Teddy Wang, a billionaire client in Hong Kong who was facing a multimillion-dollar margin call on Monday morning. Tom was shocked. Wang's margin call was the biggest he'd ever seen. He called Hong Kong immediately and roused the local branch manager, Larry Yu, from his bed to find out who this client was.

Wang was a very wealthy client in Hong Kong and his account had taken a big hit on Friday, Yu explained. Worth $50 million before the market opened that Friday, it finished the day between $8 million and $12 million in the hole. Wang had been using an options strategy to make a little extra income on his considerable holdings. It was a strategy that hums along in a normal market, but this market had turned on him. Yu said he had called Wang on Friday to tell him that unless he replenished his account immediately to meet the margin call, we would have to begin liquidating his assets to make up for the shortfall. Wang was eager to save his existing investments, believing they would bounce back. Selling now would lock in huge losses. Wang was one of the wealthiest of the wealthy in Hong Kong, a billionaire who together with his wife owned a number of high-rises in Hong Kong that made him one of the largest real estate holders in the region. He had plenty of assets to protect his positions, we were confident of that. He had collateral, but in this market and this situation, he needed liquidity. He met with Yu in person on Saturday morning and brought with him bank statements from two very large accounts to show he could cover what he owed without selling his holdings at Schwab. He gave Yu his word that the assets were under his control. And we were confident his banks could make money available to him upon his signature. Since it was the weekend, Wang left copies of the statements with Yu and promised to make good on his margin call with additional cash as soon as the banks opened on Monday morning, not knowing what Monday had in store. Yu agreed to wait. Tom Seip told Yu to stay in touch.

Barry Snowbarger, our head of trading, had arrived at the office in the middle of Sunday night to find most of the desks in the trading room already occupied. Reports started coming in from markets around the globe as each opened in turn. It sounded like a wave of selling was heading our way. Tokyo, Hong Kong, Frankfurt, London. Each one dropping precipitously as stockholders rushed to sell. Whatever would happen once the market opened in New York, it was going to be huge and we wanted to be ready.

DAWN IN SAN FRANCISCO, October 19, 1987. I remember the air was cool, the light was clear. A perfect fall day, always San Francisco's nicest season after the summer fog has cleared out. Yet all of us gathering at the office that morning felt a tremendous sense of foreboding.

I met with my executive team in the small conference room two doors down from my office. Communications, publicity, advertising, computer systems, employee morale, overtime, food, operations— there was a lot to discuss. Dave Pottruck had gotten married over the weekend, but canceled his honeymoon plans. It was all hands on deck. I had already visited our flagship retail office on the ground floor, mainly to let our employees there know that I, for one, was not panicking. Back upstairs, I talked with the team in the simplest possible terms, "Find a way through this."

Reports came to us from the New York Stock Exchange 15 minutes before the exchange was scheduled to open that there were $500 million in sell orders stacked up ready to go. Their phone lines were already jammed.

At 9:30 a.m. Eastern time the markets opened and the wave of selling from around the world hit New York. The New York Stock Exchange opened down 10%. Many big-name firms didn't start trading for hours as the specialists tried to make sense of the jumble of orders or to find willing buyers for the wave of sellers. It's hard to imagine it from the perspective of today's highly digitized world where you simply click and it happens, but in 1987, an investor wanting to buy or sell a stock called his broker; the broker passed along the information to his representative at the exchange; and that person sprinted with it to hand it off to a floor broker, who walked it to the trading station for that particular stock. There the specialist matched a buy and a sell or stepped in himself to trade for his firm if a buyer or seller couldn't quickly be found. Confirmation of the trade made its way back through the chain and the client was notified. On a normal day that happened in just minutes. That morning, the system limped sluggishly as if it didn't know what to make of all the demands. Nervous clients called back repeatedly, adding to call volume, "Did my trade go through?"

The Over the Counter Market, where unlisted stock sold, was equally troubled. Market makers who served as the middlemen between buyers and sellers, and were accustomed to making tens of cents per share on the spread between the two, saw the market move so fast that they were sometimes buying and selling at what were called quadruple-wide spreads of $5.00. It was unheard of but showed the level of panic in the market. People just wanted out and if it meant giving up $5.00 on the stock, so be it. Even at these rich levels, the risk the market makers held as buyers of stock was so high that many simply threw in the towel and stopped making a market. Liquidity was drying up. The options exchanges were unable to make sense of some of the complex trades like Wang's that were unraveling. For periods of time, options trading simply stopped on the stock exchanges.

The scene at 101 Montgomery was wild. Nothing we had ever experienced compared to that day. Our computer network, designed to handle what we thought of until then as heavy volume, was straining within 15 minutes of the start of trading as customers inundated the phone lines and flooded the branch offices with trades. Suddenly we were back in the old days before computers, taking orders on slips of paper and calculating margin exposure by hand. Trading volume surged artificially as some customers submitted multiple orders for the same trade, hoping one would go through. Out of the financial services industry's experience that day would come reforms designed to prevent such meltdowns in the future. At the moment, however, what we needed to do was reassure our customers as best we could.

Everyone at Schwab had their walking orders. If you weren't solving a pressing problem, you were on the phones helping clients. It didn't matter your title, how senior you were, what you normally did from 9 to 5—clients were job one. We called it our Swiss Army, everyone volunteering as needed.

Hugo Quackenbush, then our head of corporate communications, made the rounds to check on the branch and phone service teams and with his contacts at other companies to see how things were going. "It's a madhouse," he reported back. The panic that had hit the markets was now rippling across the country. The same circumstance we were experiencing was being played out all across the industry: a flood of trading activity where there were more people eagerly wanting to sell than there were people wanting to buy, compounded by program trading that was flooding the market with sell orders. Any reasonable match between sellers and buyers disappeared and the natural equilibrium of the market vanished with it. The market in some securities, especially the more complex ones, locked up and trades simply didn't happen. At the end of the day the 52 specialist firms at the NYSE held $1.5 billion in stock in their accounts they couldn't sell, 10 times the normal amount.

Teddy Wang was not the only margin client who found himself overextended on Black Monday. We made margin calls on hundreds of smaller accounts. When we couldn't execute trades at the exchanges, we tried acting as market makers ourselves, executing the transactions at prevailing market rates. That cost us in some cases, but it helped clients who were eager to sell and it had a stabilizing effect. We had people lining up outside our branches, hoping to make trades. We were in full-on crisis control mode at Schwab, but I knew we'd get through it. I wasn't so sure investors would recover their confidence in the markets, however, and that worried me terribly.

I'd worked too hard to convince people that investing could work for them, and I knew this crash would be temporary. I couldn't stomach the thought that millions of people might give up on investing.

Among those who were suffering in the moment were many long-time Schwab customers who had participated eagerly in Schwab's IPO just a few weeks earlier, as well as our employees. That added to my worries. Shares in Schwab, which had gone off at $16.50 a few weeks earlier, fell to $12.25 on Black Monday and continued falling all the way down to $6 by the end of the year. I had done everything I could to make sure the people who worked for me—especially those who had survived the BofA period—were rewarded with Schwab stock in the offering. Now every last one of them had taken a huge hit, myself included. It would be two years before the stock recovered, and another two years after that before the stock really started to climb—too late, unfortunately, for those who could not wait and sold out too soon to capture the rebound when it inevitably came. I don't think human nature deals very well with the patience and strong stomach investing requires. We're wired for fight or flight. Look at a chart of the S&P 500 (see page 303) over 40 years and you see an endless series of jagged peaks and valleys. Each one of those downs and ups is a moment of panic or elation. But step back for a wider view and you see the inevitable direction is up. Stick with it and ride out the emotions and you're an investor.

There is a central truth about investing: *time is on your side when there's plenty of it; it can be your worst enemy when it's scarce.*

BEYOND THE WIDESPREAD STOCK market issues confronting every brokerage in the world that Friday and Monday, we had problems unique to Schwab. We had just gone public, for one thing. Because our IPO had occurred within the past 90 days, we were still operating in the so-called prospectus delivery period. During that time, the company and the underwriters both had a keen interest in what happened to the company; both had signed off on the prospectus and would be liable if appropriate disclosure of our circumstances were not made. If something calamitous were to occur after the offering period, it would be strictly management's problem. But if it occurred during the offering period, that would be everybody's problem: the company, management, underwriters, lawyers, accountants. Our lawyers made it perfectly clear: we had no choice but to disclose any material changes—or any hint of change—in our circumstances to the investing public during those few bleak days, even if we didn't yet know what the real impact would be. We were under the microscope.

None of our competitors had that burden and so they weren't talking, except to the SEC. In public, they clammed up or fell back on vague comments about the crash having "put strains on the company but we remain financially strong and in compliance with regulatory reserve requirements." But here we were, less than a month after going public, with a responsibility to make public any new liabilities, any guess or speculation about what could happen, despite the fact that we were strong and our client assets were safe. Like the bottle of medicine that has to carry the most extreme-case warning, "This product could harm you," Schwab's disclosure had to be complete and in the most conservative terms. We were in contact with the regulators immediately to let them know what our circumstances were.

Which brings me back to Wang. We needed to get the risk he posed under control quickly because whatever losses we faced would soon be reported. Wang was in fact a very good client—not just of Schwab's but of other brokerage firms, too. He had been with us for several years, and never given us cause for concern. He had a very large portfolio of high-quality blue-chip stocks that he used as collateral for options trades he did on margin, but he got himself in trouble by trading esoteric options known as "short puts" on the options exchange. A short-put seller collects a cash premium in exchange for agreeing to buy a given stock at a fixed price at a future date. He's betting that prices will rise or stay the same, in which case the option will simply expire and he pockets the fee as a profit. As long as markets stay calm or go up, investors like Wang can make a very nice income writing short puts. But when the market declines, those puts become very valuable to the person who bought them, because the put owner has the right to sell the stock back to the person who wrote the put (Wang in this case) at the fixed price when the option was purchased. And when the market tanks significantly, like it had now, Wang was obligated to buy a lot. To protect themselves, many short-put owners will accumulate offsetting options to balance out the risk. Those who go without such protection are said to be holding "naked puts." Wang was naked.

And now it wasn't just his short puts causing him trouble, it was his margin account as well. Wang owned lots of blue-chip stocks that would normally suffice as collateral to support his margin account and his options trades. In most cases, if needed, he could sell enough to cover the losses on his short puts and then just wait it out and leave the rest of his portfolio alone. But when the market tanked, it happened so quickly there was nothing Wang could do to protect himself fast enough to avoid a margin call. The value of all his holdings had suddenly dropped, leaving him without enough to cover his short-put obligations.

As prices plunged and markets for many securities evaporated, solid, reliable information was simply unavailable and the market for those securities froze. There were crossed markets (where offers from buyers and prices from sellers move in opposite directions and are unable to match) and locked markets (where there is no difference in bid and ask prices). In a normal market you wouldn't have that. Both were signs of a stock market in crisis, a market that wasn't working. Wang was completely caught in that downdraft, and as Monday progressed, we had to sell his margined blue-chip stocks at losses while his obligation to cover losses from his short puts rose. As the day went on, his debt to us finally peaked at roughly $126 million.

Would Wang cover his losses? That was the pressing question. We knew he could. He had the means to do it through all his other holdings, bank accounts, real estate, and so on. But the question was made more urgent by our need to report every risk we faced . . . in detail. The uncertainty of when and how was hanging over us, with that looming pill-bottle obligation to disclose the exposure.

I was fuming inside that we faced this problem. We had hundreds of risk controls in place to cover seemingly every market scenario. Where was our risk control on this naked-put strategy of his? How had we let it come to this? Getting through the situation was job number one on our list; fixing the gap in our risk management process was an urgent second.

ON BLACK MONDAY, the New York Stock Exchange saw five times the volume it had on the previous Friday, which had already been a record point drop. Sensing a possible collapse of the market, late Monday, the Federal Reserve stepped in. Fed chair Alan Greenspan put out a one-sentence statement saying, "The Federal Reserve, consistent with its responsibilities as the Nation's central bank, affirmed today its readiness to serve as a source of liquidity to support the economic and financial system." Banks became more confident in the wake of the announcement and started to loan in greater numbers to specialist firms and market makers. Trades began to find a natural balance, and over the course of the week the markets returned to a steady state. The panic was over nearly as quickly as it started.

OUR PROBLEMS, ON THE other hand, weren't so quickly solved. As the week progressed, lawyers for the underwriters insisted we report the potential risk related to Wang immediately. We pushed back. Teddy Wang is just one client, we argued, this is a manageable issue. The underlying health of the company is still quite good. We still have money. Trading volume is huge. We're generating strong cash flows and profits from all the trade commissions. Capital needs are lower because so many clients are now sitting in cash and money market funds after selling their stock positions. We're weathering this storm as well as or better than many in the business. Our risk is contained, it's manageable. Plus, we argued, we were making real headway in Hong Kong. Much of Wang's losses were secured by his bank accounts and his promise to us. We can't provide an accurate report yet. Disclosing now will be misinformation, not information. We need a little more time.

The argument bought us 10 days. Ten days to collect a huge debt from a savvy, reclusive billionaire residing in a foreign country.

Speed mattered at this point. Larry Stupski was working closely with our San Francisco attorneys, led by Larry Rabkin from Howard Rice. Since Tuesday, October 20, they had been busy lining up counsel in Toronto, Seattle, Washington, and New York, working desperately to lock up Wang's assets wherever they could be found. The lawyers succeeded in obtaining a Mareva injunction, temporarily freezing the assets in both bank accounts Wang had disclosed to Yu over the weekend. The judge scheduled a hearing in 10 days. At which point, unless we could prove that Wang controlled the accounts, the injunction would be lifted. Ten days to identify those assets and get a commitment to pay us back from a man who probably had a lot of others leaning on him as well.

Word came back to me from Hong Kong that the initial face-to-face meeting with Wang did not go well. The negotiating had started and the clock was ticking.

For the benefit of all those who were depending on me, I tried my best to remain calm, as did the rest of the team. Deep down maybe I was grinding my molars, but you put the worries aside and you muscle through.

When you lead an organization, you look at the problem, make your best judgment about what needs to get done, and act.

I was confident it would all work out. In fact, I thought the worst case would be reporting a terrible fourth quarter where we would have to write off the Wang loss. But we were on track to earn north of $90 million in pretax profits that year and could absorb a sizable expense like that. And options were available to us in the event we needed additional capital to address the margin losses that Wang might not cover. Maybe not perfect options—because they meant more loans, or outside investors, less independence—but options nonetheless.

THURSDAY, OCTOBER 29, 1987—deadline day. The 10 days were up. We had scheduled a press conference at the St. Francis Hotel for that afternoon to explain our full disclosure, just as we had committed to do. A press release would go out before the markets opened. Negotiations were still under way in Hong Kong. All we knew for certain as the hour approached was that thanks to a mild recovery in Wang's portfolio, our maximum remaining liability was now closer to $84 million. That was a lot better than the $126 million we faced a couple of weeks ago, to be sure, but it still represented an uncomfortable hit to The Charles Schwab Corporation. That was the only remaining uncertainty. Otherwise, we were clear on what the crash had cost us. It hurt, but it was nothing we couldn't get past, and likely mild compared to many other firms.

With the deadline looming, Larry Rabkin, our outside counsel, wrote two press releases and our PR department prepared two scripts: one reporting the largest loss we could calculate assuming no successful negotiation with Wang; the other, a loss from which we would quickly move forward. The first spelled a serious and embarrassing setback, as the losses from Wang and others would eat into our earnings and capital, straining our financial performance and flexibility for some time; the second, a black eye for the margin losses, yes, but a future that everyone would recognize as very manageable.

Early that morning, a small group of us gathered in Larry's office to await the final word from Hong Kong. Seven thousand miles away, the relentless game of chicken that had gone on for 10 days was nearing a conclusion. The day before the deadline, both parties remained far apart, with the Wangs offering $40 million, take it or leave it, while we were holding out for $80 million and giving similar indications it was our best offer before we'd walk and take it to court.

Negotiations resumed early. Finally, a deal was struck, the team called us from Hong Kong with the news. The agreement put in place an aggressive repayment plan. We hadn't recovered every dollar Wang owed us. With a little more time, maybe we could have gotten it all. But I had no interest in squeezing every last dime out of the settlement. Better to take what we could get and close the book, rather than protracting the situation with endless negotiating and forcing us to walk into that press conference carrying press release number one. We got most of it back, a total of $67 million: $12 million immediately, another $13 million coming in two weeks, and the balance payable in equal annual installments over the following five years.

We were in a position now to announce a pretax loss of $42 million related to the market crash (including accounts unrelated to Teddy Wang). It was an amount we could manage. We would still come through the year profitably (earning more than $24 million in net income for the year, up 66% over 1986).

That afternoon, drained, we headed for the St. Francis—with press release number two. The room was packed. I felt like a hostile witness in a congressional hearing. It didn't help that we were strung out from lack of sleep and the sheer, unrelenting suspense of the past 10 days. One of the first questions from the floor was from a reporter who wanted to know what a naked short-put option was. Larry stepped forward and tried to explain. He was normally very good at that sort of thing. But not today. He stumbled through it for a while, made no sense at all, and finally gave up. It was the only time that day that I can recall hearing anybody laugh.

After that I handled the rest of the questions. I tried to be calm, sensible, and accurate and not understate the scope of our problems. My message was pretty simple: we had a big problem and it had cost us. It was an unexpected risk and we weren't the only ones who suffered from it. We had applied industry-standard risk management calculations and learned they weren't enough. Here's how we're going to fix it going forward. I was speaking not just to the press but to our customers, of course, and also to Schwab employees, whose hard work I knew was only beginning.

I've always felt that when you make mistakes, if you stand up and admit them, people will give you the benefit of the doubt.

Acknowledge and own up to problems and people will trust you. That will be helpful the next time. If you blame somebody else or try to sugarcoat the problem, you may get away with it once. But everybody makes mistakes more than once, and any leeway you might gain from fudging it the first time will quickly disappear. Explain the situation, accept responsibility, fix it, move forward.

IS THERE VALUE IN a crisis? Black Monday taught us first that our existing systems were simply not up to the demands posed by extraordinary market volume. On the eve of the crash, with the bull market in full swing, we had been averaging 17,000 trades a day. That was a lot of business for us, more than we had ever handled before without straining. Managing the ebbs and flows of customer demand had always been a challenge, but I thought we were doing a great job. I was proud of the efficiencies we had gained by dividing up the labor, deploying small armies of phone reps in the branches (whose job was to provide quotes, one after another, often repeatedly to the same clients), with registered brokers standing by, also in the branches, to execute orders.

But on Black Monday, when volume surged to over 50,000 trades in one day, our speed and responsiveness simply wasn't good enough. If you're a growth company like Schwab was, and your objective is to be the best at what you do, you've got to be looking further out. Anticipating what's around the corner. Some customers never forgave us and we lost them forever. We paid the price for years to come in their lost revenue. Worse, to my way of thinking, we had failed in the eyes of those clients. Once lost, trust is hard to regain. Ultimately that experience led us to develop state-of-the-art call centers, which could handle far greater fluctuations in volume, and eventually to pioneer the development of automated systems using touch-tone telephones and the internet. We learned from our shortcomings.

A second consequence was that we took a long, hard look at our margin lending practices. Did they adequately match the risk of the product? Did we know enough about our customers before we extended them credit? Were our collateral requirements high enough? In essence, we asked, could the Teddy Wang situation have been prevented? The defensive response is no, everyone was blindsided. Historically, the brokerage industry had relied on margin requirements set by regulatory authorities as the conservative standard for credit risk. Unfortunately, these guidelines failed us during the market crash of 1987. So the more candid position is, yes, we were too vulnerable on this particular risk, and we needed to do a much better job of managing it in the future.

To be fair, every worst-case scenario at the time assumed a sudden market decline of 5%, not 25%. What happened on Black Monday was a previously unimaginable event, which, after the fact, becomes a calculable risk against which responsible parties take steps to protect themselves in the future. It's those extreme moments when things come out of a dark closet and into the light so that you can see them. Teddy Wang exposed a hole in our defenses. Within days we imposed margin requirements more stringent than industry standards on uncovered, or naked, options positions. Those new standards were tested just months later on January 8, 1988, when the Dow Jones Industrial Average plunged 141 points, this time without a significant increase in our uncollectible customer receivables. They were tested again in the market crashes of 1997 and 2000, and yet again in 2008 when the market plunged over 50%. Each time, we had no significant losses, and no need to take the government support in the form of the Troubled Asset Relief Program (TARP) in 2008. In other words, after Black Monday in 1987, we closed the gap, and the crisis became a source of future strength. Today, we take those measures to new heights, running crisis scenarios that are far out of the realm of any prior experience, trying to make the unknown, if not knowable, at least imaginable.

Finally, beyond Schwab's walls, Black Monday paved the way for much-needed market reforms. In May 1988, I testified before the U.S. Senate Banking Committee on the need to clamp down on program trading, which I described as "the modern high-tech equivalent of our old nemesis, market manipulation. Pools of capital, moving in concert, utilizing high leverage through options and futures contracts, and very often managed by computer programs—these are the modern-day robber barons." In many cases, I argued, the money deployed by program traders belongs to Wall Street firms, which "are abdicating their responsibility to the American markets." Ultimately the exchanges all instituted so-called circuit breakers, which suspend program trading during periods of high market volatility.

Those were some of the tangible benefits that followed directly from Black Monday. We also benefited in ways that, while harder to measure, were no less meaningful or real. I want to be careful here because the company's gain was not shared by everyone who suffered through the crash of '87. We were wounded by the crash and its aftermath. We laid off people afterward, something we weren't used to doing. Those same branches that were flooded with customers the week of October 19 very quickly became deathly quiet, as investors fled the market. In fact, part of what prompted the transition to call centers was the way the branches emptied out so quickly, and stayed quiet for some time. I've mentioned that we were averaging about 17,000 trades a day before the crash. It took us until 1991, with a client base that by then had nearly doubled, to get back to that watermark. We were all stunned by the drop-off in business. Sadly, the employees who were let go in the face of reduced demand never had a chance to reap the benefits of the rebound.

But for those who remained, the crash of '87 would forever be remembered as a defining personal moment. For years afterward, people would recall the exhaustion we all experienced, the way we all came together and did what had to be done to survive, and the strength we derived from having lived through it, the camaraderie of being part of our own little Swiss Army fighting for a common cause.

NINETEEN EIGHTY-SEVEN WAS A watershed year for Schwab. The tsunami tested us and matured us. We freed ourselves from Bank of America—an act that unleashed a pent-up growth surge that carried us through the 1990s. We went public, and not a moment too soon. Had we not completed our IPO before the crash, debt would have changed our path forward in significant ways, likely limiting our independence and flexibility and certainly slowing us down during the long, sober years before investors returned to the market in anything approaching their pre-crash numbers. Then, of course, there was the crash itself, an experience I would not wish on anyone. On the other hand, so much of what The Charles Schwab Corporation has since become I trace to what we learned from that singular event. We're more conservative, cautious with managing risk. For that reason alone, I am grateful we went through it.

|||||||||||||||||||||||||||||||||||||||||||||||||||||||||||||||||||||||||||||||||||||||||||||||||

Taking and managing risk is a critical part of any successful endeavor. In business particularly, you have to have an appetite for it or you stagnate and don't do the things that delight the customers and keep them coming back for more.

|||||||||||||||||||||||||||||||||||||||||||||||||||||||||||||||||||||||||||||||||||||||||||||||||

I'm probably more comfortable than many at taking that step into the abyss when it's time to try something new and shake things up. Maybe it's in my DNA (my granddad loved his racing bets!), maybe I learned it growing up when I discovered what good things often happened when I pushed myself into the unknown. Maybe it's my dyslexia. I've seen research that suggests taking risks is a trait common to dyslexics, and why there are many successful dyslexics in business and the arts where conceptual thinking, experimentation, and pushing ahead can be so useful.

Whatever its source, the jump into the abyss is also never simply a blind leap of faith that puts everything at risk, at least not for me. You're never gambling the whole house, you take calculated risks. You've thought things through, and experience and maturity and intuition and the tests you go through give you incrementally better odds each time. Nineteen eighty-seven was one of those tests.

In many ways it was a blessing in disguise. That moment, that crisis, I think of now as the final episode in the formative stage of The Charles Schwab Corporation. In the years to come we would emerge bigger, stronger, more resilient, more innovative, more profitable, and more influential than ever before.

Sure, we'd be tested again. Many times. And will in the future, I'm sure. But we came out of 1987 independent, smarter, a better company.

||||||||||||||||||||||||||||||||||||||||||||||||||||||||||||||||||||||||||||||||||||||||||||

PART III

Boom and Bust

Even when things are going well, you can't be satisfied, because it may not last. You have to take that step out into the unknown . . . and do it over and over again. You have to imagine what people might want and then make it happen.

In my case, I knew investing well enough that I had a sense of what "someone like me" would like to have if we could simply dream it up. The customer probably doesn't yet know they would want it, so you're always just that little step ahead.

But you don't know for certain whether customers will think you got it right until you've done it. Is it useful? Does it solve a problem? Does it make life easier, better, more productive? Is it priced properly? Success all comes down to customer demand. The beauty of free enterprise is that it encourages that creativity in us. Anybody can come up with a new, winning idea. If you create a better buggy whip, odds are people will buy it.

Most important, you have to be willing to embrace client-focused innovation, even when it competes with your own existing business. Sometimes the most important competitor you confront is yourself! That's how you stay a step ahead of everyone else. You can't think just because you're big, just because you're successful, that you can't disrupt yourself. You can—and in fact in today's world, you have to.

Of course, sometimes you stumble: maybe you calculated wrong, the world changed, your timing was off—either you are too early or you weren't fast enough. All you can do is just keep plugging away, get back at it, and try again with the next idea.

20

ADVANCING THE REVOLUTION

Early in 1990, two years after the crash, Larry Stupski and I invited a team from Boston Consulting Group (BCG) to come take a close look at our operation and suggest ways we might reposition ourselves for the next stage of growth. It had been a pretty tough couple years since the crash. We had muscled through it and put significant changes in place that strengthened us and protected us from future crises. It had not been easy. In 1988, trading volume dropped 35%–40% because of ongoing investor worries. But things were starting to pick up after the November election and our new electronic channel, Equalizer, was starting to show promise. Nearly 30,000 clients were now using it to trade—a harbinger of the future. Essentially we told BCG this: we were a fast-growing company through most of the 1980s and we want to get back on track and growing fast again in the 1990s.

Hiring consultants was a bit of a tactical departure for us. I had avoided them so far, because I normally don't trust ideas divorced from execution, and consultants don't execute. It's too easy to make grand conclusions when you don't have to put them into action. Often the best answer is right there in front of you, if you know your business. My change of heart was an acknowledgment that we weren't such a young company anymore; we could no longer rely solely on our own hunches, and there was a lot we could learn from others. Still, our expectations were modest. "This is really going to be easy," Larry told Dan Leemon, the BCG partner who led the engagement (and later came to work for us). "We know what our strategy is, we just need somebody to write it down."

I would not have said that our vision was quite as clear as that. Everybody in our industry had been hit hard by the crash, and we were no exception. We laid off 15% of our workforce immediately after the crash, an agonizing decision to make just after going public. This was the team that brought us through it all. We slashed $9.1 million out of annual payroll. (I cut my own pay 50% for six months.) On the revenue side we raised commissions 10%, a bit unsettling to say the least, but it accurately reflected what the market would bear and we needed it. The good news was that the stock market was rising again, restoring to wholeness those who had stayed put and greatly rewarding those brave enough to have jumped in at the trough. (October 21, two days after Black Monday, the Dow soared more than 10%, its fourth-best one-day gain to that point.)

We know now with the benefit of hindsight that the longest bull market in history was already off and running. In fact, the late 1980s, right after the crash, was probably the best opportunity my generation was ever presented to dive into the market. It was the chance of a lifetime to make enormous long-term investing gains. But few recognized it at the time. Having just been burned, many now watched warily from the sidelines. I have now seen nine market crashes in my life, and it still troubles me that investors react this way, because it always ends the same. The market roars back and leaves too many investors sitting on the sideline missing out. Sometimes I wish I could just tie them to their chairs to help them ride out the temporary storm. To this day our advice is the same: "Panic is not a strategy, stick with your investment plan, and don't let emotions get the better of you." Heeding that advice when you're in full panic mode is just not easy. People aren't wired to be good investors.

For Schwab, investor wariness at that time meant empty branches, quiet phones, and sharply reduced trading volume. And because commissions accounted for nearly all our income, we were struggling. Key metrics such as average daily trades, net income, and new account acquisitions, while starting to move in the right direction again, remained well below the peaks we had reached in the summer of '87.

So what next? I could see that the old growth model, while not exactly broken, was in need of retooling. How did I know that? I didn't *know*, exactly, at least not in the sense that I had stacks of hard data on which to base my conclusions. I had never paid much attention to what my competitors were doing. I did not waste time thinking about how to exploit their weaknesses. Instead, I was always keyed into my own clients. To me, the trick was coming up with products and services that satisfied investor needs before anyone else did. Get out ahead and others would be playing catch-up. If I could succeed at that, then I could safely ignore my competitors.

The only way that works is if you have solid firsthand knowledge. I got mine by spending a lot of time in the branches—talking to customers, watching what they were doing, trying to understand what they were thinking. And because I created Schwab to be the kind of firm that I would want to do business with, I always paid close attention to my own changing needs and habits as an investor. If I've been right more often than not over the years, that's probably because I've always been my own best customer.

Steve Jobs famously said customers don't know what they want; you have to show it to them. Any entrepreneur who is out there coming up with new ideas will say something similar. Innovation springs from that internal voice saying this is a great idea, the next big thing. People will love it. Market research and testing can play a role, but they're no substitute for good gut instincts and simply building something you yourself would love to have.

THE FIRST THING BCG did was interview the top 10 or 12 people in the company about our supposed strategic consensus. To everyone's surprise the responses were all over the map: We're here for the *little* guy; we want to move to the *big* guy. We're here to do equity *trading*; we're here to provide equity *services*. Branches are the key; we've got to figure out a way to get away from the branches. The point is, there was no consensus whatsoever. BCG then proposed we back up a step or two and do some basic analytical work. Among the questions we considered: How many individual investor households are there? How much wealth do they have? How much income? What is the lifetime value of a single account? What kinds of investments are attracting assets and what kinds are losing assets? What is our cost structure? How can we improve our profitability?

What did we learn? First, that while Charles Schwab had grown a lot since 1975, our business model was essentially unchanged. We still served mainly independent investors, individual investors who didn't need or want advice. Our best customers were active traders who generated consistent commission and margin-balance revenue; in effect, they subsidized the less-active customers. (BCG's term for clients who traded once or twice then disappeared was "flashbulbs." They tended to be referrals from full-service brokers who didn't want their business.) We made our money executing transactions, cleanly, cost-effectively, and without sales pressure. It was a proven model and had served us well for 15 years; so well, BCG was telling us now, that we had probably captured about as much of that market as we were going to get. We basically had two choices going forward. Find new customers—for example, those looking for advice, which meant competing with full-service Wall Street brokers. Or find a way to sell new products and services to our existing, self-sufficient customers.

Second, BCG's research underscored how clearly we fit the classic profile of a discounter—low prices, low operating costs, high volume, economies of scale, the whole bit. Technology was a key part of that picture because it let us process transactions faster and cheaper than our competitors. More than that, it was central to our mission. With each new technological advance, we provided a level of service a cut above other discounters; *and* we brought our clients one step closer to my ideal of direct, unmediated participation in the market. Our newest piece of that puzzle, deployed in October 1989, was a platform we called TeleBroker, by which clients could obtain quotes, check balances, and make trades (for a 10% discount) using a touch-tone phone. As the first to provide this automated service, we got a big bump, in terms of both new accounts and notoriety.

Third, we learned that for most of the 1980s, the position occupied by individual stocks in the larger investing universe had been shrinking. Shrinking in terms of supply in the market (LBOs were partly to blame for that, by breaking up public companies and taking their equity out of play), and what's more, shrinking as a percentage of individual investor portfolios. Congratulations, BCG said to us: In a deteriorating environment for stocks, you guys have been growing. Great work. Good luck keeping it up! But here's the really good news, they said: While individual stock ownership is falling, mutual funds are on the rise. Furthermore, we think the popularity of funds will continue growing. In fact, we would hazard a guess that the 1990s might actually be the decade of the mutual fund. If you guys want to keep growing, you need a new pony.

That was critical intelligence, though as it turns out, partially flawed. We soon found that individual stock ownership wasn't going anywhere but up in the 1990s; BCG was plain wrong to suggest it had reached a plateau. But BCG was definitely not wrong about the surging popularity of mutual funds and was right to push us to capitalize on that trend.

I HAD HAD MY eye on mutual funds at least since 1984 while still part of Bank of America, when we introduced Mutual Fund Marketplace, which was a way to buy almost any no-load mutual fund through us by paying a transaction fee. It was basically a discount brokerage service for mutual funds. I wondered if we should also be offering low-cost, efficiently managed funds of our own. I liked index funds in particular: they were smart choices, especially for investors unwilling to devote a lot of time to research. They passed the would-I-buy-it-for-myself? test. Index funds make no attempt to outperform the market—as the index rises and falls, so, too, does the index fund—which turns out to be an excellent strategy for outsmarting most actively managed mutual funds. That's still true. Recent research shows that between 2007 and 2016, just four actively managed stock mutual funds were able to rank in the top 25% of performance for seven years. None made it to eight years. And being able to pick that fund out of the pack consistently? Impossible.

I also had a hard time with the idea of Schwab hiring armies of analysts and portfolio managers to produce actively managed funds we would then market to our own clients. That felt like a betrayal of our mission. It was too close to what traditional brokers do, promoting stocks they've underwritten and mutual funds they manage with empty promises of outsized returns. I was afraid that if we started down that road, we'd end up like everybody else. Instead, in 1991, we launched the Schwab 1000, our first stock mutual fund. Schwab 1000 was an index fund; each share represented a stake in each of the 1,000 largest US corporations. One purchase and you tapped into the growth of the US economy. You were part owner of the largest and most successful companies. We were on to something big as an early entrant into index investing. Indexing was cost-effective for investors and relatively straightforward to manage; it scaled easily, it performed in logical and consistent ways, and it made a great center-piece to an investor's portfolio. In retrospect, it's clear that we didn't push in that direction hard enough and ceded the indexing territory to Vanguard for far too long.

BCG's overall conclusions: what we had built at Schwab was a lean, scalable brokerage machine, well tuned to deliver services to in-dependent investors. ("A wonderful, fabulous, efficient factory," was one of the phrases Leemon used to describe how we operated; also, "The goose that's laying the golden egg.") BCG's recommendation: Don't kill it. Don't complicate the cost structure by mimicking full-service brokers. Don't go after clients who need a broker's advice. Don't do anything that might compromise Schwab's reputation for being fair, independent, trustworthy, consistent, innovative, and a good value. On the other hand, *do* leverage what's already in place, including technology and the branch network. *Do* offer new prod-ucts and services appropriate to your existing client base. *Do* ramp up advertising to attract new accounts and build scale.

The upshot was a one-page document, widely distributed among our employees, called *Ten Steps into the '90s*. Step number 1 was "Profitable Growth," for which Larry Stupski, our chief operating officer, set an annual goal of 20% top-line growth with a 10% profit margin. (Funny thing about goals: they drive results. Years later, deep into the most prosperous decade in Schwab's history, Larry wondered aloud, "Why do you think we grow so much every year?" Dan Leemon, who by then had left BCG and joined us as chief strat-egist, had a ready reply: "Because you won't accept anybody's plan if it doesn't adhere to that standard.")

Number 6, "Information Platform," involved creating a system for gathering and analyzing data about our business; in other words, no more hunch-based decision making. Number 8 committed us to building more branches, and so on.

|||||||||||||||||||||||||||||||||||||||||||||||||||||||||||||||||||||||||||||||||||||||||||||||||

There is nothing like a goal to focus your mind and focus your efforts. It's true if you're building a business or getting through school.

|||||||||||||||||||||||||||||||||||||||||||||||||||||||||||||||||||||||||||||||||||||||||||||||||

But what strikes me most about the list when I look at it now is how many of the steps—4 out of the 10—had to do with strengthening the brand and expanding our appeal with new products and services aimed at our existing customers. Number 7, "Broaden Products," was probably the most important in that regard. It followed the finding that individual stocks were losing ground relative to other investments, especially mutual funds. We knew that our clients were already big buyers of no-load mutual funds. The challenge we faced was persuading them to consolidate their holdings with us. Our stated goal—pretty ambitious when you consider that all we had at the time was a small collection of money market funds—was to capture 25% of our customers' fund business.

As it turned out, we had the means to blow that goal right out of the water already in our possession. All we had to do was unlock its potential.

OUR CLIENTS PLAINLY HAD a huge and growing appetite for mutual funds. So we took a close, hard look at the economics of the fund industry, searching for an opening. The no-load fund universe in those days was basically composed of three giants—Fidelity, Vanguard, and Twentieth Century. Everybody else was made up of hundreds of smaller players fighting for attention in the listings of *Money Magazine* or *Barron's* or the *Wall Street Journal*. The key challenge for the little guys was distribution. It was a game of advertising, customer service, and distribution, and all that was expensive. But as a fixed cost, advertising, for example, scales quickly. Every time you double sales, your per-unit advertising cost drops by half. Meaning the bigger you are, the better you can afford the costs of distribution. We looked at the numbers, noted that our brokerage revenues already put us in the same league with the giants of the mutual fund industry, and arrived at a conclusion: The little funds are going to be driven out of business by the big ones. With scale, we can distribute more cheaply than they can. So they should be willing to pay us to distribute. From that insight came OneSource, the most successful new business we built in the 1990s.

Best of all, we didn't have to build it from scratch. The structure was already in place. We had tried to sell the marketplace idea on the convenience factor—easy transfers between funds, next-day postings to your Schwab account, all your funds on one monthly statement, less paperwork at tax time; "500 no-load funds, one 800 number," was the tagline in the ad we ran once a week, buried in the lower left-hand corner of page C2 of the *Wall Street Journal*. Some people thought it was a valuable service and willingly paid the fees. But frankly, not many. Schwab clients, if nothing else, hated fees. The main reason they had come to us in the first place was to save on commissions. Now here we were saying, *You can buy this Janus fund through Schwab and pay us $70, or you can pick up the phone and call Janus and buy the same fund for free.* Most chose the latter, and I didn't blame them. We had created the highest-priced no-load funds. Being the most expensive place to buy no-load mutual funds was not a good market position for us, which is why I never promoted Mutual Fund Marketplace beyond that one little ad in the *Wall Street Journal*. I felt it muddied our message.

Not surprisingly, Mutual Fund Marketplace never gained much traction. In 1990, when BCG surveyed our clients, only 25% even knew it was possible to buy no-load mutual funds from Schwab. As best we could determine, some 90% of our own clients' mutual fund assets resided in accounts they kept elsewhere. I felt that if we could

offer our clients a compelling reason to consolidate their fund holdings with Schwab, the potential for growth was staggering. Especially given our projections about where fund ownership was headed
in the 1990s.

John McGonigle, a young VP who had joined us recently from
Bank of America, and later went on to run our mutual fund business, felt the same way. John was one of four Schwab employees
assigned as liaisons to the BCG consulting team. He was deeply involved in the research and analysis that resulted in the Ten Steps,
and when it was all over, Larry Stupski tried to recruit John to work
on number 6, the new information platform. But John had other
ideas. Was it possible we were at an inflection point in the mutual
fund business? Could we get fund companies to pay us so we could
eliminate transaction fees and this marketplace idea would take off?
John thought maybe that day was near, and if so, it was a once-in-a-
lifetime game changer. The potential was huge for us and for investors. He pleaded to work on that. David Pottruck interceded on his
behalf ("I'll make sure Larry doesn't get too mad"), and John, with
David's guidance, turned to the task.

John and his team encountered skepticism at every turn, and
that was before we even thought about trying to sell fund companies on the idea. We knew going in that the margins would be
thin—25 to 35 cents for every 100 dollars invested. "Let me get this
straight," Larry challenged John. "We have this nice little business
(Mutual Fund Marketplace) selling no-load funds to our clients.
And they pay us a transaction fee. We put transaction fees in the nu-
merator and assets in the denominator to see how much we're earning as a percentage of assets. Works out to about 0.60%. So you're
saying we should trade in a 0.60% business for a 0.25% business and
you're going to make it up on volume?" Well, yes, that's what John
was saying. Larry was right to be concerned.

Essentially we were talking about a leap of faith. To succeed, this
new business would have to grow to be many times larger than Mu-

tual Fund Marketplace. Larry had other concerns. "If we take away the per-trade charge," he wondered, "won't trading go up?" Good point, no one else had thought of that. Trading costs are a drain on profits. The economics only worked for us if customers didn't go crazy jumping in and out of funds, trying to time the market. So John added a short-term redemption fee to the program, payable on shares held less than 180 days. (The fund companies had the same concern; the redemption fee was useful in aligning our interests with theirs. Later, that policy was reduced to 90 days.)

Larry's pushbacks sent John back to the spreadsheets several times. Finally, in the spring of 1991, John and David Pottruck came to Larry and me with a full-blown proposal for what at the time they were calling the Schwab No Transaction Fee program—terrible name, but we fixed that later. *Here is why the economics are not going to be as bad as you think,* they explained. *Here are the steps we've taken to mitigate the risk. Here is how much scale we think we can get.* Of course, no one knew for sure what the scale of the operation would be. It was more like, *We don't exactly know, but here's what we think.* Larry, with his phenomenal analytical mind, kept pushing, even at this late date. It was his role to ask hard questions. Building this new capability was destined to consume half our technology budget between 1991 and 1993; by mid-1996 our total investment would top $150 million. Larry needed to know we weren't just plowing ahead with stars in our eyes.

For most of the meeting, I listened. My role was to embrace risk when I saw an opportunity for a huge reward. I've always tried to encourage my operating people to make big leaps that could have a significant impact on the company's bottom line.

Whenever such opportunities arise, my instinct is to leap *now*, before anyone else does.

This was a service that people were going to use, obviously; I knew *I* would use it if it were available. *Let's do it*, I thought. *Right now. Even if we're not yet completely sure how it will make money.* So after Larry had asked all his questions, when the room fell silent and everyone was waiting for me to speak, I had only one question: "Why is this going to take us so long to implement?"

John was a little taken aback. "Well," he said, stumbling, "we need to run pilots to make sure we've got the messaging down because it's kind of a confusing message for clients. You know, 'No-load funds, we don't charge a transaction fee.' How do we brag about a benefit most people haven't thought to ask for yet? And while we're at it, we've got two other big and important things we've got to do. We have to build a system to track how long the funds are held in clients' accounts so we can charge the market timers a fee, and we need a system to bill the fund companies."

Again, market timers were investors that jumped in and out of a fund quickly depending on what the market was doing, hoping to profit from short-term market movements. The funds didn't like them. The quick in and out created tax issues for other shareholders and a host of management headaches in what were designed to be longer-term investments.

"We'll also need time to persuade the fund companies that this concept of no-load funds writing checks to brokers doesn't violate existing regulations," John reminded us. "If you're giving us the thumbs-up sign, great, we're ready to get going. But we've got a lot of work to do. It's going to take us a while."

If John thought it was a tough sell internally, that was before he started peddling the service to outsiders. *Before you say we're crazy—* that's how John always began his pitches to the fund companies— *just listen for a moment. We think we understand your economics. We think you have a huge distribution challenge. We think we can solve it for you—for a price.* Initially, he got a lot of pained looks. The no-load fund families were caught in a classic vise between fear and greed.

They were living in a tidy little world of their own design, controlling everything from the manufacturing of investment products to their distribution. They enjoyed a direct relationship with their customers. Now here comes Schwab, proposing to insert itself in the middle of that cozy relationship. The fear the funds faced was that of losing control. But fund managers are not stupid. They understood that for a mere 0.25%, here was a chance to offload the distribution, shareholder servicing, and record-keeping pieces with all the related headaches and open the floodgates to potentially enormous asset inflows.

Even so, John worried that the only funds willing to sign on were small funds desperate for distribution, possibly because they weren't performing well. In which case we'd be stuck offering funds nobody wanted, and we'd never attract star funds to the program, and the whole thing might never get off the ground. John, Dave, and Dan Leemon came up with a solution. We would invite only the top 20 fund families, measured by Schwab client assets, into the Mutual Fund Marketplace. We offered them an exclusive deal: sign up now to be a "charter member" of our program, and we promise that it will cost newcomers more than the "charter member" rate.

We launched on that basis on July 20, 1992, with 80 funds from eight "charter member" fund families: Janus, Dreyfus, Neuberger & Berman, Invesco, Founders, Berger, Stein Roe, and Federated. By year-end we were handling 2,700 mutual fund trades per day—a decent start, although as John had feared, we had a hard time explaining the benefits to investors. It wasn't until a year later—when we expanded the lineup to over 200 funds from 20 fund families, including Twentieth Century, Oakmark, Strong, Benham, and Baron, and we changed the name to OneSource—that sales really took off.

And an amazing thing happened: Fidelity launched a competing program, modeled after ours. Fidelity was the biggest, most successful fund company around. It already offered its clients a full lineup of proprietary no-load funds covering every conceivable investment angle, funds on which it earned closer to 1.20%. Why did Fidelity want to bother selling competitors' funds and only make a sixth of that? We were stunned.

Fidelity's countermove was a sign that we were on to something big; that investors, once aware of the alternative, would no longer put up with the inconvenience of knocking on a different castle door every time they wanted to add a new fund to their portfolio. "We have to give investors what they want," is how Fidelity executive Paul Hondros explained their decision to *Fortune* magazine. "If we don't, we'll shrivel up and die." Once Fidelity got into the game, the press started paying attention. Now they had a horse race to cover. We ramped up our advertising, always with a focus on the funds themselves; OneSource—where you could actually buy all these great funds—was almost an afterthought. People responded in a big way. We soon realized that OneSource was the most powerful account acquisition tool we had ever come up with. From 1993 to 1995, assets gathered by way of OneSource rocketed from $8.3 billion to $23.9 billion. Yes, the margins were thin—but in terms of asset growth, OneSource was a stunning success, attracting hordes of new clients. And because they were *our* clients—the fund companies did not even know their names—we got all their other business, including their stock trades and their cash balances. In fact, you could track our progress toward meeting our various internal goals just by watching our ads. When we fell behind in top-line growth, we ramped up our OneSource advertising and new accounts came pouring in. When profits lagged, we advertised our brokerage services, encouraging traders to come our way.

ONESOURCE WAS NOURISHED IN one unexpected way, by Schwab's growing network of independent financial advisers. We fondly called it our accidental success. That network was not something we set out to create. In fact, it may be the only business ever jump-started by a compliance officer. One day in 1985, Guy Bryant, our chief compliance officer, walked into Tom Seip's office and dropped a computer printout two inches thick on Tom's desk. "This printout represents people who have powers of attorney over a number of brokerage accounts," Guy said.

"So what?" said Tom.

Guy explained that he had to review the form from time to time as part of his compliance duties. And what he expected to find were guys who had power of attorney over a bunch of family accounts. That's pretty common, running money for parents or siblings or children. But here we had people who didn't appear to be related, spread all over the country. He showed the paperwork for a guy who had 300 different accounts that he had power of attorney over. He needed to find out what was going on.

Well, we started calling all these guys and lo and behold, we stumbled upon an embryonic industry. They were like brokers, offering advice, placing orders, and handling record-keeping for their clients. Except instead of getting paid by commission, they charged an annual fee based on a percentage of their clients' assets. The more money they made for their clients, the more they got paid. Turns out an awful lot of them were executing their clients' trades through us rather than Dean Witter or Merrill Lynch because they liked our service. Plus they didn't have to worry about us trying to steal their accounts. Tom Seip was intrigued. He said to Dave Pottruck when all this came clear, "Dave, give me a little bit of money and a couple of guys and we'll see if we can make a business out of it."

So we started courting the financial advisers. I was skeptical at first. My whole focus from day one was on independent investors, people like me who didn't want anybody's advice. But I knew there were always going to be people out there who needed help, who didn't know about asset allocation, and who didn't have the time or inclination to research stocks and mutual funds. And I liked the business model the financial advisers had, eschewing commissions in favor of an annual fee. They had figured out a way to help clients who needed advice while avoiding all the sordid contradictions and potential for conflict of interest inherent in the traditional broker model. That was something I could get behind. I had always thought the Wall Street brokers who delivered accounts to financial advisers owned the financial advisers. I was wrong. The financial advisers wanted their independence from the Wall Street firms and their conflicts, and they thought they could attract clients who also sought independent advice for a simple account fee. I figured we were small enough and nimble enough that we could customize our services for these guys and the result would be good for everybody. And it was. The financial advisers became, in effect, a national sales force for Schwab, reaching thousands of clients we could not, bringing us millions in new assets.

Once we came out with OneSource, the financial advisers just swarmed to it. Although not at the expense of Mutual Fund Marketplace, which completely surprised us. They recognized the value in Mutual Fund Marketplace; they didn't feel stupid paying us a transaction fee to handle all the back-office functions on their behalf and issue the statements. They liked having access to the full universe of mutual funds, including those not part of OneSource. As we became better known as the premier one-stop shop for mutual funds, both businesses blossomed. The more funds we offered, with or without transaction fees, the more we made the financial advisers' lives easier, and the more opportunities they had to impress their clients by delivering winners, especially previously overlooked winners—the more obscure, the better. In fact, we noticed that the small and midsize load fund companies were getting squeezed off the shelf at the wire houses in spite of having good performance records. We were able to convince several of these companies to waive their loads and offer hundreds of their funds to fee-based advisers through an offering we called "Institutional One Source," which further enhanced the value clients could get from their advisers. I argued that OneSource was the key technological development—the killer app—that transformed financial planning from a cottage industry into a fixture on the financial services landscape. Within a year, advisers had invested more than $1 billion in Institutional One Source. The enthusiasm of the financial advisers, combined with the fund companies' desire to be plugged into a vibrant, growing distribution channel, was a powerful combination. The financial advisers became the levers that made OneSource go.

FIFTEEN MONTHS AFTER THE introduction of OneSource, Tom Seip and John Coghlan, who was enterprise president for the adviser business, met in New York with Barton Biggs, the legendary chief of asset management at Morgan Stanley. OneSource had just popped up on his radar and Biggs wanted to know more about it. In a story later recounted in *Fortune*, "Biggs listened carefully while Seip and Coghlan laid it all out for him. Then he put down his coffee cup. 'Gentlemen,' he said, 'it's time for me to retire because this program will change the world of mutual funds as I know it.'" Biggs was dead-on. The mutual fund supermarket had arrived. Power no longer resided with the manufacturers—that is, the fund managers. It had shifted to the distributors—our OneSource, Fidelity's FundsNetwork, and to a lesser extent the other fund supermarkets that followed. "Investment management becomes the commodity," is how Biggs described the new reality to *Fortune*, "and the proprietary asset is the ability to distribute."

Not everyone welcomed the new reality. It put pressure on entrenched powers—brokerages with their in-house funds and the big fund families like Fidelity and Vanguard.

OneSource advanced investor choice and opened up the market. New funds clamored to get on board. It spurred competition among fund companies and brought fund expenses down. It spurred the

|||||||||||||||||||||||||||||||||||||||||||||||||||||||||||||||||||||||||||||||||||||||||||||||||||||

I have always believed in giving investors choices, and with those choices the freedom and power to make their own decisions.

|||||||||||||||||||||||||||||||||||||||||||||||||||||||||||||||||||||||||||||||||||||||||||||||||||||

growth of mutual fund research and ratings outfits like Morningstar. It lifted deserving fund managers like Ron Baron, Garret Van Waggoner, Bill Berger, Paul Stephens, and many others from relative obscurity and made them known to a wider public. (In fact, Ron Baron immediately connected the dots and began investing aggressively in Schwab stock. As recently as 2017 he considered it one of his greatest investments, making his fund's shareholders over $1 billion in stock appreciation.) It broke down all the old artificial barriers—mountains of paperwork, transaction fees, misplaced loyalty—that once bound investors to nonperforming funds, and it opened a clear path for rational decisions based on the only factor that matters: performance. OneSource, as much as its parent, the discount brokerage industry, was about empowerment. It advanced the revolution.

21

LIFE INTERCEDES

On January 11, 1992, around 7:00 a.m., the phone rang at my home in Atherton. It was Larry Stupski's wife, Joyce, and she sounded terribly upset. Larry was in the hospital. He had apparently suffered a heart attack while playing basketball at the gym on Friday night. He was no longer in immediate danger, she said, but was facing bypass surgery and, at best, the prospect of a long recovery. I didn't ask when or if he might return to work. But I knew as I hung up the phone that Larry's future—and with it my future—was suddenly up in the air. You can plan all you want, but sometimes life intercedes.

Larry's heart attack made sense afterward to those of us who knew him best. Larry was intense, and always all in, to put it mildly. I hired him in 1980, at a time when we were growing so fast that I really felt I had to have a drill sergeant on staff, someone to whip the back office into shape, hold us all accountable, and prevent the kind of careless mistakes that could have landed us in hot water. That was the best personnel move I made during the formative years of Schwab. Larry was everything I was not: obsessively analytical, dispassionate, highly organized, confrontational, and more than a little scary. He was known to simply stand up and walk out of meetings if he decided somebody was wasting his time. He spoke very slowly, very precisely, without an expression that anyone could read. He was given to long, pregnant pauses; his staff learned, sometimes the hard way, to make absolutely certain he was finished talking before they chimed in. Whereas I was the one who might wander into your office, tossing out thoughts and ideas, Larry was the one who came by afterward, making sure you followed through. Larry did not have a marketing bone in his body, but that was okay. He counterbalanced me perfectly. Throughout the years with Bank of America, as I was drawn increasingly into struggles that had nothing to do with running Schwab, Larry kept us growing. In time he emerged as my undisputed number two and presumed eventual successor as CEO.

David Pottruck had quickly become a central member of our management team. David was an entirely different type of person than Larry, maybe not as cerebral, but he kept more in his head and could think faster on his feet. In many ways he was also more like me: a marketer, an idea person. I thought of David as additional ballast on my side of the ship, someone who could do the things I could do but that I could no longer handle all by myself. That said, David was by no means my clone. I have often been described as mellow; no one has ever described David that way. David was a lot more expressive than I was, and a great communicator.

Both were still young—Larry was 46 when he had his heart attack; David was 44. I thought the three of us made an ideal team. As founder, I was part visionary, part exhorter. David conveyed the company's vision to the troops with great passion. Larry executed. Larry was my only direct report, and that's how I liked it. If you have too many people reporting to you, then you have to worry about competing interpretations of your intent. With just one, you can be very broad in your exhortations, even vague, but only if you trust the person beneath you the way I trusted Larry. We all worked so well together for so many years that I was probably late in recognizing what had become, by the early 1990s, a fierce competition between Larry and David. It's not that I couldn't decide which one to choose; it's that I hoped I never *had* to choose. One of my strengths as a leader is my willingness to surround myself with people who are smarter than I am, or at least have skills that I don't; one of my weaknesses is a tendency to avoid confrontation. Both my strengths and my weaknesses were on display as Larry and David fought hard for the unofficial title of Chuck's Favorite Son. How was I going to figure this out without losing one or the other? I wanted them both. They each had great attributes. The whole thing was becoming a major distraction. As founder, these were decisions I had to make all by myself. As CEO, there really was nobody I could talk to about such things. I'm sure neither of them was happy. I know that David in particular was fed up with all the uncertainty, to the point where he may have been exploring opportunities outside the company. I was afraid I had already lost him.

Then Larry had his heart attack. Two days later he had bypass surgery and two weeks after that, he was telling me he was ready to come back to work. But we both knew that things had changed. I hired a consultant, Joe Cutcliffe, and Larry and I spent several days alone with him, holed up in a suite at the Mandarin Oriental Hotel, going over organizational charts and talking about how to proceed. I was letting Larry tell me what he wanted to do. He was very clear that while he had no intention of quitting, he could not remain in his current role. I'm sure his doctor was telling him that he had to find a job that didn't come with so much stress. Together we kept drawing and redrawing the charts, writing in names and crossing them out again, shuffling and reshuffling the deck. Finally, we decided, *This is the way it's going to be done.* Then we brought David into the conversation, and later the rest of the management team.

David's title had been president of the brokerage business; basically he ran sales and marketing, and anything else having to do with revenues. Larry was president and COO of the company; he ran systems and operations, finance, and human resources. Larry reported to me and everyone else, including David, reported to Larry.

With the reorganization that Larry and I worked out together, David took over as president and COO and Larry moved into the newly created role of vice chairman, a title he held until his retirement in 1997. Essentially Larry was removing himself from day-to-day involvement in the company's affairs and David was moving up to fill the vacuum created by Larry's withdrawal. There were some who were dissatisfied with the result. Barbara Wolfe, who was our trusted head of HR and Legal, essentially the caretaker of the values of the company, thought she should have a crack at the top job. When it didn't go that way, she sued us in NASD arbitration, feeling there was bias in the decision. It got ironed out in arbitration and Barbara left the company.

Larry's illness and subsequent reassignment was a turning point in the history of Schwab. Had he not become suddenly sidelined, I might never have given David the additional responsibilities he went on to fill for many successful years. As it turned out, David was especially well suited to step in at a time in the firm's history that called out for innovation, risk-taking, and growth.

THANKS TO ONESOURCE, WE quickly shot past our stated goal of capturing 25% of our clients' mutual fund assets and kept right on going. OneSource worked two ways for us: it generated fee income, which is generally more predictable than commission income; and it gathered assets, both from existing clients who brought us their mutual fund business and from new clients attracted to Schwab specifically because of our mutual fund supermarket. And, of course, it revolutionized the ease of investing in mutual funds. The inflows were astonishing. Total customer assets topped $100 billion by February 1994. In fact, asset growth was probably the most compelling theme of the 1990s. But OneSource was only one factor behind our growth.

It was a period full of growth and innovation for Schwab and the industry. In 1991, we created our first Schwab managed equity mutual fund, the Schwab 1000, which was an index fund that invested in the 1,000 largest US companies; in 1993, we expanded internationally with a new office in London; Canada came in 1998; in 1994, we offered a Spanish version of TeleBroker, our phone-based automated voice-recognition trading system; the Schwab Corporation was added to the S&P 500 in 1997; and in 1999, we provided after-market-hours trading on the NASDAQ and launched the Schwab Fund for Charitable Giving.

And there was our push into Individual Retirement Accounts, or IRAs. It was one of those examples of turning old assumptions on their head and seeing the competitive landscape change as a result. IRAs had been around since 1974. The basic concept—saving pre-tax dollars for retirement—was immediately appealing to investors, but didn't really gain traction until 1982 when Congress made the traditional IRA "universal," allowing any working person under age 70 to contribute up to $2,000 per year tax exempt. At that point IRA assets took off, mushrooming from about $5 billion in 1982 to about $725 billion in 1992. IRA season is early spring, same as tax season, and builds to a crescendo on April 15 as last-minute filers rush to take advantage of the IRA deduction. In March 1992, about a month before the deadline, Jeff Lyons, then a marketing VP in charge of customer acquisition, was sitting in a meeting, daydreaming, as he recalls, when he had an idea. OneSource was due to hit in June, and rollover IRAs were starting to become a big factor—there were a lot of assets in play. Suddenly Lyons thought, *Why not take the annual fee off the IRA account? Make it free.* I loved his idea!

We had a $22 fee for IRAs. Such fees were standard in the industry. Getting rid of ours now would be painful, not unlike eliminating the transaction fee on mutual fund trades for OneSource. But Lyons saw an opportunity to try something bold, break away from the pack, gain some notoriety, and with luck, open the gates to a flood of new accounts. If it worked the way he thought it would, the growth in assets would more than make up for the loss of annual fees. David was immediately enthusiastic, but wary. He worried about losing so much fee income at precisely the time of year when those fees start rolling in. He calculated the cost at $9 million. Not a huge number in a year in which our revenues would exceed $900 million; but that was $9 million that would otherwise drop straight to the bottom line. So David argued for a threshold of $25,000 in IRA assets. Above that, your account is free. Less, we still charge.

My first thought when David and Jeff brought me the proposal was, why bother with thresholds at all? Why not just make it free for everybody? Here was another one of those ideas that made immediate sense to me as an investor: I knew I would open an IRA at Schwab if Schwab was the only firm that didn't charge me a fee. I didn't care about losing income in the short term. What was $9 million against an opportunity to acquire new accounts and build our asset base? In the end, we set the threshold at $10,000, which put our projected short-term loss closer to $5 million; that seemed a reasonable compromise. We calculated that plenty of people with IRAs that size would be intrigued enough to come our way, and possibly bring other business with them when they saw what we had to offer.

Now we had to move fast. Already it was the middle of March 1992. The IRA deadline was less than a month away. Practically speaking, we had about two weeks—two weeks from harebrained idea to approval to implementation, including a full-fledged advertising and direct-mail campaign. Miss the deadline and we'd have to wait another year to test the concept. Needless to say, we did not miss the deadline.

The Schwab no-fee IRA succeeded beyond all expectations. I never imagined it would be the industry leadership issue it turned out to be, or such a powerful magnet for assets. We opened hundreds of thousands of new accounts that first season and blew past all our estimates. Looking strictly at the revenue generated by new IRA accounts, we made up for the loss of fees in less than one year. It was another example in a long line that proved how motivating lower costs can be.

||||||||||||||||||||||||||||||||||||||||||||||||||||||||||||||||||||||||||||||||||||||||||||||||||||||||||||||

A simple but important truism: all else being equal, price matters.

||||||||||||||||||||||||||||||||||||||||||||||||||||||||||||||||||||||||||||||||||||||||||||||||||||||||||||||

As OneSource did with mutual funds, the no-fee IRA thrust us into the middle of a market long dominated by Fidelity. We thought there was no way Fidelity would cut its fees. Fidelity's IRA business was already huge, generating about $35 million in annual fees. But in the end, even Fidelity had no choice; after a year, they matched our pricing. But by then it was too late. As with OneSource, we had first-mover's advantage.

THE INVENTION OF ONESOURCE, the development of our independent financial adviser network, and the introduction of the no-fee IRA, all of which complemented one another, transformed our business model in the early 1990s and proved vital to our continued prosperity. The days when we could get by on commission income alone—when we could charge $70 to execute a stock and still undercut the competition—were behind us. A new breed of deep discounters was emerging. Commissions were dropping fast—a trend that, though I did not know it yet, was about to accelerate dramatically with the emergence of the internet.

What I did know was that competing solely on price was becoming an increasingly dicey proposition. The fact is, we had never been the least expensive option, even in the early days. As an investor myself, I had always been willing to pay a little extra for better service. That was one of the principles on which I had built the firm, and if anything, that principle was becoming more important to us, not less. The effect of all the new products and services we introduced in the early 1990s was not simply a more diverse revenue stream; it was also a more diverse customer base.

I had started Schwab as a streamlined brokerage for active traders; it was fast becoming a financial service hub for mainstream investors. And our team was changing. New leaders emerged as Larry stepped back. That was an important lesson—often there are strong people and new ideas just waiting for their opportunity to shine. You think you are dependent on one person or one team and then the unexpected surprises you.

22

THE NETWORK

My old office at Montgomery and Sutter, on the 24th floor where I started the company in a 4,000-square-foot space, was catty-corner to Dean Witter's home office. On the ground floor they had a little amphitheater open to the public. In the pit of the amphitheater was a giant chalkboard covered with stock symbols and prices. All day long, while the market was open, runners scooted back and forth between the phones and the chalkboard, updating prices. It was a fascinating spectacle. Some people hung out there all day in front of the chalkboard, and I could easily understand why. Being in that amphitheater gave you the illusion of being right there on the trading floor in the middle of New York City and all the action. But, of course, it was only an illusion. By the time the prices went up on the chalkboard at Dean Witter they were already old news, already known to market insiders, already processed, profited from, and discarded. The gulf between reality as depicted on the chalkboard and the true reality of the market was as wide as the gulf separating individual investors from big traders and market makers. The amphitheater was only that, a theater; reality lay elsewhere, hidden and inaccessible.

I found myself remembering that old Dean Witter amphitheater years later, on the day I finally grasped the full potential of the internet. It was Monday, December 4, 1995—five months after the founding of Amazon.com, four months after Netscape became the first major internet IPO, and right before Trade Plus, a little-known regional brokerage, reinvented itself as E*Trade Financial.

||||||||||||||||||||||||||||||||||||||||||||||||||||||||||||||||||||||||||||||||||||||||||||||||||||||||||||||||

Technology for me is a means to an end. I get excited about some new gadget or software when I can see how it might foster a deeper, faster, more direct connection between my company and my customers, or between my customers and the market.

||||||||||||||||||||||||||||||||||||||||||||||||||||||||||||||||||||||||||||||||||||||||||||||||||||||||||||||||

It was a surprising new wrinkle our technology team had discovered that brought David Pottruck and me to a meeting with William Pearson, one of our young tech guys who was part of Beth Sawi's electronic brokerage development team, at the invitation of Dawn Lepore, our chief information officer. "You've got to see this," she said.

Just months earlier in July, we had launched our website, Schwab .com. It had been a huge jump into the future—but essentially was still just an online brochure. Very cutting edge, mind you, but not the internet capability we think of today with the ability we have to inquire and transact.

So there we all were, staring at a computer screen while William sat at the keyboard. Beth had been in charge of marketing and recently took on a team dedicated to bringing our brokerage business into the internet age. It was only a demo we watched that day, something the techies had cobbled together just to give me an idea how trading on the internet might work. We had recently built a capability to streamline processes for our service teams. The team had realized it was possible to make it work for clients as well. We had been experimenting with online transactions now for a couple of years, with something called "Equalizer" that sent clients' trades directly from their computers to Schwab's trading system through AOL and CompuServe, but it was cumbersome and required some dedicated technology and lots of phone time to transmit data. (Like lots of Schwab's early brands, Equalizer was meant to send a clear message: the client's access was now "equal" to the pro's.) The internet was still in its early days, especially in terms of business uses, but everyone was poking around the edges trying to figure it out. "You mean to tell me we can do that through the network?" I said. "Through the internet network?" I didn't really believe it. The world barely knew the term and here it was putting investing right at the client's fingertips. What about security, privacy, and reliability? All those millions of account balances and Social Security numbers and buy and sell orders rattling around in cyberspace? I couldn't imagine how so much sensitive information could possibly be protected. But they were confident; they said it could be done. Not immediately. There were still bugs to work out. But we could make this work.

YEARS EARLIER, RECOGNIZING THE revolutionary role that technology could play in our business, we had wanted to make it clear to everyone in the company as well as to our clients that we were all in on tech, so we had launched a stand-alone organization called Schwab Technology. We kicked it off with a special event that featured Milton Friedman as a guest speaker on future trends. We announced a new online financial planning tool (that turned out to be a dud—far too complex for most users); created special arrangements for clients to access their accounts through CompuServe, the emerging leader in home online connectivity (now defunct); and launched something called SchwabLine, which brought market news right to your desk (too expensive, news was slow, we shut that one down). We brought in a brilliant guy named Bill Gillis to head Schwab Technology, but with a "my way or the highway" approach, he eventually clashed and left. Dawn had now replaced him. In other words, we were trying as many things as we could to get ahead in technology. Not all of them were working but we kept pushing forward—knowing the future was coming at us fast, and the future was all about technology.

The team had been working for some time to create a way for our service representatives to connect directly into the highly complex mainframe system in an easy-to-use intuitive way on their desktops. And doing it using new technology . . . the World Wide Web. It eliminated a whole step in the processes of getting stock quotes, checking margin balances, inputting client trades. It just so happened, they realized, that if they could do it for our reps, it wasn't a leap to do it for clients.

My head was spinning. I saw potential for huge cost savings. At the time, we were spending a fortune on dedicated phone lines and 800 numbers for StreetSmart, our second-generation computer trading program that had replaced Equalizer. With StreetSmart, clients accessed our network directly, with Schwab footing the bill for online access. Once trading shifts to the internet, we realized the cost of access switches to the customer, since they are paying for that already for their personal internet service. There was no incremental expense— for us, or for our clients. Moreover, our software and communication expenses go way down. (Anytime we updated StreetSmart, we had to mail thousands of new disks—at a cost of about $1 million— then brace ourselves for a flood of customer-service calls from all the people who got tripped up on the installation.)

Finally, the client gains complete access to account information and market data twenty-four hours a day, seven days a week, from any computer with internet access anywhere in the world, thereby narrowing the gulf between market insiders and ordinary investors. It wasn't the theater I saw across the street through my office window, it was the real deal.

I also saw a chance to grab an advantage in the marketplace. As it turned out, we would not be the first discount broker to offer internet trading; that distinction went to K. Aufhauser & Co. in 1994, which was later acquired by Ameritrade. Then again, we were not necessarily the first broker to execute a discounted trade, either; I don't think anybody's ever figured out who that was. We just ran with it and grew faster than our competitors did—and by investing rapidly in growth, I think it's fair to say we took the biggest risk. I figured we could do the same with internet trading. Fidelity's internet program was a year behind ours. Meanwhile, the traditional brokers were so far behind as not to matter. Merrill Lynch and the others were terrified of the internet and how it could undermine their business model. Everything the internet promised—24-hour access, full transparency, abundant (and ultimately free) news and research—was anathema to the business model of the old-line wire houses and their self-assigned role as market gatekeepers. Later some in the industry equated internet investing to giving someone a loaded gun. I thought that was paternalistic and an act of self-preservation, which I also knew couldn't last.

By the time I left the conference room that day, I was ready to terminate the experimental phase of Schwab's internet plan and proceed immediately to implementation. I knew what we had was not yet operational, much less a perfectly developed product.

||||||||||||||||||||||||||||||||||||||||||||||||||||||||||||||||||||||||||||||||||||||||||||||

I have never believed in waiting around for perfection.

||||||||||||||||||||||||||||||||||||||||||||||||||||||||||||||||||||||||||||||||||||||||||||||

I also knew that the internet was going to be huge for the markets, huge for investors, and huge for Schwab. Better to go to market too early with the best we could come up with than too late with the best we could possibly do. Something like 85% ready is usually enough for me. Then you fine-tune as you go along. I just knew that I wanted to get Schwab in the game as soon as humanly possible. Back in my office, I tracked down Beth Sawi at the Claremont Hotel in Berkeley, where she was holding a planning session with her internet team. "Beth," I said, when she came to the phone, "we've got to get this thing moving faster."

At first she didn't grasp my urgency. The group was making good progress, she assured me. Everything was on schedule. There was lots to do, and many exciting opportunities, and so on. "No, no, Beth," I said, interrupting, "you don't understand. I want it done. I want the customer offer on the web. How soon can you get it done?" There was silence at the other end of the line. I knew what was going through Beth's mind. I also knew that she was a reliable leader, and enough of a marketer to understand that speed was more important than perfection. First quarter '96, she finally said. For all I knew, when Beth said first quarter she was thinking March 31, 11:59 p.m., Hawaii time, but even that was an audacious goal. Not even four months to develop, test, and implement a World Wide Web trading capability. I said, "I'd like it by Valentine's Day," and Beth returned to her meeting. "Guys," she announced to the room. "I just talked to Chuck. Everything has changed."

THE TEAM DUBBED IT "Project Cupid." It was going to be a huge leap for us, but at least we had a running start. Catering to self-directed investors and early adopters is part of our outsider heritage. (It is no coincidence that the online trading revolution was led by three firms far removed from Wall Street: Ameritrade in Omaha, E*Trade in Palo Alto, and Schwab in San Francisco.) We were the first to offer touch-tone trading with TeleBroker and the first to update TeleBroker with reliable voice-recognition software. We tested a handheld gizmo called SchwabLine in the mid-1980s. It delivered market news and portfolio updates and printed them out on adding-machine paper. Pretty neat but way too expensive, plus the news wasn't always fresh and the printer never worked very well. In fact, we tried a lot of things that didn't work. For a while it was one failure after another. But that never worried me. Innovators should expect failure, it's part of the process. As head of the organization, it was my job to encourage experimentation, not punish failure.

Each time we failed we learned something and so resumed growing from a higher base. We were the first in our industry to build a network that allowed clients to walk into any Schwab office or call any Schwab broker on the phone and place an order that in turn was entered directly into our company-wide network. Equalizer extended that capability to the client's home computer—as long as that computer was running our software and the client called in to one of our dedicated lines. CompuServe provided us with a private network that made it possible. StreetSmart, which ran on Windows, was an extension of Equalizer and so popular that at its peak it had about 200,000 users.

So we had a history—a culture of innovation—that helped prepare us for the internet. We also had a solid, leading-edge IT platform, already in place. That was another legacy of the crash of '87. Our computers did not hold up well on Black Monday; we knew we had to be better prepared the next time. That failure led us into a big tech initiative in the early 1990s, code-named SAMS. Ostensibly, it was an acronym for Schwab Architecture and Migration Strategy, but really we named it for Sam's Grill & Seafood Restaurant in San Francisco, where much of the after-hours planning and dreaming took place. We ended up trashing the Quotron terminals and putting more powerful and versatile workstations on everyone's desks. We installed an internet protocol (IP) network, which back then was a big deal; we were betting—correctly, it turns out—that IP would become the next standard. The whole thing ended up costing about $125 million. That was a lot more than we had set out to spend, but I saw no other choice. After all the number-crunching—the revenue projections, the cost-benefit comparisons, the anticipated future needs analyses—Larry Stupski and I took a step back and asked ourselves, "What are we really trying to achieve?" Given our company's historic reliance on technology, can we afford *not* to spend whatever it takes to protect our lead and project it into the future? In the end, we were glad we did. Without SAMS in place, moving to the internet would have taken a lot longer than it did and been far more costly and complicated than it was.

Among the final triggers for us was a curious fact David picked up somewhere and shared with us at an off-site in early 1995: for the first time, sales of PCs had surpassed sales of television sets. That got us thinking hard about our electronic brokerage strategy. When we looked at the competitive landscape, a few scary features jumped out at us. We worried about AOL, already the dominant online service provider and plainly interested in breaking into financial services. Silly as it seems now, we also worried about AT&T, with its new credit card division and deep pockets. Mainly, though, we worried about Microsoft, especially when Bill Gates made a play to acquire Intuit, initially offering $1.5 billion and ultimately agreeing to pay $2.3 billion. Microsoft was obviously trying to get its hands on Quicken, and so gain access to Quicken's huge base of loyal, financially articulate users. That definitely worried us. We knew Gates was keen on leveraging his dominance with Windows to stake out a position in banking and brokerage. It was not hard to imagine Microsoft and Intuit controlling the desktops of our clients, and undercutting us on price. We were still charging $70 a trade with a 10% discount for using StreetSmart. We knew there was extra margin in those prices; it would not have been hard for Microsoft to charge even less for online trades and still make money. The more we looked at it, the more we saw ourselves as a big, fat, tempting target. I had people asking me, "Chuck, how would you like to be working for Bill Gates?"

Thankfully, nothing ever came of the proposed Microsoft-Intuit merger; the threat of a Justice Department antitrust action stopped it. In the end, Microsoft failed to emerge as a major player in financial services. Same with AT&T and AOL. But at the time the threats felt real, and they spurred us to act. I felt our best hope lay in moving fast, in coming up with a serviceable online product that we could offer our clients at a price that was low enough to generate excitement and dissuade others from entering the market.

As the role of the internet grew, we began to understand that financial services was tailor-made for this new medium. What the internet does better than anything else is execute transactions and deliver data. There is simply no better way to deliver financial services than via the internet. Today, that has extended to mobile, putting your entire financial life in your pocket wherever you are. So the internet was a natural for our industry. What's more, given our history at Schwab—our comfort with technology, our *clients'* comfort with technology, our commitment to breaking down barriers between individual investors and the market, our marketing prowess—we felt that dominance in internet trading was ours to lose.

How could we not be a part of the coming revolution? I know that's how Dawn Lepore and Beth Sawi felt. Sure, it was a huge leap of faith into the unknown. But they saw it the same way David Pottruck and I did: we had no choice. This would be a vast improvement on the client's experience with investing. It changed the game. Here was a chance to capture the lead in a thrilling new world of online financial services, even as that world was just coming into focus. There may well have been no more dramatic turning point in our history.

THE PERSON BETH SAW I relied on to execute her pledge to deliver a working internet trading application by the end of the first quarter 1996 was Gideon Sasson, an Israeli who came to us from IBM. Before that he had worked at MCI for 10 years, going back to the early days of the internet. I was in no position to evaluate Gideon's tech credentials—that was a task for Beth and Dawn. My only question the first day we met was, "Are you an investor?" It was a question I asked everyone I hired.

"Yes."

Right answer.

One of the first areas Gideon looked into when he arrived was our primitive email system. We were having a lot of problems, and the system kept crashing. We thought the issue was too many emails. "What do you call too many?" Gideon asked. Forty company-wide, he was told. "You mean like 40 an hour?" No, 40 a day, that's how primitive our email setup was at the time. "*I* get 40 emails a day!" Gideon said.

Obviously, we had a lot of catching up to do. Our web page at the time was an electronic brochure with no transactional capability. Gideon looked at proposals from IBM and Netscape and three or four other companies that wanted to help develop our new site, but none of them was willing to commit to our timetable. They were also outrageously expensive. Gideon didn't know a lot about Schwab yet, but he was familiar with the computer systems and software we had in place and he knew what else was available. He thought the deadline was tough but not crazy. In the end, he decided we could do what had to be done ourselves. Looking back, that was the right decision, and the implications were huge. Not only did it allow Beth's and Gideon's teams to meet our deadlines at a fraction of the cost, but more important, it marked a new era for Schwab as a self-sufficient technology powerhouse. We weren't renting our technology capabilities anymore, we owned them.

Gideon hired a couple of consultants to fill in the gaps, but basically he relied on creative folks with technical know-how who were already working at Schwab. By the end of February, we had a functioning application. By the end of March, just under the deadline, we launched. It wasn't the Valentine gift for our clients I'd hoped for, but close. And maybe in a perfect world, we would have waited longer. I know that Gideon and his colleagues in operations would have liked a little more time to work out the bugs. But again, I was looking at it from a marketing perspective. I wanted a great product, too, eventually; but right now what I wanted most was a product.

That first month we didn't even advertise. The system was still shaky, and we didn't want to overload it. Still, we had 100,000 clients who somehow found their way to our website and started trading. Too often they had trouble logging in, and once in, it was almost always slow-going. The system kept stalling out. That was the story line for months to come. Fortunately, the phone was always a backup for clients. We kept adding capacity, and with more capacity came more activity, and so the need for still more capacity. It was a while before we had something we could be proud of. But we just kept working it and getting better—more capacity, more functions, and greater ease of use. It's easy to take these capabilities for granted today, but we were inventing as we went.

Our clients had a lot to learn, too, even just about using computers. That's what made it so expensive, the long customer-service calls that had nothing to do with trading stocks and didn't generate a dime in revenue. I remember sitting with a customer-service rep one time. He had a client on the line and was saying to him, "Do you see such and such on your screen?" He saw that. "Now, do you see the box?" He didn't see that. "You don't see the box? Let's go through it again. Upper-right corner." After 15 minutes, he finally found the box that, when he clicked on it, expanded his screen and revealed the information he'd been looking for. Mission accomplished. But that was a 20-minute conversation. Zero revenue, nothing to do with investing.

Pricing was a huge challenge. A sudden, rapidly escalating price war had broken out, spurred by newcomers like E*Trade. We found ourselves occupying a price point well above our least expensive competitors. That had to change. We knew that ultimately our costs would come way down, and when they did, we could make money charging less than $70 for internet trades. (A lot less, as it turned out. The advent of internet trading accelerated a 30-year trend during which trades, once fixed and expensive, have essentially become commodities. In many cases today, trades are "free.")

But we still had a booming business based on the old model. We couldn't just toss that aside. So we compromised; we came up with a two-tier schedule. If you were willing to pay full freight, then you could still trade the old way, either in person at one of our branch offices or on the telephone. And by paying full freight, you had access to all our services, including, for example, unlimited calls to our phone reps. Otherwise, you could pay $29.95 for online trades and forgo the additional services. We named our new offering e.Schwab.

Part of the justification was that we assumed sophisticated e.Schwab customers had little use for telephone calls anyway, since so much of what they needed—quotes, trade confirmations, balance inquiries, and whatnot—was available online. If they still had questions, we invited them to contact us via email. That was a big mistake—one of those ideas that are conceptually brilliant but horrible in practice. What we soon learned was that helping customers via email is three to four times more expensive than with a phone call. Customers wrote to us asking simple questions such as, "Can you tell me when that dividend is due?" Well, which dividend? That's another email. We had to have all our responses preformatted for legal reasons, and the preformatted responses never seemed to fit the questions exactly. Plus we still didn't have the capacity to handle a business-size flow of email.

Bottom line: our e.Schwab customers loved online investing, but they hated the limits that came with e.Schwab. They felt like we'd shunted them into a service ghetto. We used to let them have only two or three phone calls a month, and we kept track. Everybody in the branches had access to detailed customer records and was supposed to not answer questions from e.Schwab customers who exceeded their monthly allotment. Which irritated both the branches and the customers, of course. It wasn't right, plus we were losing market share to smaller brokers like E*Trade and Ameritrade that offered fewer services, perhaps, but also fewer rules and lower prices.

I was going crazy, and David was, too. In December 1997, we had appointed David to co-CEO from his position as president and chief operating officer, and he and his leadership team were deeply committed to getting this transformation right. He was a marketing guy like me. "Don't be afraid to sacrifice revenues if that's the price you have to pay for market share."

In 1997, we talked about doing away with service restrictions for our $29.95 online customers. It was a big decision, a bet-the-company idea. You could argue it would prompt a mass migration to internet trading, costing us revenue and hurting our stock price. We all knew it was going to be costly, no one was arguing with that. The strategy team estimated a year-one hit to revenue in the hundreds of millions. We just had to be confident that while it was not going to be profitable in the short run, it would be profitable in the long run. And so on January 1, 1998, we eliminated the e.Schwab distinction and brought low-cost online trading to all Schwab customers, with open access to branches, phone help, and all the services available to any Schwab client. Online investing was now the norm, not the exception. And why not? As far as we could see, it was the future.

OUR TIMING WAS PERFECT. Trading volume soared—from an average of about 60,000 or 70,000 trades a day in 1997 to almost 100,000 in 1998. Assets held in customer accounts leapt from $354 billion to more than $490 billion, a 39% increase from 1997. We passed through 1.3 million online accounts at the end of January, up from 638,000 the year before. The wind was at our back. Americans were becoming more deeply engaged in investing with each passing year, in part because of the growth of 401(k)s and IRAs, and no doubt reflecting the excitement of a dynamic economy. All those growing retirement accounts taught people to pay attention to the market at precisely the time when stock prices were rising across the board. Every time you looked in the paper, you got more positive reinforcement. Then you had all those maturing baby boomers, a huge demographic bubble of people just reaching that age where enough of them actually had money to invest. Information was plentiful, ideas were everywhere. Just a huge confluence of events and contributing factors that made the late 1990s a great time to be in the brokerage business and the perfect time for something as engaging as online investing.

And it was a turning point for Schwab. On December 28, 1998, with total client assets surging toward an astonishing $1 trillion, we achieved a milestone I would not have even aspired to when I started. Our market capitalization, a measure of the total value placed on our company by the investing public, reached $25.5 billion, surpassing Merrill Lynch. Merrill Lynch, of course, had once aspired to bring Main Street to Wall Street. As we were passing Merrill by, we were finally becoming exactly that—the brokerage for the Main Street investor.

Which is not really how we started. As much as I've always believed in bringing the power of investing to the masses, Schwab began as a brokerage for individual investors who by definition were sophisticated investors: people who were not scared of the stock market, who preferred to go it alone because they believed they knew better than any broker what was best for them. The little guys came to us in large numbers much later, with the advent of online trading. Those investors were attracted to a new kind of service—delivered privately and efficiently online, and with easy access to research—that coincidentally arrived in the midst of a historic stock market boom. The Dow hit 5,000 in November 1994; 6,000 in October 1996; 7,000 in February 1997—on its way to a high of almost 12,000 early in the new millennium. New investors swarmed the markets, and Schwab was a prime beneficiary.

While we were adding internet services, we were also aggressively expanding our branch network. That was by no means the obvious way to go. In fact, it was the subject of a huge internal debate. Would the whole industry migrate online? Was our branch network now obsolete? Many people thought so. I disagreed. I knew from that first experience with Uncle Bill in Sacramento what powerful tools the branches were for attracting new accounts. People may prefer ultimately to trade online, but they liked to open their accounts in person. They wanted both: a sophisticated online trading tool and a nearby office with our name on the door. And that's the way we chose to go. The strategy distinguished us from everyone else in the industry and helped drive our revenues to new heights. It's no accident that Schwab today is many times larger than online firms that lack our national branch network. Where else could the little guy open an account with a few thousand dollars at a neighborhood branch, go online, start trading, and join the investor revolution?

I'M ENORMOUSLY PROUD OF the way Schwab opened up the markets to newcomers and helped transform legions of savers into investors. But as time went on, I began to worry about some of what I was seeing. Many of those newcomers grew and learned over time, developing into sophisticated independent investors much like we had been serving all along. But many others floundered.

|||||||||||||||||||||||||||||||||||||||||||||||||||||||||||||||||||||||||||||||||||||||||||||||||||||||||||||||||

Investing well is hard work. Not everybody has the time or inclination to go it alone.

|||||||||||||||||||||||||||||||||||||||||||||||||||||||||||||||||||||||||||||||||||||||||||||||||||||||||||||||||

As long as the market kept rising, everybody was happy. But when the market finally collapsed, as markets always do, I would have to reevaluate certain basic assumptions about who we were and what services we could offer our clients.

23

UNLIKE ANYTHING I HAD
EXPERIENCED

The run-up to the millennium was a period of unprecedented growth and prosperity for Schwab. Every year we went through our planning exercises, and every year we asked the same question: Can it really be as strong next year as it was this year? And every year it was even stronger. We were making money hand over fist, thanks mainly to active stock traders—those who trade several times a month, if not every day. And we were spending it, adding new services and upgrading our capacity and systems at breakneck speed. It's true that every extra dollar that was coming into our money market funds was also lucrative; ditto for the dollars accumulating in our OneSource mutual funds. But active traders—and there were so many of them during the bubble—were the main drivers behind an enormously profitable era in the company's history.

In response, our employee ranks swelled almost tenfold—from 2,700 at the beginning of 1990 to over 26,000 in 2000—and still we could not keep up with demand. Our managers felt understaffed; our employees, overworked. In retrospect, it's obvious that we went too far with adding staff, but at the time we saw no other way. Should we have dialed back our marketing and stemmed the flow of new customers? That would have been difficult in the extreme for someone like me. I have always been focused on growth, even when it brings chaos. I simply could not have conceived of lowering our sights, even temporarily. You go along for years, normal ups and downs, some minor trembling, and then it's like an earthquake hits, a major earthquake, and for the first time you appreciate how much more powerful 8.0 is on the Richter scale than 6.0 or even 7.0. We needed more capacity, period, and so we hired, and hired, and hired some more.

It was a time of incredible creativity. The internet, coupled with rapid advances in computing power, was making all sorts of dreams possible for entrepreneurs all over world. We were at the beginning of a new era, like the industrial revolution before, or the creation of mass transportation or broadcast media. The future was wide open. It was barely two years since launching our own internet capabilities and we were assessing what it could do. After reviewing our business plans in early 1999 with Dan Leemon, our head of strategy, I sat down in March and scribbled notes for what I thought we should be developing when it came to the internet. I called it the *Schwab Portal* and imagined a website that offered the best of everything a client might need. Investing, insurance, banking, sure, but also travel services, technology support, clothing, sports equipment, you name it. All in a completely secure and privacy-protected environment. A relative newcomer in Seattle, Amazon.com, was launching similar plans, expanding from online book sales to other products. Today, what can't you buy on Amazon? With so much growth happening in our core business of investing, we didn't pursue the Schwab Portal idea. I often wonder what would have happened had we pushed it forward. But the coming bear market had different plans for us.

The period from spring 1999 through late 2000 was unlike anything I have ever experienced in all my years studying the market, and by then I had seen my share of manias and market bubbles. What happened to valuations, what happened to investor psychology, what happened to the dot-coms, to Wall Street, and to business ethics—it was truly bizarre, way out of line with reality, and we were right in the middle of it all. You never saw Schwab running those crazy ads about hitchhikers buying their own islands; that was never what we were about. But when internet stocks became *the* topic around the office watercooler, when CNBC became the hottest network on cable, and everywhere you looked, dentists and cabdrivers, house-wives and college students, were embarking on new careers as day traders, we felt the impact as much as anyone else. It was like a fire hose blasting right through the front door; new accounts just came pouring in. Client assets briefly topped $1 trillion in August 2000. Average daily trading volume surged as high as 350,000. Meanwhile, we were hiring people as fast as we could to maintain a high level of customer service in the face of unprecedented demand. We were also plowing our earnings back into the business by expanding capa-bilities such as after-market-hours electronic trading, wireless stock alerts for pagers, one of the first wireless trading platforms—we called it Pocketbroker—for what were then called "wireless enabled cell phones" (today, just "your phone"), access to private equity of-ferings, and electronic trade confirmations that enabled a completely paperless experience for clients. We had expanded internationally in Japan, Australia, Canada, and the UK. And in two of our biggest moves, we announced the acquisition of U.S. Trust, the 150-year-old wealth manager, and purchased a Texas company called Cybercorp, an advanced technology platform for active traders.

Did I worry? Of course, I worried. I knew full well that we were in a bubble, that what we were experiencing could not possibly last. As early as 1996, Alan Greenspan, the Federal Reserve chairman, had warned of "irrational exuberance." But the stock market was raging, everybody wanted in on the action. What could we say to our clients? Don't invest? We put out lots of well-reasoned informa-tion on how to be a smart investor, but manias are manias and you can't slow them down. I insisted we put out a press release when the Dow Jones hit 10,000 to remind people it's just a number. I've been an investor during every thousand-point mark the Dow has reached, and while the milestones make great headlines for a day, it's the return on investment over a lifetime that people should focus on and often don't, or can't, because of the emotion involved. "I urge investors to look beyond today's numbers to the future," I said. "Make sure that in this world of fast markets and quick turnover, you've got an investment plan that's built to last. Keep things in perspective and plan ahead."

A group at Stanford University had invited me to speak at a gathering in 1999 about my perspectives on the markets and economy. The "new economy" was on everyone's mind. Jerry Yang was there to talk about Yahoo and its explosive growth, Meg Whitman was representing eBay. I told the attendees the story of my first experience with a bubble in the early '60s when bowling products were all the rage, and how the current situation had a similar feeling of frenzy to it. Weeks later a bowling ball arrived at my office from Stanford, engraved with something I had said to the group, "Can the magic last?" The ball sits in my office today as a good reminder about market euphoria.

Even our own stock went nuts, which, by the way, had the opposite effect our compensation structure was designed for. We had a fair number of long-term employees who had accumulated big piles of company stock. The reason any company awards stock to employees, of course, is to promote loyalty and commitment to the cause and the future. But as Schwab stock hurtled toward $50, the effect was the opposite. People started quitting, cashed in their options and their 401(k)s, and, in many cases, retired as millionaires. I don't blame them. The opportunity was hard to ignore. But it made things tough for those of us who stayed. We lost many experienced people.

Part of the underlying problem we were about to face was hubris.

||||||||||||||||||||||||||||||||||||||||||||||||||||||||||||||||||||||||||||||||||||||||||||||||

**We were all a little guilty of assuming that since things
were going so well, we must be geniuses.**

||||||||||||||||||||||||||||||||||||||||||||||||||||||||||||||||||||||||||||||||||||||||||||||||

Hubris is a common trap successful people fall into. We figured that our model—combining state-of-the-art internet trading with a national network of brick-and-mortar branches, coupled with the industry's largest network of independent financial advisers, and a rapidly growing retirement business—must be the real reason we were succeeding. Well, it's true, we did have a terrific model. But Schwab's relationship to the market then was like a sailboat's to the wind. When the wind blew hard, we went fast. During the late 1990s, the wind was blowing 100 miles an hour. Even when average trading volume reached an unprecedented 350,000 trades a day, we didn't stop to celebrate. Instead, David and his planning group were talking about doubling payroll to 50,000 employees so that we could execute a million trades every day. It was a colossal undertaking. Already they were hard at work building an infrastructure to accommodate all those extra bodies—renting office space, buying chairs and desks and computers, ramping up capacity in every conceivable way.

In hindsight, one obvious overreach was in our real estate portfolio. The brokerage business was cyclical. Starting every January and continuing through tax deadline day in April, we got very busy, and it strained our capacity. During the late 1990s, with business booming, the problem was especially acute, and in 1999, David came to me and said, "I want to make sure that we don't have this problem again." With that he embarked on an unprecedented expansion. I flew down to Austin on May 8, 2000, to preside over one of the openings. I'll never forget being taken on a little tour of the office park. My host wanted to show me all the "buildings" that were ours. In some cases those buildings were little more than construction sites, and already we were signed up for long-term leases. Later someone showed me a picture of a Schwab employee on the cover of a real estate trade magazine. He was being honored by the brokers for signing so many leases. *Oh my god*, I remember thinking. *What kind of disaster have we created for ourselves?* You never want your real estate person on the cover of anything. It was totally out of control, and we ended up paying a steep price for our enthusiasm, for years to come. Unwinding all those leases eventually cost us well north of $400 million. That was almost as much as we paid out in severance to all the people we had to lay off.

THEN IN LATE SPRING 2000 it happened. The wind died and our sails sputtered. Almost overnight, everything was quiet. Suddenly we found ourselves handling a mere 200,000 trades a day, which shocked us until it dipped below 150,000, then 100,000. As quickly and inexplicably as the incredible bull market of the 1990s had begun, it was ending. Like any market top, the precise timing of the bursting of the tech bubble is identifiable only in retrospect. We know now that the NASDAQ peaked at 5,048 on March 10, 2000. But who knew it at the time? All we knew then was that valuations were seriously out of whack. A return to some kind of normalcy was inevitable. But just as it had taken us a while to recognize the liftoff for what it was, we did not mark the finality of the crash until much later, when it was fully upon us.

Meanwhile, the uncertainty played havoc on our planning. As trading volume declined, earnings fell, and our own stock price retreated, we took what in hindsight were clearly inadequate measures to try to stop the bleeding. We could have handled a 15% or 20% decline in volume. That much was built into our budget forecast, and we had a contingency plan in place to address it without layoffs, mainly by reducing bonuses. But we had no plan for a 70% drop, and that forced us into survival mode. David and I each took

50% pay cuts, the executive committee took a 25% cut, and on down the pyramid. But that was not nearly enough. All our great training programs and educational programs had to go, too. It was incredibly painful but absolutely necessary. We could not have survived with our current cost structure.

We had frozen hiring, cut salaries, slashed budgets, encouraged job sharing, and enforced mandatory days off. But it still wasn't enough. At the end of March 2001, we announced our first round of layoffs, cutting more than 2,000 jobs and slimming down further through attrition. It was a shock to the system. Yet it had to be done. I remember at one particularly somber meeting of our leadership team, seeing the looks on everyone's faces as they realized the personal enormity of what was in front of them, I said, "This is what we're paid to do, people. I know it is hard. I know it is going to be terrible. But this is what we're paid to do."

Schwab hadn't gone through this before, and I felt terrible and wanted to be able to do something for those Schwab employees we had to let go. Helen and I put $10 million into a fund for laid-off employees to help with tuition if they wanted to go back to school and study for another profession. The program was administered by the San Francisco Foundation so that it was impartial, and many people took advantage of it and went into new careers that way, some into teaching, some into law and medical care. Over the years I've gotten letters from people thanking us: "it made it possible for me to go back to school . . . into nursing . . . I went into teaching" . . . a whole range of new beginnings. Why did we do it? We just wanted to, I suppose. And we were fortunate enough that we could. Just like it had seemed right to try to make employees whole again after the sale to BofA when so many saw the value of their shares shrivel up, or how my father, a tough-minded guy who believed people needed to take personal responsibility, was always the first guy putting a dollar bill in that basket coming around at church. It just felt right.

We struggled with those layoffs and the retrenchment. But we'd had our reasons. Reasonably good ones given the past experience where slow trading markets came screaming back and you'd better be prepared with capacity or your service suffered and clients left. But it was different this time and I knew who was responsible: I was, David was; everybody at the top of the organization who had failed to plan effectively was. And I felt terrible that others were going to have to pay for our mistakes with their jobs. Of the 2,000 we laid off in the first round, most were junior employees in the call centers. Of course, we wanted the people who stayed to be proud of the company they worked for, and we wanted to avoid survivor syndrome, where employees start thinking, *I hate this company. I'm embarrassed to work here.*

We also wanted the people we laid off to be willing to come back to work someday if we needed them back. So we tried to make it as painless for them as we could. We were over-the-top generous with severance. We worried about questions like, How do we notify people? Do we let them go back to their desks? Do we turn off their email? Do we let them say good-bye to their colleagues? We sweated all that stuff, probably more so than companies that had more experience with layoffs. But we were not selling dog food, we were selling financial services. Our business required empathetic, concerned, able people to serve our clients, and whether they were coming or going, they had to be treated with generosity and respect. I think our approach paid off. We got through that first round okay. But that was only the beginning. Unfortunately, we led our employees to believe that we would be back on track faster than we were. I was as surprised as anyone that the recovery took so long. In 2000, we thought, *It's getting bad, but bear markets don't last that long.* The average bear market lasts around 11 months. Then we thought, *Okay, it's early 2001, things will start to get better soon.*

But by mid-2001, a half year into the new millennium, I could see that it was not nearly enough, that we had to keep cutting. The future of the company as I had envisioned it was on the line. On

July 24, 2001, as was my habit when I had an important message for David, I sat down to think things through and then scribbled a handwritten note to share my perspectives. *I feel that we need to realign ourselves once again closer to the current market environment,* I began. *We've been making progress, but, unfortunately, it appears another point of decision has been reached.* Normally I gave David a great deal of latitude in running the company. When he became co-CEO, I fully expected he would one day have the whole job to himself, at which point I would retain the chairman's title. So I felt it only fair that during this transitional period, he be given plenty of authority to act as he saw fit. But sometimes I felt I needed to give a nudge. This was one of those times. *I would give Bob [Rosseau] the direction to shut down Aust. and Japan,* I wrote, *and move the remaining intl. organization to Steve's [Scheid's] group, cutting a layer of mgmt out. . . . I think we need to close Austin [call center] . . . and consider Orlando. . . . All other overhead areas need another 10%–14% shrink. I hope these kinds of decisions will set us up for a full recovery, and return our remaining team to full compensation, plus bonus opportunities. Let's discuss.* I signed the note, "Chuck," and carried it down the hall to David's office.

ON AUGUST 30, 2001, we announced plans for a second restructuring. The plans included reducing our head count by roughly an additional 10%, letting go another 2,000-plus employees and contractors, which, together with previous cuts, put us at about 25% below where we started going into the millennium. We also cut facilities, backed out some of our technology, and took a hefty charge of $225 million for the year to cover it all. Losing great people, who had contributed so much and worked so hard for clients, was enormously difficult and painful. Treating those employees with concern and respect was an absolute priority, and we offered the same transition assistance program—including severance pay and benefits, tuition stipends, a special stock option grant, and a hire-back bonus—that was available for those involved in the earlier layoffs. Behind the scenes, the wheels started moving to divest ourselves of operations in Australia and Japan. We put the chill on the idea of new acquisitions.

YOU CAN'T CUT A company to greatness. We had taken lots of expenses out by now, painful as it was, and I knew we had to think forward and find new ways to grow and be more important in our clients' lives.

If you boiled the Schwab business model down to its essence, you could say we found areas in financial services where people were being underserved, where their experience was a compromise between getting what they needed and having to pay excessively for it. Other times the compromise was making things harder than they need to be. Think high-cost investment advice, for example, or nickel-and-dime "gotcha" fees or banker's hours. Our business was based on finding ways to break compromises. That was the magic behind lower trading costs, 24-hour phone service, local branches, no-fee IRAs, and internet trading.

We'd been making changes at breakneck speed, especially since we freed ourselves from the constraints of a big bank in 1987. And now, in the midst of all the cutting we needed to do as the dot-com crash was on us, a *bank* was exactly what was on my mind. My experience at BofA had shown me the importance of retail banking in the consumer's everyday life, and how a checking account met the most basic and necessary need: managing a person's daily finances. Banking was at the center of everyone's lives. It was also an area where consumers faced plenty of compromises. That was the opportunity!

I had pushed hard for it back in the late '90s. A bank?! Others on the leadership team thought it was a bad idea. They pushed back hard every time I brought up the idea. Many of them came from banking themselves and had a distaste for it. I understood that. Traditional banking required huge scale and expensive systems to manage the risk and regulatory hurdles. The basic refrain was that there was little in the way of business return for checking accounts. I could understand all that if I was asking for a *traditional* bank. But they didn't see the bank I had in mind—an online investor's bank that would be attractive to our clients, make their lives easier, and encourage them to do more business at Schwab. It could be a game changer for clients, and we could earn some revenue on the cash balances they held while managing the money very conservatively. If we built that bank, I said, customers will come.

By 2001, I had heard "no" so often that I finally put my foot down and told Steve Scheid, our CFO, "Just go build a bank." I insisted we assemble a team to scope out the requirements and come up with a business model that would work for us. To his credit, though he hadn't been a fan of the idea up to that point having been in retail banking himself, Steve said, "If we're going to do a bank, let's do a great one."

We put together a small team—Joe Martinetto, who represented finance for the retail client enterprise (and later became our chief financial officer and more recently chief operating officer), Dave Martin, our treasurer, and Scott Rhoades from finance—as the project leads to put it all together. I had standing monthly meetings where we hashed out the details. Do we buy an existing bank and build from there? Do a joint venture? Or start a new bank, a de novo bank, as they call it? There were arguments in favor of all three approaches, but I liked the idea of a de novo bank. It meant a clean slate, no existing client base or infrastructure or existing loans—all of which could pose risks. No, I wanted a fresh start, something unique and designed with our investor clients in mind.

After months of meetings and fleshing out a plan, Joe and Scott presented it to the board in December 2001 and with the board's approval we were off to the regulators with an application. It would have all the elements I wanted. It would be simple, with online access. No national branch network. Quick and easy mortgage loans. It would integrate into a client's investment accounts for maximum convenience and include free checking, free ATM withdrawals (from just about any other bank's ATMs), free transfers between accounts, and none of the BS around returned checks and "gotcha" fees. No nickel and diming. Other banks hit you with a $3.00 charge if you used their ATMs and weren't their customer (we would just rebate that back—creating an instant worldwide no-fee ATM network). Most banks charge $35 per returned check and make a tidy amount as a result. Customers absolutely hated that. We would add a feature I thought was brilliant, helping you avoid bounced checks by creating a minimum balance feature. You'd always stay at the level you set by pulling cash from your brokerage account when balances in your bank account got too low. It was a safety valve. Because it was an integrated account, you'd always have a minimum balance, so you'd never have a returned check. And we would have no monthly or annual fees and you would earn interest on your balance. And, of course, the most important feature, it was a bank, a safe place for people to put their checking and savings with FDIC insurance. Only a bank could offer that level of security. It was too important a piece of every client's financial requirements for us not to be able to solve it for them.

In April 2003, we received regulatory approval and launched Charles Schwab Bank, the first bank designed exclusively with investors' needs in mind. Within six months we had to revise our business plan because the bank took off so quickly, blowing past our three-year projection. Average checking account sizes during that first year were over $30,000, surprisingly high for any bank, let alone a new one.

As the decade unfolded and the financial crisis of 2008 created a rush to safety among investors and brought trading levels down dramatically, the bank would prove to be Schwab's saving grace because interest revenue made up for lost trading revenue. It has remained one of the most important elements of our business model to this day and will continue to be into the future.

Sometimes you have to push hard when you have a strong instinct and just ignore the naysayers.

NOT ALL OUR DECISIONS during that difficult period were great ones. In the heat of the moment it's easy to make unwise decisions that you don't think all the way through. That's never an excuse, just a fact of life. We were turning over every stone to save on expenses. A little later in 2002, we decided to eliminate the 401(k) matching contribution for all Schwab employees. That was my call and I know now that I made a big mistake. It's true, we had been extremely generous for many years. Over the past decade we had awarded over $500 million in matching retirement funds to our employees. Eliminating the match saved us about $50 million in 2003. But it sent the wrong message, to our employees and our clients alike. In our 401(k) business, clients couldn't believe we had done something like that. Walt Bettinger, who was leading it after we had purchased his firm in 1995, was inundated with client calls questioning our integrity. For more than a quarter century I had been trumpeting to the world the virtue of saving for retirement. Now here I was eliminating a major retirement incentive for my own employees. I was trying to avoid more layoffs, but I should have found another way.

A lot of difficult decisions were made and now under way, and we thought with a sense of relief, *OK, we're in good shape now and things in the market will start to get better soon.* Then came September 11.

I was working at home that morning, participating in a conference call with the PGA Advisory Board, when the first plane hit. I thought it looked like a little Piper Cub . . . a terrible accident. When the second plane hit, I realized along with the rest of the world that it was something far worse than an accident. First I called to check on my daughter Katie in New York, then left for the office. My thoughts were for our employees in New York. We had a small office on the main floor of the World Trade Center; luckily, they all got out safely before the towers crashed. But even 3,000 miles away, rumors were flying about possible attacks on the Golden Gate Bridge or other Bay Area locations. The markets were closed and to be safe, we shut down our San Francisco offices and sent everyone home.

We were back in business the next day, but, of course, the world had changed. I believe it is important in situations like this to connect with our clients and help them maintain a long-term focus rather than reacting in the moment—which is an essential skill as an investor, but a very hard one to master emotionally. I sent a letter to all our clients sharing some of my thoughts: I said that Americans could be proud that their financial system absorbed the shock and continued working; that despite the terrible tragedy of September 11 and the destruction it caused near Wall Street, the stock exchanges had reopened just four market days later on the following Monday and by the end of that first day of trading, the New York Stock Exchange had handled a record-volume trading day, and the NASDAQ a near record day. This was a testament to the men and women who labored tirelessly to ensure that the system worked. I reminded clients that the market volatility and declines after the market opened, while stressful, were in line with historical patterns. National or international crises always spark sell-offs, but the drops reverse eventually, often within a short time frame. While the markets were extremely active and volatile during the week, buy orders outnumbered sell orders among Schwab clients . . . a good sign of long-term confidence in our economy.

Those calming sentiments were important. But before September 11, 2001, it was still possible to believe that an economic recovery was imminent. After September 11, no one had any such illusions.

So the "long term" in *long-term investing* had become more meaningful. It was clear to me that stimulus was needed to get the economy buoyed and growing. I lobbied the government heavily to act speedily with economic stimulus and distributed an open letter to the president and Congress in early October. We put on town halls for investors where they could hear from and meet with the Treasury secretary and express their views directly.

By year's end, the Dow had fallen more than 7%. Things went from bad to worse in 2002: the Dow lost more than 18%, driven in part by scandal on Wall Street that highlighted the many conflicts of interest that still existed between investment banking arms of the major Wall Street players and their brokerage businesses. Over the preceding two years, America's capital markets were turned upside down by revelations of corporate malfeasance, accounting fraud, and conflicted advice. I always knew that research coming from Wall Street was, if not 100% biased, certainly more than zero. After the dot-com crash in 2000–2003, it became obvious to everyone that Wall Street had terrible incentives for pushing the public into riskier stocks. Stock recommendations by the most reputable firms in the world were shown to be more about smoothing the relationship between investment bankers and CEOs than about providing sound information to ordinary investors. I was incensed about it and wrote an opinion piece for publication that suggested simple solutions that would sound familiar today: more disclosure, greater transparency, accountability at the senior-most executive levels of financial services firms that serve the general public.

SOMETIMES IT'S BEST TO simply take the situation as an opportunity rather than rail against it. Our approach had always been to find bad situations in financial services and try to turn them into opportunities for disruption where we could make life better for the investor. We heard about a firm in Chicago called Chicago Investment Analytics whose system was based on taking the entire market and sorting stocks into As, Bs, Cs, Ds, and Fs. Obviously, the A and B stocks you'd want to buy and the D and F stocks you'd want to sell. Cs were one you'd hold. And their system was based on a very objective methodology of sorting through all the data of companies, earnings reports, and any public information available and forcing an equal number of buys and sells.

I thought this might be a really interesting thing for our clients, an objective way to give people some help without conflicts. So in the midst of the Wall Street scandal, we bought Chicago Analytics and launched Schwab Equity Ratings, an objective stock assessment system that challenged the conflicted Wall Street ways of recommending stocks.

We also launched Schwab Private Client, our first foray into wealth management services, and an approach that put greater objectivity into investment advice by paying Schwab Private Client investment consultants salaries, not commissions, so they'd base their advice on individual needs, circumstances, and objectives, not their own pay.

Individual investors were disillusioned. They needed to invest for the future, but after the dot-com bubble, Enron, and other events, they had deep misgivings about the conflicts inherent in the way traditional brokers delivered research and advice. Because we didn't have an investment banking business, we didn't have the conflicts that often arose from trying to serve corporate clients, who needed a firm to raise capital by selling their securities to retail investors, *and* individual investors, who were entitled to advice based on their personal needs. The way to avoid this conflict of interest was pretty simple and clear: put individual investors at the heart of the business and do what's right by them.

We landed on the June 3, 2002, cover of *BusinessWeek* after a team of us made the media rounds in New York on May 16 to announce our new services: "Schwab vs. Wall Street: With the big firms reeling, Charles Schwab is pushing to win over their disgruntled investors," with a cartoon of me on the cover wrestling the Wall Street bull to the ground. I have to admit, I liked that one! It pretty well summarized what we've always been about.

I also participated with President George W. Bush at his economic summit at Baylor University in Waco, Texas, to provide the perspective of our clients, average individual investors who wanted to see the economy goosed out of its doldrums. I flew there to the meeting with my great friend Mike Boskin, who had been chairman of George H. Bush's Council of Economic Advisors during his presidency. Mike was also a premier economics professor at Stanford's Hoover Institute. We spent the flight talking about things that could give the economy a needed boost to get it moving.

A couple hundred people gathered for the summit in the university auditorium to present thoughts on what could be done. As it turned out, I was seated next to President Bush, whom I know personally. George knows Helen's family, the O'Neill family from Midland, Texas. My brother-in-law Joe and his wife, Jan, introduced George to Laura Bush in the backyard of their home many years before. So we were friends. But I was honored to be sitting right next to the president for these presentations. When my turn came around to present, the thrust of my message was that we needed to lower capital gains rates on stock buying and selling, and we needed to reduce the taxes on dividends. Both of those changes would encourage people to sell appreciated stock and encourage companies to put out more dividends. Much of that money would be spent and would help trigger economic growth. After I finished my comments, President Bush said to me, "You know, that's a pretty good idea, Chuck." So the next thing I knew I was asked to share the idea in Washington, D.C., with a couple of different groups, including a discussion we held with the president and a dozen or so clients in Schwab's Alexandria, Virginia, branch. One of them said, "I'm retired and this could really help me increase my income." Another said he would love to save more and this would give him the incentive to do it. Eventually the idea was turned into legislation and a reduced capital gains tax on stocks and tax on dividends was passed.

In March 2003, the markets dived lower still following the Iraq invasion. Average daily trading volume plummeted to new lows, and the layoffs we had planned at Schwab continued apace.

Finally, inevitably, we started laying off senior management in our third restructuring. After all the other layoffs, we were left with too many officers and not enough troops. That was one of the toughest things I have ever had to go through in my business life. I never lost my commitment to the cause, but it was heartbreaking to be around, just heartbreaking. We all suffered. One of the hardest parts for me was having to accept that maybe we were no better than those cutthroat firms on Wall Street that are always hiring and firing. Schwab is not populated with hard-nosed, kick-butt cost cutters. We are growth junkies—people who thrive on change and adaptability and the next new thing. And we're proud of what we stand for. But now I felt ashamed. Employees were embarrassed to tell people where they worked because the person you were talking to might be an ex-Schwabbie who might resent you for being one of those lucky enough to survive the cuts.

As CFO, Chris Dodds was right in the thick of it. He had five or six people in his hometown of Piedmont across San Francisco Bay tap him on the shoulder and say, "Aren't you Chris Dodds?" He knew why they were asking. "I got laid off in round two," they might say, "and it's really been a struggle. It's really a tough job market." It was just very hard on all of us. We had to say good-bye to so many good people who had helped us build a great company. "It's not that you're no longer needed," we told them. "It's just that we can't afford to have you around anymore." I'm sure that was little consolation.

All told we lopped off about 30% of our payroll, at all levels of the company, and reduced our head count by almost 50%. I hoped to never have to go through that again.

DAVID HAD BEEN CO-CEO since January 1998, when in January of 2003 I persuaded the board to give him his chance to lead on his own. Frankly, I was afraid of losing him. I had been hearing from the HR people that he was thinking about making a move, that there were headhunters on his trail. I did not want David to take the next step forward in his career with some other company. We'd been through some fast times together since David became co-CEO. With the board's approval, I promoted him to CEO effective at our annual stockholders meeting in May 2003. The timing may seem odd. We were deep into our retrenchment phase, still not finished with layoffs, still not sure when the long-anticipated recovery would begin. But frankly, I had already given David a lot of latitude to operate the company as he saw fit. Moreover, I had spent much of the past two months attending to my daughter Katie, after a terrible fire at some friends' apartment in New York City. Katie got through it—but it was touch-and-go for a while. The fire took place in March of 2002. She was in the hospital for five weeks. I was in New York the whole time, occasionally checking in with the office but otherwise totally focused on Katie. When I finally returned to San Francisco, it seemed like the right time to cede the reins to David. And truthfully, the transition had been carefully under way for some time. I believed David was the guy who could take the company forward into the future. He had everything going for him and, like me, believed deeply in what we had built and how we stood out from the crowd.

When I look back over David's 20-year career at Schwab, I see so much talent and many accomplishments. David was an extremely effective executive. He did so many good things for the company, always with a spirit and an enthusiasm unmatched by anyone else on the management team. David was instrumental in thinking about branding and getting us on the major networks with advertising. And the whole strategy of combining online trading with an extensive branch network—he believed passionately in it and championed it above all others. The cost of opening and operating so many branches (at the peak we had almost 400) was phenomenal, but I also know it's the main reason that we had multiples of the client assets of even the largest of our internet-only competitors.

David was also a wonderful communicator, such an important tool for a leader. But I've learned over the years that someone who is the best leader at one point in a company's evolution may not be the best at another time. In an environment where we were growing at a rapid pace, there were challenges all their own, and David had been very strong at helping to guide Schwab during the late '80s and '90s when we were rocketing forward. But suddenly we hit a new reality, where the entire investing landscape was slowing; pricing pressure was on, and we were putting the brakes on growth. Suddenly you're looking every which way to identify where your growth will come from and what expenses you can eliminate. That's an entirely different challenge for management and requires a different approach. Switching hats like that isn't easy.

A new price structure was put in place in 2003. It was a striking example of how we were disconnecting from our clients. Fidelity had just announced new lower commissions. We had to respond. Unfortunately, what we came up with was a multitiered scheme that was so complex that even our own employees could not understand it. It came with a long, complicated fee schedule that hit hardest on our least affluent customers, those with accounts under $250,000. It looked like we were telling them we didn't want their business.

Again, we have never been the cheapest discount broker, but we have always tried to offer our customers the most value. When investors didn't think of us anymore as a great value, I felt we lost our identity. (We spent the second half of 2004 and on into 2005 aggressively rebuilding that identity. All told, we would cut prices eight times.)

The pricing problem became apparent to me at our annual Chairman's Club meeting, where we celebrate the individual successes of our managers each year. Our meeting in 2003 took place in Jamaica. It didn't feel very celebratory—there was a real pall underlying the company's mood at the time. Senior management had a planning meeting one morning and a young executive, John Clendening, made a presentation about how far out of the market we were in terms of pricing. I couldn't believe it, but there it was staring back at me. I came to the realization that we had to drop our prices dramatically if we were going to succeed. I'll always thank John for his candid analysis of our situation.

We had lost our focus. Those higher prices raised a lot of revenue, but they also covered up our inefficiencies. And they weren't driving growth in a way that would build a stronger future. In the end, they obscured the need for real structural reform until it was almost too late.

IN THE YEARS SINCE, I have asked myself, *Is there anything I could have done earlier to prevent so many layoffs, to avoid such a deep, company-wide retrenchment?* Certainly I had misgivings at key points along the way—for example, when we were adding all that office space.

I'm all for growth, as I've said repeatedly. But I also have an entrepreneur's natural reluctance to spend, a wariness of overcommitting to fixed costs.

I was definitely afraid we were getting too far ahead of ourselves. Our international expansion had always been saddled by the complexity of managing each country's regulations. It was like getting into a new line of business each time. We simply could not duplicate our business model in these foreign jurisdictions because of their laws about financial services and how they protected the banks. We did not want to form a bank in each country.

And our expansion into investment banking and research arenas, which on the surface seemed a good diversification move, shifted us away from our core of serving *individual* investors. I occasionally shared my misgivings with David, but I had to be careful. I never wanted to undermine his authority. Anytime I had anything negative to say to him, I said it in my office, with the door closed. Then he did what he thought best. Which was how it should be. I *wanted* David to play a greater role. The whole co-CEO thing was never meant to be more than a transitional stage leading to David's ultimate ascension to CEO. David had done a great job in so many ways. The company had grown and thrived with his leadership during our rapid growth phase, and into the dot-com age and bubble. Unfortunately, there was this new reality now . . . and it was proving to be a very different beast.

||||||||||||||||||||||||||||||||||||||||||||||||||||||||||||||||||||||||||||||||||||||||||||||||||||||||

PART IV

Second Act

The life of a business goes through cycles. An idea is new and the company grows and that growth begins to decline as the business matures and new competitors enter the fray. You fight the decline with new ideas and the cycle begins again.

At times, you just have to shrink the organization so that you can grow again in a new way. When you do so, it's absolutely essential that you reduce your costs. Get the cost of doing business down to a level that is sustainable, especially if you need to reduce prices to maintain your competitiveness.

So many people you see in business throw up their hands and can't do it, or don't want to do it. It's too painful, too unpopular. They don't have the vision and determination to do what's needed. They end up selling the company voluntarily, or someone comes along and takes it away.

In my view, when you're in that kind of situation, you can't act fast enough or aggressively enough to get back on track. I expect that's where a lot of management teams go wrong when faced with a big change in their environment. They don't recognize the need for change and don't address it quickly. They're too attached to the things they built, the strategies they concocted, too worried about the consequences of change.

A turnaround requires a very critical eye, and it needs to be done when you still have the wherewithal to get it done. Wait too long and it gets that much harder, you don't have any cushion left. You flounder, or worse yet, you find yourself suddenly out the door, with a new owner taking over who is more than willing to act boldly.

In fact, I believe there are cycles to so much in our lives. From our careers to our relationships, sticking your head in the sand in the face of a challenge or setback just isn't an option. You need to address the challenge and move forward.

24

A VERY DIFFICULT DECISION

In many ways, 2004 was a tale of two companies. The year had started with promise—we had reduced head count and offered new services to clients—but then the investing environment deteriorated, price competition heated up, and all that hard work we had done in the last few years to cut costs and develop new innovations just wasn't enough. We were strong financially, that was never an issue. But looking forward, it was clear we were struggling to grow, and Schwab has always been a growth company. It's what enables us to invest back in the client with new products and services that make their investing experience better and what makes them recommend us to their family or friends, adding further fuel to our growth. Now we were doing things to solve *our* problems that created difficulties for our *clients*. Our prices weren't competitive, and we'd let some nuisance fees creep in. Walt Bettinger, who was then leading the branch network, called them gotcha fees, which, as I mentioned earlier, we tried to avoid. We'd gotten harder to work with. We made our struggles into our clients' problem, and that couldn't stand.

Companies are motivated to grow. It's what I love about investing. The great companies take that growth and reinvest it in smart ways for more growth. We had been through tremendous periods

||||||||||||||||||||||||||||||||||||||||||||||||||||||||||||||||||||||||||||||||||||||||||||||||||||

You capture a little piece of the action by owning shares in businesses.

||||||||||||||||||||||||||||||||||||||||||||||||||||||||||||||||||||||||||||||||||||||||||||||||||||

of growth. In the '70s, fueled by the unique low-priced service we provided to self-directed investors, we grew quickly and reinvested in those capabilities to scale up. In the '80s, we benefited from the high demand for our type of service that came as investing became something the average American realized they should, and could, do on their own. When they realized they didn't have to depend on the old-guard Wall Street firms to do it.

We were still starkly different from most of the brokerage industry and could depend on a strong return from our rapidly growing commission profits. In the '90s, we reinvested the profits from that growth and grew staggeringly fast as we rode the dot-com boom and used new technologies like the internet to give investors greater control and convenience. In retrospect, it was clear now that we had squandered an opportunity to reinvest those earnings. We could have eliminated competitors then with bold pricing moves, and that haunted us later. By 2004, we had wandered too far afield and I was intent on getting back on track. We needed to do more, to act boldly.

In the spring of 2004, one year into his tenure as CEO, David came up with a plan to shed some of our ancillary businesses. He was bitterly disappointed by our lack of progress; we all were. The year had started with such great promise. In January, our average daily trading volume had hit 215,000, a number we had not seen in years. Maybe, we hoped, the worst was over. Then volume collapsed. Our cash flow remained strong, but during the second quarter of '04, our pretax profit margin slipped to 16.3%, or about 30% below the standard to which we had become accustomed during the late 1990s. A lot of factors were involved, including the spillover from an acrimonious presidential election and the depressing effect of the Iraq war on people's willingness to bet on a sustainable recovery. The whole industry was suffering, but none more so than us.

David was feeling the weight of the crisis on his shoulders. He was concerned the ideas behind our new institutional research subsidiary, SoundView Capital Markets, were not working out. That was quite a reversal. At David's urging we had just paid an enormous price for SoundView, more than $300 million. We had only owned it for a few months. Initially, we had all been very excited about the role within Schwab as a subsidiary offering unbiased research to institutional investors. But suddenly it was not looking very good at all. The costs of operations were huge, with its high-paid employee costs, and the strategic benefit to a firm like us just didn't make up for that. A big about-face now felt like floundering.

By mid-2004, David came to me with deep frustrations. He was confused as to which way the company should go. Then he said, *I think we ought to consider selling Schwab.* I was shocked. This turning point completely changed my mind about his ability to direct the company to a better future. It was a seminal moment for me. I had no interest in selling the company, ever. That was an absolute for me. I did that once with Bank of America and it was something I never envisioned doing again. Our values meant to me we could never be in someone else's hands. Our values and culture would be destroyed. Independence was a must for me.

There were other signs of trouble as well. A recent survey of employees showed morale was low, especially among our population of officers—it's a particularly bad sign when your leadership ranks are that unhappy and concerned about the future. People had become cynical, a toxic situation in any organization. There were executive departures that had me and other members of the board worried and signs of some dysfunction among the management team. But by far the worst—a symptom of how deep the troubles were—our client satisfaction measures were atrocious. Our clients have always been the heart of our business. Their unhappiness was the worst sign imaginable.

The crisis that had brought us all to this day was a long time building and hadn't been without some big attempts to address it along the way. The dot-com crash in 2000 brought a sudden end to boom times in the brokerage industry and we had fallen hard. Because we had been growing so fast—and meanwhile planning so hard for even more growth, and making huge investments in people and real estate in line with those plans—it had taken us almost two years to face up to the new reality. By 2003, after three agonizing rounds of people cuts, we had finally accepted that things were not going to get better anytime soon, and that in order to return to health, we had no choice but to drastically scale back operations.

> For a company that was built around the idea of putting our clients first, above all, fixing Schwab for the future meant rediscovering our identity, our sense of purpose as a company, our mission.

Ultimately that meant biting the bullet on a host of cuts. It meant, as Chris Dodds repeated often over the ensuing years, reducing our tolerance for complexity. We had to get to the heart of the matter if we were going to turn things around. We had to face up to the harsh reality that we had lost our connection with our clients. To move forward, we needed to step back toward what had made us strong in the first place. That meant redoubling our focus on clients.

ON MONDAY MORNING, JULY 19, 2004, the board of The Charles Schwab Corporation was meeting in the executive session to work out the final details of a decision it was about to make.

David Pottruck, our CEO and my handpicked successor, sat in his office and waited for the executive session to end. He was scheduled to present his management team's strategic blueprint to the board and was waiting for the call to join the meeting. Since then I've heard from others that David had sensed what was coming. He certainly knew that the company was struggling and it was under his leadership. An extended executive session of the board first thing on the agenda couldn't be a good thing.

I knew what was being discussed and joined them shortly after they started. Many on the board weren't happy about our situation. The Friday before, on July 16, Nancy Bechtle, a longtime board member, called me in Montana where I was playing in a golf tournament to say with some urgency that the board needed to talk to me. The board was scheduled to be in San Francisco early for the Monday meeting, so I suggested we should all meet at my apartment in San Francisco on Sunday, the day before. I flew back from Montana and we met at about 4:30 in the afternoon. Most of the board was able to come, fortunately.

I give a lot of credit to Nancy for initiating the discussion about their dissatisfaction with David's leadership. That takes clear thinking and toughness. The SoundView acquisition and liquidation had made it crystal clear to some that Dave was the wrong guy to take us forward. We bought it and, as I mentioned, within months we were selling it. Not that selling was a bad choice, but the flip-flopping and lack of foresight wasn't good. It underscored how bad we were at assessing the acquisition and what capabilities they brought to Schwab. To me, it was an example of thrashing around. Things had come to a head.

That Sunday afternoon, we went around the room and everyone had an opportunity to speak. At the end of the meeting there was agreement that David's run as CEO needed to end. The board members turned to me and asked if I'd return to CEO. I said, of course, the company meant everything to me. I certainly wasn't inclined to simply turn things over to someone from the outside, and there wasn't yet a candidate ready internally. I said I would do it for two more years. I hadn't had any intention of doing this at my age, but circumstances had changed.

On Monday morning, the board completed the nonmanagement executive session and asked me in to join them as they reaffirmed the agreement of the prior evening that David would be asked to leave and I would become CEO. Frank Herringer, our lead outside director, and I walked to my office, where Frank sat and waited while I went down the hall to David's office and asked him to join us.

Sitting at my conference table, I let David know about the board's decision—that they would like him to retire from the company. David welled up some and said, "No, I shouldn't retire. I need to tell the truth and say I've been fired." I tried to counsel him and say he might be better off taking the retirement path for his own reputation. But he refused. David was very clear that he wanted to address the reality head-on, and he wanted to be direct and open about it. No sugarcoating. He wanted it to be clear in our public communications that the board was letting him go. It wasn't the typical way this kind of thing was done and would make it a little more dramatic, but we accepted it. He didn't want to go out on a pretense.

We included a comment from David in our announcement the next day, "For nearly 30 years, Schwab's top priorities have been its clients and stockholders. And for 20 of those 30 years, I've been privileged to be part of the Schwab team, working with Chuck and some of the most talented, dedicated people in the investment world. But the last few years have been difficult in the securities markets, and I accept the Board's decision that it's time for me to step aside. It's been a great journey."

David acknowledged later in interviews that he felt he had come at the monumental task of reducing costs and unwinding things with some reluctance, when he needed to be tougher. "If I had it to do over again," he said, "I'd be so much tougher." There's no question it's hard to switch gears from builder to dismantler . . . but sometimes it's the only path forward.

SO IT WAS THAT I found myself on the morning of July 19, 2004, about to turn sixty-seven years old, back in charge of the company I had founded roughly 30 years earlier. Not the position I expected to be in at this stage of my life, but one I was ready to embrace. I was plenty busy as chairman and was happy to go on that way. But when you see the company that you've built from scratch struggling, you can't sit by. At least I couldn't. It was my baby, and I wanted to do everything I could to fix it. What else could I possibly be doing that's more important than this?

In my mind, the company had—still has—an important purpose in life that goes back to our beginning: trying to help ordinary Americans put money aside, to invest, to build resources for their future—resources for educating their children, for educating themselves, for their long-term well-being. Ultimately, in our society, we're all going to have to live upon saved and invested resources to continue a good standard of living.

Social Security is at best a minimal standard of living. If you want anything beyond that, you've got to be an investor.

Someone from the outside wouldn't see it that way. Anybody who would take over the company would change its visions and values and purpose. They would try to extract so much more out of the hides of our clients, through increasing prices, cutting services, or adding fees. I couldn't stand the thought of that.

Those first few weeks following David's departure and my assumption of the CEO's duties were hectic, nearly a blur. I felt it the moment I walked back into the boardroom on July 19 after Frank and I talked to David. The fire hose of decisions was aimed at me now. It's a completely different experience being the CEO and I could feel it immediately.

Frank Herringer, former chairman of the board of Transamerica Corporation, a longtime friend and member of the Schwab board of directors, had been very blunt and honest about my return. When interviewed by *Fortune* magazine sometime later, he acknowledged he wondered at the time whether I was willing to take on the change that was required to engage again as a CEO. He understood the scope of what was ahead. "I had a big question about whether Chuck was really ready to do this," he said.

DAVID HAD BEEN ON the agenda of the July 19 board meeting to present a Strategic Update that outlined where we were on the restructuring process. Chris Dodds, our CFO, stepped in to make the presentation at the last minute in David's absence after the executive session. Chris and his team had been critical to its development and pushing hard to make some stark changes. He walked us through, highlighting point by point, how the business model that had been built in anticipation of a certain environment—a steadily advancing stock market, asset growth equating to revenue growth—was wrong for the current environment, where people weren't trading much and internet competition was driving commissions down. He described how we needed to take dramatic steps to change it. It was clear that we had an enormous task ahead. After he finished, George Shultz, former secretary of the Labor, Treasury, and State Departments under President Reagan, director of the Office of Management and Budget, and president and director of the Bechtel Group during his career, said to Chris, "That was one of the finest presentations I've ever heard."

It was a stark road map for sure. But clear. We knew that we had a lot of work to do in two critical areas.

One, complete the top-to-bottom streamlining and restructuring begun under David that Chris outlined in the board presentation; and two, something I felt was even more important: restore our spirit, that powerful sense of mission that informed the founding and subsequent growth of Schwab.

And that meant we had to reconnect with our clients: cut our prices, cut our source of revenue in the short term, to grow. That is an incredibly hard decision for any business to make. It represents an enormous leap of faith . . . or true confidence. Better if it's the latter. We knew that trading was becoming a commodity and would be priced that way. The internet had changed everything. At the peak of the internet bubble, trading revenue was over 40% of our total revenue. Those days were rapidly coming to an end, and that was fine with me. The value in our relationship with clients, and hence our revenue, would come through other products and services such as advice, mutual funds, income solutions, and banking. We had to evolve to thrive.

I'M CONVINCED THERE ARE times when a founder is the only one who can force the big, often painful steps that need to take place in a turnaround. At least if you want to do it in a way that maintains your culture and sense of purpose. People trust you in a way they can't with others. They know you're acting with the company's founding values front and center, and they are able to line up behind the tough decisions, and even suffer themselves, when it's in pursuit of a shared vision. And there's the confidence factor—a faith that you know a way out of this predicament. We've seen that happen at Apple, at Nike, at Dell, at Starbucks. Each benefited at crucial moments from a founder stepping back in to push for hard changes. This was one of those times: people needed to understand that our founding principle—total empathy for our clients—was still the driving force behind the company and would lead us forward. People could line up behind that, I knew it.

Which isn't to say folks weren't in shock—especially David's direct reports, the Schwab senior management team. Spirits were low, and I knew I had to do everything possible to keep people focused on the path ahead. That night, Helen and I had the executive team and board to dinner at Kokkari restaurant. It was time to start looking to the future.

25

WE'VE GOT THIS

On day two back as CEO of what I optimistically believed was going to be a difficult but doable two-year process of turnaround, I sat down in my office on the 30th floor at 120 Kearney Street with our chief financial officer, Chris Dodds, to review the situation.

Beyond the broader executive leadership who played a crucial role in the days and months that followed, I had a relatively small team of people whom I was going to rely on in a big way, day-by-day, during the process. One was our chief legal counsel, Carrie Dwyer. We were going to be bold, and I wanted to be sure I had someone by me with a very strong knowledge of the company, and of securities law and regulations.

Another was Jan Hier-King, who was the head of Human Resources. HR has never been my passion; you'll recall it's the one subject I failed miserably at in business school. But we were about to look at the organization from top to bottom and hers was a crucial role. Jan had been with us many years and worked a variety of leadership roles in those areas herself. It wasn't an easy job. At one point down the road, I heard people started calling her "Jan *Fire* King" because she had to be involved in letting so many people go. The stress would be enormous.

The third was Chris Dodds. Chris had been with the company since the days we bought ourselves back from BofA and went public. A smart, articulate, no-BS guy who understood the business inside and out, Chris could get things done, and he cherished what Schwab stood for, just as I did.

Chris and I sat down and reviewed the enormity of all that had to be done. I said that it was clearly going to be hard, but it was doable, that we'd made tough decisions before, and we could do it again. In my mind, we had this one chance to turn around and save the company or it shouldn't be ours to save. We didn't deserve another chance after this. Chris said, "Chuck, I couldn't agree more, all we have to do is do it. We've got this."

There had been a two-day meeting scheduled that week with Bain, the consulting firm, as part of the planning process that was already under way. I decided to go ahead and have it. Bain was hired to examine our company and to recommend to us ways we could combine and trim down. That two-day session was an important kickoff. We hired them to look at our whole cost structure at the company from top to bottom, and I thought they did a wonderful job at structuring that review. I wanted to look at the current organization and emphasize a few things right away. First, that our focus should be on the client, that it's got to be made simpler, and that we've got to decentralize. I also wanted people to own their own world in terms of profit and loss, and I wanted to measure people on their ability. And to make it all work, I wanted a very intense focus on revenue generation. That's what was going to pull us out of the mess I felt we were in. I was setting the stage for big changes, and I wanted them to know that. My sense was that people were feeling a little shell-shocked at this point. We'd already been through three very big restructurings since 2000 and people thought, *We're not done?* As I looked into it, the answer was pretty clear, "No, not even close."

One of the examples that stuck out like a sore thumb and where we had let things go astray was something called Personal Choice. Personal Choice was an array of different account types designed to serve different client needs—almost like the varying bundles of services you can get from your cable company, each at a different price. I thought it was a crazy mess. Too complicated, too hard to explain and understand, too expensive for the client.

Based on those initial meetings, the Schwab team, led by Chris Dodds, with Steve Ellis and Manny Maceda overseeing the heavy lifting from the Bain group, figured out what the structure would look like moving forward. We set up five or six operating groups for analysis. Each group included Bain and a senior person from Schwab leading the team and looking line by line: how we did it, how much it cost, how efficient it was. One of the big *aha!*s for me about Bain's approach was that they wanted not just a simple consultant perspective but to have a senior businessperson to head up each of the work groups. They wanted people who really knew the business. And so in a dispassionate way, where we were part of the thinking and immediately aligned, at the end of their work they came up with a plan to cut over *$650 million* of expenses over 18 months, about 15% of the expense base I inherited as I came back as CEO.

The plan was clear; it was just a matter of execution. We agreed on three things: first, we had to get our prices fixed—they were out of whack with the market, and we had too many fees. That wasn't Schwab. It wasn't what we stood for. So we were going to cut prices, and simplify them. We weren't just a "discount broker" anymore, but we sure as hell were going to be all about value. Price matters. It's that simple to me. Second, restructure and streamline the organization for greater accountability and efficiency, by cutting expenses and getting rid of things that didn't provide client value and the right return. That in turn would improve our margins and return on capital. And third, reconnect with our clients. Pricing was a major part of our problem on that one, but we had to find out what else might be going wrong there and fix it.

WE HAD BUILT UP our bureaucracy to a shocking extent and we had added businesses that didn't . . . *couldn't* have the kinds of returns we needed. And it was simply too complex. When I took a hard look at what we had become—with our two corporate jets, our swollen management ranks, and our bloated bureaucracy, even after so many layoffs and cutbacks—I was reminded of nothing so much as the old Bank of America. Back in the early '80s, we were the lean profit-making machine and BofA was the dinosaur. Now we looked like a dinosaur, too. Lowering operational costs was key, given the still-gloomy operating environment and the need to pay for all the commission and fee reductions I immediately undertook. First thing I did was reorganize our top management in such a way that we could really measure the performance of the key revenue-generating units—brokerage, mutual funds, banking, financial advisers, and so on. The heads of each unit were given much more responsibility for pricing, customer service, and marketing within their own domains. I wanted to be able to pin down those managers and demand accountability. Chris added to "We've got this," a new line: "Who's got this?" Each leader was charged with two fundamental tasks: increase revenues and decrease expenses. I was trying to bring into focus the critical elements of our business and, in so doing, give more responsibility to people who were dealing with the customers every day.

This was a huge cultural shift. Establishing decision-making rights was new. Now, if you had accountability, you were going to have decision authority. The person running the adviser business, the person running U.S. Trust, the person running retail . . . they had decision-making power because they also had the responsibility for revenue growth and profitability in their business. Support enterprises? That's what they became. That was a big change. Support groups had grown into power centers with their own agendas and that had to change. If the client enterprises didn't want it, or couldn't afford it, it was no longer going to happen. A support group's job was now to support the businesses and run as efficient a factory as they could.

So I flattened the organization. We had too many executives at the top and a host of complicated titles. I let a number of executive vice presidents go, each of whom was responsible for at least 500 or more people through their chain of command. It was part of the whole consolidation. All were members of the executive leadership team and were significant contributors. But I knew I had to start at the top. You couldn't make any moves if you started below. Start at the top—that's where you change things.

Then I set up two important councils: the Cash Council and the Marketing Council. They were the two most important levers I had at the time: Cash because it was a crucial source of revenue for us. We could earn a small spread on the cash clients kept at Schwab by investing it in very safe short-term investments. I had monthly meetings with anyone who touched cash in the company. With cash so critical in our financial picture, I was so glad we had the Schwab Bank in place. Marketing was the same: I had all the heads of the businesses together in one room to be sure we all had a common idea of what we were saying to clients and prospects. I had the damnedest time with marketing. People were arguing, decisions took too long, there were turf problems, and yet I knew marketing was the key to refreshing our image and attracting clients. I was not happy with the marketing results and I felt that decisions needed to be streamlined. The Marketing Council became the place to do that: get everyone who needed to be involved in the same room and make decisions. "What does this company stand for?" I said repeatedly. "We have to make that crystal clear again!"

OF MAJOR CONCERN IN any major transition is reassuring everyone that you have the process well in hand: employees, clients, shareholders, everyone. You have to be calm and in control and crystal clear on your intentions. Just as communication had played a central role when launching Schwab, I knew it had to play a central role when fixing Schwab now. Our struggle hadn't gone unnoticed. We had been *Forbes* magazine's company of the year in 2000 at the height of the dot-com bubble, the top-ranked securities firm in *Fortune*'s Most Admired listing in 2000, 2001, 2002, and ranked fifth in *Fortune*'s 2001 Best Places to Work. But by the middle of 2004, our brand and reputation had slipped and we'd fallen off those lists. I needed to talk to clients, financial advisers, employees, and reporters, and do my best to reassure everyone with a stake in The Charles Schwab Corporation that despite the temporary upheaval of a transition like this, we were going to be just fine. I wasn't bluffing; I knew we could turn things around.

That job started the day I took over when announcing David's departure. In an email to all employees I laid out our vision: *Our task is to return to growth and reaffirm the principles on which this firm was founded—to serve serious investors and continue to drive innovation in the financial services industry. . . . We must also follow through on our commitment to lowering costs. Every one of us is responsible for doing everything we can to drive efficiency and reduce costs. I know it's not easy, but the benefits to the firm—and to shareholders, clients, and ultimately all of us—will be huge. I founded this firm to offer a different—and better—value proposition to our clients and to the marketplace.*

A little less than three months into the turnaround, I knew enough about the shape of our plans to get out there and announce them to the world. I didn't want anyone to have any doubts that we were strong, getting stronger, and knew exactly what it would take to succeed. A turnaround is also a great opportunity to telegraph what it is that you stand for. People are paying attention—tell them what really matters to you. On October 5, we held a luncheon for New York media—I had some credibility with the press, but given our condition there was a lot of skepticism.

In a small meeting room in the bowels of a downtown Manhattan hotel, I walked them through the details of our plans, highlighted current successes, shared examples of new marketing, and laid out very specific markers that they could use to measure our success. The markers included increased client satisfaction; growth in new accounts and assets; double-digit revenue growth even in a down market; a pretax margin of greater than 25%; return on equity of 15% or greater; annual revenue per employee of $300,000; and revenue per dollar of client assets at 0.5%. During times of doubt, you need to be very clear, unequivocal. It was a high bar, but there was also a clear message . . . *we've got this*. But you could see the doubt in their eyes. To this day I wonder if the reporters who were there realize that we did pull it off, exactly as I outlined it that day.

We also needed to let clients know what was under way as well, and make sure they knew we were rock-solid safe and completely focused on their needs. I did town halls, small-group meetings, and one-on-ones. In August, we sent a letter to every client assuring them of our financial health, our commitment to them, and our availability to help them with their investing needs. It was reassuring to me to see how confident and trusting our clients were. Most weren't aware of management changes, and their experience with us was simply through our client service staff. At one luncheon in Chicago I was seated between two clients. One turned to me and handed me an envelope. With all the noise around us, I didn't hear what he said. In the moment I assumed it was probably an article or something I should read. I tucked it away in my jacket pocket. A couple of hours later as I was flying to my next meeting, I opened the envelope and out fell a check for $430,000. He had simply been handing me a deposit! Now that's trust. Needless to say, I made sure that check was deposited as soon as we landed!

IN NOVEMBER, WE HELD our annual leadership meeting and reviewed how much we had already accomplished. We had reorganized the company to give greater responsibility and accountability to the leaders of our businesses; spans of control—the number of people reporting up to each leader—were expanded, decreasing layers between employees and their leaders. We made hard decisions and said good-bye to many colleagues. Only 2 of the 10 members of the March Executive Committee remained and we had eliminated the "vice chairman" role completely. Our officer population was reduced by about 30%. We had reduced head count an additional 11%. In August, we had signed an agreement with UBS to sell them our Capital Markets business. Much of the proceeds were offset by charges we needed to take to close up shop. But we were free of that business, and clients were assured great trade execution through UBS. We had traveled the country and listened carefully to our clients who told us they wanted two things: lower prices and stronger personal relationships.

By year-end, things looked even better. We had a clear and simple business strategy; our prices had come down and were competitive again; operating costs were down; and capital returns were improved. We brought in $17 billion in net new assets, bringing our total client assets back over $1 trillion. Revenue was up 8% year over year, and we had booked nearly $350 million in annualized savings from our cost-savings initiatives. The board and I felt our shareholders deserved some attention after what they had been through, and we raised the dividend 43% and repurchased stock to the tune of nearly $400 million.

If I characterized 2004 as a defining year for Schwab, where we committed to turning the company around and setting it on a new path, 2005 was our get-it-done year. I felt we were creating something new and exciting, while staying true to our roots. It took enormous effort and sacrifice and commitment. Every business faces a challenge like this at some point: you've made a strategic mistake, or the environment has thrown you a curveball such as a recession, or a new technology comes along that disrupts your old way of doing business. It is easy to let circumstances take you down if you don't act decisively.

> **There can be lots of reasons you need to act boldly and quickly. I think this is exactly where many great companies stumble. They get stuck in a rut and fade away, or they try to transform and fail.**

I wasn't going to let that happen to us.

While we continued on the path we started in 2004, I still felt it was important to remind people what we were up to and why. We kicked off 2005 with an open letter to clients. I wanted to leave no room for doubts about our financial strength or our focus on improving their experience. There are times for slick ads, and there are times for clear, heartfelt commitment and promises. This was one of the latter, so we took out full-page ads in all the major papers with a personal New Year's thank-you from me to our clients.

By now I had the themes of our turnaround very clearly articulated throughout Schwab as well. I defined what Schwab stands for in three simple terms: *value, performance,* and *service.* I repeated it every chance I had. I knew I couldn't say this enough or say it too broadly. It became a mantra. I sent a detailed white paper out to all employees that described these themes and how they connected to the changes we were asking employees to put in place on a daily basis. *Value* was giving you more for your money. *Performance* meant helping you be a better investor and reaching your goals, whether that was through our advice, great tools for independent investors, or the convenience of easier investing. And *service* was the experts and professionals who focused on you. I took the themes on the road, visiting branches to talk to our clients, meeting with the press, and visiting our service centers.

We also looked for a high-profile opportunity to showcase the plan and progress we were making. Good advertising and articles in daily newspapers or interviews on TV were one thing, but it felt like a feature story from one of the major business magazines could help to make our case. So when Betsy Morris of *Fortune* magazine asked if she could meet with me to discuss the change, I agreed. Some people advised against it. "Too soon." "Wait until the turnaround is done." "It'll just focus on the negatives." There was any number of reasons to say no. But I knew that a good story requires some tension, and we had enough progress under our belt that I felt we should take the chance. In retrospect, the piece focused more on David's departure than we'd hoped; it made for a more dramatic story, I suppose. But the underlying theme was clear: we were fixing Schwab.

We still had some pricing adjustments to make, and so we dropped account service fees for investors with smaller accounts and followed that with new $12.95 trade commissions, a 35% reduction. That cut was aimed squarely at average investors, people with $50,000 in assets at the company. There were still some lower tiers available for especially large or highly active trading clients, but we were now in much better fighting shape to win business in the heart of the market. I signaled to our competitors that this might not be the end, saying in our press announcement, "We've said we will be *relentless* about creating the best value for individual investors." It's a phrase that was prescient and proved to have great significance over the years to come, all the way up to today as prices have continued to come down. Then, with a huge sigh of relief, on September 15 we eliminated account service fees and order-handling fees, some of the last residual "nuisance" fees that I had desperately wanted to get rid of.

ALL THE MANY SEEMINGLY little steps we had made over the last few years had added up. But there was still much to unwind. It's like the proverbial frog that doesn't know he's being boiled if you turn the temperature up in small steps. We had added too much complexity and distraction in the previous five years, and so the changes kept coming as we undid those decisions. We still had so much to do to improve the experience our clients had at Schwab. And there was our biggest move yet, one that took us forward into the future. We needed to change our service model, going all in from a transactional focus to one focused on personal relationships.

26

IMPLEMENT IT ALL

By the turn of the millennium, far more Americans owned stocks and mutual funds than ever before in our country's history—more than half, actually, and the percentage rose fast for families with higher incomes. The stakes were high for these families. Their investments weren't just fun money. They were investments for a future home purchase, for a child's education, and above all, for retirement. In 2006, the first wave of baby boomers turned 60; about four million more would follow in 2007 and every year thereafter for a long time to come. Those new retirees were far more vulnerable financially than my generation. By and large they didn't have pensions. They didn't trust they could count on Social Security. Their medical costs were spiraling ever higher. All these factors put unprecedented pressure on people to take charge of their affairs and take steps to secure a strong financial future.

That's a heavy burden. Frankly, it's probably too much for most people to bear on their own. Investing is complicated, and financial education is woefully inadequate. As for Schwab, there was a time when I could build a nice tidy business providing savvy investors with the tools they needed to make their own decisions, and then get out of their way. But assuming I wanted this company to keep growing, that was no longer enough. I felt there were too many people still being sold the wrong products and paying too much for them. They didn't have adequate diversification across asset classes such as stocks and bonds and foreign investments. They may not have understood what asset diversification was. They didn't have easy means to know how much they were paying for the services they got.

|||||||||||||||||||||||||||||||||||||||||||||||||||||||||||||||||||||||||||||||||||||||||||||||||

Successful investing is not easy, that's the bottom line. It involves so much of your emotions, your sense of self-worth, your ego.

|||||||||||||||||||||||||||||||||||||||||||||||||||||||||||||||||||||||||||||||||||||||||||||||||

Investing isn't easy. Success often requires getting help. I wanted us now to be the ones providing that help.

THE SEEDS FOR OUR transformation had already been planted. In late June 2004, the month before he left, David asked Walt Bettinger to lead the branch network and the service centers. By then, Walt was a Schwab veteran, but he was also an entrepreneur like me, having started his own retirement business, the Hampton Company, in his 20s. We had bought Hampton in 1995 to expand into the retirement plan area and Walt had committed to stay with us and run it. In the midst of the crisis in 2004, he was given the assignment to rethink our retail branch strategy, as it suffered with client defections and some of our best-performing employees departing for better pastures.

Walt's first step was pretty simple, always a good sign to me. And he moved fast. Another good sign. He got names of the last 50 significant clients that had left Schwab and a list of 50 branch employees and started calling them. He hit the road and visited over 100 branches, met with members of senior management, and fairly quickly started to hear the same things over and over. While on those plane rides from city to city, he drafted a memorandum that walked through what he learned and what he thought we should do.

When I saw the plan just a week later after David's departure, I saw in it a clear path forward. It was all about recasting the way we interact with our clients through the retail organization, with a focus on relationships, local where possible. It was a new mentality that depended on encouraging entrepreneurialism for our employees, all with client satisfaction at the core. The evidence Walt presented made it clear that despite the trends in our industry toward automation and self-service on the internet, relationships were the strongest predictor of client satisfaction, and we needed to advance our abilities in that area. We've always used marketing to drive growth, but we needed to strengthen the personal relationships clients had with us to augment good marketing, he said.

It was an *aha!* moment. It crystallized for me the idea that we had to make another major change in what Schwab would be for our clients. I agreed it was what we needed to do. I told him to do it, *implement it all.*

We started Schwab to help self-directed investors make inexpensive transactions without the oversight of some commission-driven broker. That was probably 5% of the market—independent and knowledgeable about investing. The other 95% of investors needed different levels of assistance, and that's where the financial consultants came in. I wanted to do it completely different than Wall Street. Our financial consultants didn't make commissions, they were salaried. They got bonuses based on numbers of clients and assets that they were serving. It had nothing to do with commission production. Walt took on the assignment to basically retrofit our retail branch strategy. He and his team spent the rest of that year fleshing out the plan, putting the pieces in place while we worked to back out of the misguided Personal Choice service. We had taken people who had come to Schwab because they were fee-averse and self-directed and enrolled them into a fee-based solution. It was a mistake that we needed to unwind while we cut prices. Those were two of the biggest themes that Walt reported back from his client and staff interactions: our prices were too high and the fiasco of Personal Choice was alienating clients and employees alike. The team was also hearing that the compensation structure and incentives weren't promoting successful client relationships in the branches, and the people who were working in call centers felt that being a great service person had lost its value to the company. He and the team were going to change that and make it right to be all about service again, "the nobility of service," they called it.

Walt had an enormous task ahead of him. Rethink the service model. Rethink what our sales culture should look like. Redefine roles. Change the comp structure. Right-size the branch network, even right-size the branches themselves. Operationalize a transformation to build deeper client relationships and do it in a cost-neutral way. No increase to the budget.

I encouraged Walt each step of the way and signaled my support for the strategy. He needed to bring so many people along with him. He wasn't running the entire retail organization at that point. This was a big undertaking and everyone needed to know we were aligned on this and he needed to know that I had his back. When I tapped Walt to take on the larger role of running the entire retail organization later in the year, that sent a very strong signal that we were on this path and we weren't getting off. This was the right direction. We'd have to make some adjustments along the way, but this is where we had to go.

I'VE SAID THAT WALT comes from an entrepreneurial background. Does that matter? There are great executives with all sorts of backgrounds. But I think the experience of building a company from the ground up gives urgency and a sense of ownership that are often hard to find in people who have never had to play all the roles an owner does, from chief salesperson to check writer and envelope stuffer. Because Walt had spent most of his time at Schwab running the retirement business separately from the rest of Schwab—it was located in Ohio, not at headquarters in San Francisco—he also had the advantage of an outside-in perspective. He could make decisions without a lot of historical baggage. If he had to make hard hiring or firing decisions, he was more likely to do it based on the merits, not on personal connections. During a meeting once, he told me he had a list of senior-level, long-tenured people who would be let go as he restructured and asked if I wanted to take a look. It was a reasonable request, assuming I may have had personal connections with these people. But it was best that my connections not cloud whatever was the right thing to do, and I told him that he should do what needed to be done and what he believed was right. All of us had to let go of many incredibly talented people who had done nothing wrong. We just had too many. And I valued his outside perspective. I think it helped make cleaner choices.

THE FIRST THING WE did in our transformation to a relationship model in the retail sales and service organization was assign each of our clients with at least $250,000 in assets to an experienced financial consultant. Someone who kept an eye on your account and called you up to ask, for example, "Your asset allocation is 90% in technology, is that really what you want?" Or, "You've got all this cash just sitting there doing nothing, would you like to put it to work? How about a short-term bond fund? Or a high-yield CD?" Each of these consultants had no more than 300 accounts. They didn't earn commissions when a client traded, and they had zero incentive whatsoever to get you into a particular stock or mutual fund. But they did have a stake in the game. If you were a happy customer—if you made more money and you kept your account with Schwab—then they benefited as well, by earning some of the money Schwab earns on customer assets. That way everybody's interests were aligned. We did this carefully to ensure the client still knew their relationship with a financial consultant was an additional aspect of their total relationship with Schwab. We weren't trying to create a traditional firm where the broker "owned" the client. This was a new way of doing things: financial consultant as the door to a world of resources. We tested the new approach in a handful of branches. It was available for clients who wanted it; there were plenty who didn't, and that was just fine. The results were terrific. Satisfaction scores went up immediately.

We couldn't offer that level of service to everyone, not yet. Longer term we planned to offer relationships with all our clients, building on the success of financial consultant relationships we were launching now, delivering personalized service through a mix of one-on-one, dedicated teams, and a personalized web and phone experience. Walt's team mapped out a plan to expand Schwab's physical presence—but cost-effectively—and they also focused on improving processes to make it easier for clients to do business with us on the phone, with less wait time and faster resolution. We were already more than transaction specialists and we were going to push that much further.

Things were progressing well and I determined that Walt was ready for a bigger role. Frankly, I thought he had the potential for the biggest role, CEO. I had taken on the CEO role in 2004, committing for two years to the board, but I could see that two years could extend a bit further. Still, a successor was on my mind and certainly on the board's. Jan Hier-King brought up the topic regularly and I was probably curt with her about it. "Jan, I'm not ready for the pine box yet!" I said once in exasperation.

At one point she suggested using a consultant, and I made it clear:

my successor should be someone from Schwab. "You can go ahead and do that, hire a consultant if you need to," I told her, "but I prefer internal candidates. I want someone from the inside."

There is something special about the culture and values we had put together here, and it takes time to understand, and it takes time for me to have the confidence that our CEO embraces it. Tough to do for an outsider.

27

TALK TO CHUCK

"What does Schwab stand for?! We need to make it crystal clear."

I had said it repeatedly through the end of 2004 and I was saying it again, this time to Becky Saeger, who had taken over as Schwab's chief marketing officer. "We've got our act together now; we're firing on all cylinders; *this is the time to be bold*," I said. Taking the cue, by January she and her team had reviewed advertising agencies, and by early 2005 we were sitting with the marketing team in a conference room at 120 Kearney with Euro RSCG, the agency that had won our account, as they went through the pitch for their proposed campaign.

"*Talk to Chuck*. It telegraphs everything. It's a promise that when you pick up the phone, or go online, or walk into one of your branches, you're speaking to someone who does business the way you do, Chuck."

The room was quiet and I could tell everyone was waiting for my response. They'd put tons of thinking and work into this idea and they knew it was risky. They were asking me to put my name out there in a pretty casual way. "Chuck," not "Charles." And they were assuming people wouldn't take it literally, that they'd know "Talk to Chuck" now meant all of us at Schwab, not just me.

I could see this was a huge leap at personalizing the brand and making a statement to investors that we were here to create a relationship. Not just a great place to make a trade or buy a mutual fund, but somewhere that could help you think through your investments and a place with a straightforward no-BS approach. A place with a personality; a place with a consistent approach; a place unlike the rest of the industry.

They'd taken my request seriously and pushed us far from where we were. And here I was again, being asked to put my name out there and they knew it was a big ask. I flashed back to the day in 1976 when Richard Kreuzer and Dee White showed me the photo with my arm draped over a file of daily trades and suggested we use that smiling young face to drum up business. I thought again about what friends would think, *Is Chuck on some kind of an ego trip?* And I admit, the casualness of using "Chuck" to represent such a serious business took me by surprise and made me a little uncomfortable. I used Chuck with family and friends, not on the company masthead.

Thinking out loud, I asked, "Could we use *Talk to Charles*?"

But I knew the answer before the question came out of my mouth. "It only works if it's Chuck," one of the Euro team said. He then went on to read some more lines.

"Want a great stock tip? Don't listen to stock tips. Talk to Chuck."

"Waiting for the market to come back? The market's not waiting for you. Talk to Chuck."

Everyone's eyes were on me as he read line after line. Each one was a challenge to rethink some of the long-held clichés of investing, and to come to Schwab for a different perspective. It was clear how well this could work. One of the Schwab team said they thought the approach sounded personal, like a plea from a friend. "Talk to Chuck" was at once consistent with who I've always wanted us to be for investors, a bit of a renegade from the crusty style of most of Wall Street, a place that appealed to independent thinkers. At the same time, it was a big step forward for us because it stated for the first time that we were here to help clients with the financial decisions they had to make. Honestly, we weren't yet thought of that way. As much as we had evolved since I started Schwab, people still thought of us mostly as a place to conduct discounted trades.

I could see the campaign had the potential to lift us out of the pack. It was an idea that could last: when it comes to your money, don't take the status quo for granted.

"So you're going to take us to another level, Becky?"

She smiled and said, "Yep."

"Okay. Go for it," I told them.

MONTHS LATER WE GOT another surprise as we gathered again with Euro to review ideas for television ads they had developed to accompany the print campaign. Huddled together in Becky's office with a team from Schwab, the Euro team described how challenging people's thinking would be used in television ads, too, with a twist.

"The television advertising environment is full of noise, too much clutter, people are simply tuning it out," one of them said. It was a challenge Schwab was up against in particular. The research showed that people couldn't distinguish one investment firm from another. It was a vast sea of sameness. Lately our brand had suffered a decline in a measurement called "differentiation"—how much people thought we stood out from the pack. That was largely a result of other firms taking the lead in pricing during the years 2000 through 2004. We were changing that with our new lower prices, but we still needed help to stand out.

"How do you break through the clutter and the noise and create something that will capture the viewer's attention. How do you get them to really listen?" one of them asked, and then they ran some footage from a recent movie as an example of what they wanted to do. We watched in silence, mesmerized, as an almost eerie 60 seconds of animation rolled by. It featured a *cartoon* of a real person. It was a technique called rotoscoping, where a computer takes actual footage and turns it into animation. It was arresting to say the least, and it forced the viewer to hang on every word. One of the leaders in our retail business said what everyone was thinking. "This is way out there. Isn't it a risk we'll turn people off? Or undermine the seriousness of what we're talking about?"

It was a risk. But I could see how this could work. No one could say these ads wouldn't capture the viewer's attention and make them think. We needed to take some risk. We needed to move forward. And I didn't want to wait.

"This is brilliant," I said. "Go for it."

Over the ensuing months the ads proved to be powerful at breaking through all the clutter and getting our message, our personality, and our point of view on investing out there. There were critics, people who called them creepy, gimmicky, beneath the dignity of investing. But in the marketplace, they were working. New accounts started to climb rapidly, our brand measurements improved.

About a year later as I walked across the golf course at the Pebble Beach Pro-Am tournament, someone shouted from the gallery, "Hey, Chuck! I want to talk to Chuck!" We were getting noticed. It felt great.

28

A JEWEL

By the end of 2006, the fruits of our efforts were clear. We could boast we had tightened up financial controls, delayered the bureaucracy, reduced a lot of loose decision making, and improved efficiency; and our new marketing campaign was humming. It was finally a clean slate. Profits were up, customer assets were rising, client satisfaction scores had increased, the strength of our brand had improved, new accounts were up 20% over 2005, and the stock was on the mend. By August, it had doubled from its opening price on July 20, 2004, when we'd started the turnaround. We were back on our feet and competitive again.

There was one final piece before I could say the turnaround was complete. On November 20, 2006, we announced an agreement to sell U.S. Trust, our ultrahigh-net-worth wealth management subsidiary, to Bank of America for $3.3 billion in cash.

At the time we announced its acquisition six years earlier, people called us the odd couple. Schwab was the original discount broker, a West Coast technology-enabled innovator and low-cost democratizer of investing that served the average American investor. U.S. Trust? It was the first trust company in the United States, designed to handle the most complex levels of personal finance and intergenerational wealth management, a 150-year-old private bank founded by a group of ultrawealthy New York businessmen, including Marshall Field and Erastus Corning. A private bank they built for the richest of the rich, themselves and those like them. At the time of our acquisition, U.S. Trust could boast that each of its largest 500 accounts had over $50 million in assets. Many families had had accounts there for multiple generations. U.S. Trust and Schwab looked like white gloves versus working gloves. As Randy Smith at the *Wall Street Journal* put it, "Here comes the mini version of the AOL-Time Warner deal."

I liked that kind of reaction. It got attention and made a bold statement about Schwab and where we were headed. It was our stark differences that made the marriage possible and so important for us both. The management team at U.S. Trust knew they needed to form an alliance to be able to grow, but they didn't want to be consumed by another private bank. Their goal was to be the dominant national brand in wealth management. Their ability to maintain operational freedom was very important to them. They thought joining forces with Schwab was an ideal solution, leaving them a large degree of independence in their area of expertise, high-end wealth management services, while benefiting from our expertise with technology and marketing. And this was the peak of the dot-com boom after all; they were in need of some "modernization."

As for Schwab, we were moving forward with our plans to expand into wealth management and evolve away from our discount brokerage. The need was pressing. At that point, we had to stem the steady flow of clients who were leaving us when they had accumulated significant wealth and weren't finding the services they needed with us. U.S. Trust brought new expertise and capabilities that would vault us forward on that path.

———

SO WHY THE ABOUT-FACE now? Why was it that just six years into this marriage and two years into my return as the CEO I was intent on selling U.S. Trust? I guess we were an odd couple after all, a mismatch that wasn't going to resolve itself.

We thought U.S. Trust was compatible based upon their high-end clients and the capabilities they had. I truly believed in the potential. But later, after becoming chairman of U.S. Trust in 2005, as I dug into it more deeply, I began to see the challenges of merging two very different cultures. Theirs was structured around salespeople and the incentives that went with that. Very different from Schwab. Call it *strike one.*

I always like to taste our own cooking, so immediately after the acquisition I had asked to set up my own U.S. Trust account. "Great. I'll find the best person . . . some are better than others," U.S. Trust's president told me. In other words, that old Wall Street chestnut, you'll get *our best guy.* The company had been built up across the country through acquisitions, and each followed its own methodology that varied from office to office, person to person. No consistency and certainly not a scalable model.

I had thought they had a U.S. Trust point of view, so everybody pretty much got the same outcomes based on established asset allocations, and there wouldn't be large deviation of this sort. What I began to see is that just like going to a traditional brokerage, you get the advisory perspective of *your guy* or *your gal,* not of the whole firm. At U.S. Trust, your allocation was chosen by your adviser, not a strategy and investment committee at the bank. Returns weren't consistent. Not a systematic U.S. Trust approach that was repeatable across offices and clients. New York investing one way, San Francisco, Minneapolis another. A confederation at best. And I thought, *That is not what I want to see. A model where some clients would be up 10% and others might be down as much.* And for the client it depended on *his guy* and the luck of the draw. *Strike two.*

But back in 2000, we'd made the deal and had been working hard to make it a successful marriage. Then Schwab hit the hard patch in 2001–2004, and we really had to focus on costs and revenue and growth. For U.S. Trust the pressure was on to grow. New leadership was put in place, they acquired State Street's private asset management business to expand their footprint and capabilities, but none of it was having the degree of impact we needed. They were a drag on earnings, and there were even rumors in the press that we might be thinking of selling them.

By 2005, after a little under a year back in the CEO role at Schwab, I could tell things needed to change. I was looking at my options. I asked Jan Hier-King to set up a meeting at their offices in New York to see what I could learn. "Let's meet for lunch at the office dining room," their CEO suggested, which sounded great to me. I think I may have been picturing the cafeteria at our offices in San Francisco and appreciated the chance to pick up on the vibe you can get with employees buzzing around you. What's the level of energy? How are people interacting? Do they look happy, enthused? But this was a different scene. We sat down to a very formal lunch in their dining room with white linens and fancy table service. It became a metaphor in my mind for the mismatch we had. *Strike three.*

It was just at that point that Peter Scaturro, a former Citibank executive, sent me a letter. In it, he described U.S. Trust as a "jewel," which he said could be a huge success, "if it had the right leadership." Peter had been running Citibank operations in Japan, but he had left under a bit of a cloud following regulatory issues there. I checked into Peter's background with Sandy Weill, whom I knew from my Bank of America days when he had made a run at leading the bank. He gave Peter a clean bill of health. Sandy assured me the Japan issue was none of Peter's doing.

On May 8, I invited the board of U.S. Trust to my apartment in New York and let them know I thought that Peter should come in as the new CEO and kick-start some change. Peter made a presentation about his plans. The board agreed. The next day a team of us arrived at U.S. Trust unannounced to let them know that Peter was being appointed their company's new CEO. The U.S. Trust team was surprised . . . but once a decision like that had been made, there was no point in waiting around to watch the paint dry. It would have been just hours before rumors starting flying around. So we acted fast.

Peter brought in very capable new management over the following months and was aggressively trying to expand the business. They had a lot of success at turning the revenue picture around. But unfortunately, expenses were growing just as rapidly. We were looking at every asset we had at Schwab with serious scrutiny on its financial performance, and we simply were not seeing the progress we needed at U.S. Trust to fit our model.

Things came to a head at a meeting with me, Chris Dodds, and Peter's management team. We described to them the need to turn their business model into something that was economically attractive for the company (it was barely earning its cost of capital). They argued U.S. Trust offered so much in terms of brand halo and intangible value and the service model was so different for their wealthy clients that the economic requirements should be different in their case. None of which added up to me or Chris.

I gave Chris the go-ahead to start looking into selling it. He brought in a team from UBS led by a very capable banker, Olivier Sarkozy. Chris and Olivier put together a number that they thought was realistic, and while Chris and I were at a client event in Washington, D.C., in October, a phone call was scheduled with Bank of America. Ken Lewis, their chairman and CEO, was on an acquisition tear at the time, building the largest bank in the United States.

We sat in an empty cavernous room big enough for about 400 people and there were two chairs, a small table between them, and a phone. Our voices echoed. Chris handed me a number and I called Ken. He said he was very interested. "We'd prefer not to run an auction, Ken. We want a quick transaction so that we don't face a drawn-out process that leads to deterioration of value if customers and employees get wind of it," I told him. "We're willing to give you the first look if you could meet what we think is the right price." And we gave him that price on the phone: $3.35 billion. Ken really wanted U.S. Trust. For the right buyer, it *was* a jewel. It just wasn't right for Schwab. He was more than game and said a team would be there for due diligence in 48 hours.

Here I was in yet another big potential deal with Bank of America! There were some bumps along the way—there usually are with such a big sale—but by November 20, 2006, we had a final signed agreement.

SO IN THE END, you could say it all worked out. We made a tremendous sale, and BofA added a significant asset to their wealth management capabilities, and the clients at U.S. Trust had access to new resources that BofA could offer. A win-win-win. But there is a lesson in it about acquisitions: understand the culture you're buying, really figure that one out. Is it compatible with yours? Or do you have an opportunity to transform their culture so it aligns with yours? We had none of that. Forcing our compensation structure on them, for example, would have meant we'd lose the whole company; every one of the relationship managers at U.S. Trust would have walked if we tried to bring them in line with the Schwab compensation system. And there was a difference in values. U.S. Trust had a New York–centric view of the world based on their history and wealthy clients and a disdain for discount brokerage and all it stood for. "At U.S. Trust," they reminded us, "it wasn't unheard of to walk the client's dogs if that's what was needed." And if we couldn't align, we weren't being true to the Schwab way, which was about consistency of approach, efficiency, lower cost, total engagement of the customer . . . we didn't have a lunchroom with white linens.

Acquisitions aren't easy. Many fail, or at least fail to meet their original promise. We've made a few over the years that have turned out well—Mayer & Schweitzer, The Hampton Company, Windhaven Investments, Thomas Partners Investments, Compliance Solutions, and optionsXpress—but we avoided big mistakes by passing on hundreds of others. It's certainly an important part of running a company, watching for those big potholes. You get so confident about things, willing to do anything to acquire companies, but you still have to do your analysis to see, "Does it really fit?" In my experience, the biggest potential problem is always culture.

‖‖‖

PART V

Time Tested

I learned early on that if I was going to succeed, I needed to find people whose strengths and capabilities complemented mine. Where I was conceptual and enjoyed developing new products and marketing ideas, I relied on others who had strengths in managing people and implementing complex initiatives. The sooner you recognize your strengths and weaknesses, the faster you can create a team that accounts for those.

All good leaders have to be humble about their own potential and their skill level and really honor the skills and capabilities and intelligence of the people around them. Delegate. Give good direction without overdefining it. That gives you leverage to do so much more than you could on your own. It also lets people know they are crucial parts of the team.

There's no one perfect leader. You can be an extrovert, an introvert, a bit of both: it doesn't matter. But you have to have real substance, content knowledge that you've mastered. You just can't fake it. And that takes hands-on experience. And then being able to teach other people about it, and why it's important and how to execute on it. At the same time, you have to have a degree of openness, letting people know that these things are important but that there is flexibility.

It's amazing to me the creativity that comes back to you when you find people with passion and you give them lots of responsibility. It underscores my confidence in human energy, creativity, and spirit. When people are focused and committed, with the right sponsorship, they flourish.

29

YOU HAVE TO BE OPTIMISTIC

By the beginning of 2007, so much was finally in place at Schwab and going well. Clients brought new assets to us at nearly double the rate of the year before. We launched a new checking account that paid significantly higher interest than most competitor accounts and were planning an "Investor First" credit card; both were designed to make Schwab a one-stop financial services provider for investors. We continued to cut prices as we'd been doing since 2004, dropping account minimums for Schwab mutual funds to just $100 to build up our base of younger, beginning investors. Our management team was strong. Walt Bettinger was doing a great job and was recently promoted to president and chief operating officer.

I felt I had more time to devote to public policy and my passion for investors. President Bush asked me and I agreed to chair the President's Council on Financial Literacy. Knowing how to manage your personal finances is a critical skill for every American. Managing your cash flow, the role of debt, the power of compound growth, making the most of investing—they are all important to understand to build financial security. It's a scandal that we don't require an education in the basics at all levels of school curriculums. In today's world, what more basic life skill is there?

I spoke at the Treasury Department's Conference on U.S. Capital Market Competitiveness. I knew there would be plenty of voices speaking about industry problems, but what about the backbone of the whole system, the individual investor? Their role and importance was so often overlooked. Individual investors provide staggering amounts of investment capital, which keeps the cost of capital low, productivity high, employment high, and inflation in check. America had made policy decisions over the past 30 years to put individuals in greater control over their financial futures and to carry greater responsibility for their success. Nearly 57 million American households owned equities . . . IRAs alone totaled more than $14 trillion. And with things like automatic enrollment in 401(k) plans, those numbers were increasing. Their participation in the capital markets also encourages American companies to be innovative. America is built on a history of people taking risks, exerting their choices, and having the ability to make decisions for themselves. Capital markets have been made more vibrant by individual investors participating: people who took chances, rewarded innovative companies, and brought passion and enthusiasm into the markets. I talked about individual investors and what they needed. Based on what I saw at Schwab, they want a few basic things from the system: fairness and a level playing field, low cost and efficient access to the markets, information that will help them make investment decisions, and conflict-free advice. Investor confidence was directly related to whether they could count on those things in the market.

I didn't realize then how soon that confidence was going to be severely tested.

DESPITE SCHWAB'S PROGRESS, THERE were ominous signs that not all was right. There was a wobbliness in the economy that had me concerned. It was one reason I had been so anxious to wrap up the U.S. Trust sale quickly in 2006. You never know what the market is going to throw at you.

|||||||||||||||||||||||||||||||||||||||||||||||||||||||||||||||||||||||||||||||||||||||||||||||||||||||||||||||||||||||||||||||

If you've made a decision to sell something, my advice is to move fast; there is nothing but risk in waiting.

|||||||||||||||||||||||||||||||||||||||||||||||||||||||||||||||||||||||||||||||||||||||||||||||||||||||||||||||||||||||||||||||

As I watched things get worse that spring, I remembered an instance a couple of years earlier, talking to my caddy during a round of golf. He had recently bought a house "on spec" and was trying to borrow additional money on the equity that had built up since. We talked about the process and I asked him what he told the banks about his income. I expected his income hadn't changed much since he bought his house, and I wondered how he'd get approved for a larger loan.

"I don't need to," he said. "I just use one of these new '*liar loans.*' They don't depend on documenting any income."

These were "NINJA" loans, as they came to be known: "no income, no job, no assets." It was amusing and we had a laugh about it. It was pretty clear that an extreme amount of credit was sloshing around the housing market. People were treating their homes like cash registers, borrowing against their houses as the paper value rose, buying homes as investments for quick turnaround, over and over again as the price of real estate climbed. The banks had encouraged it: they made a lot of money in the process. Money on fees, on points, on appraisals, on interest rates. The government pushed the dream of home ownership for everyone and drove mortgage debt wider and deeper into every part of the country and at increasing levels of risk. The contagion spread. It wasn't contained to the people borrowing the money and the banks loaning it. It crept into every corner of the financial system. The banks and investment groups found a way they could leverage it further. Credit swaps, collateralized mortgage obligations, synthetic-this, leveraged-that—I don't think most people understood them, but the credit agencies slapped triple "A" credit ratings on them. Then institutions bought them thinking they were great stuff based on those ratings . . . as it turned out those ratings were meaningless. Triple "F" was more like it.

Big cracks started to show early in 2007 as the real estate bubble began unwinding, particularly all the investments tied to subprime mortgages, which had flourished over the last few years, like my caddy's NINJA loan. In early February, HSBC, the giant global bank, announced they had set aside nearly $11 billion to cover subprime debt they were worried was at risk. The value of real estate was dropping, and the market for those loans was going south, and the banks and investors were left holding the bag. In April, WaMu, Washington Mutual Bank, the largest savings and loan association in the US, disclosed nearly 10% of its loan holdings were in subprime debt, which began their steady slide into receivership and eventual sale by the FDIC to J.P. Morgan Chase. Bear Stearns shut down a hedge fund, and then on August 9, European money markets froze up temporarily. It was an ominous sign.

Like bubbles will, this one was now bursting. The financial markets were suddenly gyrating, massive institutions were cramping. I was sweating bullets that the U.S. Trust sale hadn't yet closed. On the first Monday of July 2007, I got a call from the finance department telling me that we had just received a wire transfer for $3.3 billion in cash from BofA to close the sale. I rushed downstairs to the finance department to personally pick up the wire transfer confirmation. It was such a large transfer it was broken into two pieces. They were the best-looking things I'd ever seen, $3.3 billion, right there in my hands. I was elated. The deal was finally closed. And just before all hell broke loose around us.

———

MIDSUMMER 2007, COUNTRYWIDE FINANCIAL, which had special-ized in subprime loans, needed to be propped up and got support from BofA; in September, the British bank Northern Rock required government support from the Bank of England following the first run on a bank there in over a hundred years. It eventually went into receivership. Here in the US, in November both Bank of Amer-ica and Legg Mason, the asset manager, propped up their money funds with cash infusions. The federal government initiated a huge $150 billion stimulus package in January of 2008 to try to help. Still, things got worse. The country was now in full recession. J.P. Morgan Chase purchased the failing Bear Stearns in March, and then Indy Mac, a purveyor of subprime mortgages, collapsed in July.

In September, we experienced one of the worst months in US fi-nancial history. Fannie Mae and Freddie Mac, the giant government-sponsored organizations that were created to expand the availability of residential real estate loans, were both put into conservatorship; Lehman Brothers, the fourth-largest investment bank in the coun-try, filed for bankruptcy; AIG, the giant insurance holding company, was bailed out; Bank of America bought the once storied Merrill Lynch to backstop it from financial free fall; and Americans learned a new term, "too big to fail."

On September 16, 2008, I was in London when news hit that the Reserve Primary Fund "broke the buck." Breaking the buck is when a money market fund falls below its normal $1.00 per share value. Money market funds, while they are investment vehicles, not bank cash, and thus not guaranteed, had been a stable part of the financial landscape for decades. Investors expected them to maintain their value. They had become a linchpin to the economy, providing a source of funding for corporations to pay their bills and payroll by issuing commercial paper. The Reserve Fund held paper backed by Lehman Brothers, and when Lehman had filed for bankruptcy the day before, the fund's value dropped to $0.97 per share. People saw the Reserve Fund struggle and panicked, with billions of dollars getting pulled out of money markets. The federal government had to act before the panic shut down the economy; Treasury secretary Henry (Hank) Paulson was on the phone with contacts in the industry to figure out what would be best. Hank was the right person at the right time for that job. He knew all the big banks from his days running Goldman Sachs and had an intuitive feel for what needed to be done.

I spoke to Hank from London late one evening my time and shared some ideas for extending government credit to the money market funds in the industry that may have needed it. He was in full crisis management mode and I expected he was practically living on his phone. In the end, he and his team came out with a bold plan to simply guarantee the full $1.00 value of money market funds. A sensible approach that eliminated any concern that more funds would break the buck. It stopped the run on money markets on its heels.

One crisis averted. But the broader financial meltdown was still under way. It was like Whac-A-Mole, the amusement park game. One problem solved, others popped up. The market for commercial paper froze, putting pressure on businesses that needed that short-term credit to operate. On October 3, President Bush signed the Emergency Economic Stabilization Act, which included the Troubled Asset Relief Program, or TARP. The program promised to help restore stability to the credit markets and the banking system by buying assets that banks and other financial institutions were otherwise unable to sell. We supported it wholeheartedly, but Schwab was in a healthier and stronger position than many banks, with a strong and flexible balance sheet, plenty of available cash, and strong credit ratings. Walt and I were concerned that taking the TARP funding signaled the opposite, and after some discussion, the board agreed. We announced we wouldn't participate. In the end, we were one of the few large banks that didn't, and it sent a strong signal to our clients and potential clients about our confidence and stability. In retrospect, I think it is one of the reasons so many new clients came to Schwab during the crisis and in the years that followed.

Of course, we weren't unscathed. A fund we managed became popular during 2006 and 2007 and then suffered a decline in value as the housing industry unraveled. The Yield Plus fund was small in comparison to other funds in our mutual fund complex. It carried mortgage-backed securities, which were all highly rated and offered a nice yield. The fund was popular for people with a need for an income-oriented investment; no one knew those assets would become poison as the credit crisis took hold. I had believed in the fund so much that my family was one of the largest investors in it. Schwab ended up settling lawsuits that included significant client reimbursements (though not for me or any Schwab employees, of course). And some of the investments we held in our bank lost money during the crisis, all of which we were able to recoup from the banks that had sold the underlying securities in the first place. These securities had been sold to us with inaccurate prospectuses that didn't make clear the riskiness of the holdings and had now declined in value.

ON SEPTEMBER 29, 2008, the Dow dropped 777 points, its biggest drop ever, which after a few head fakes back up, didn't stop dropping for another six months. We know now that by the beginning of March 2009, the stock market hit bottom. From its peak at over 14,000 on October 9, 2007, the Dow Jones landed at 6,507, a 54% decline in 17 painful months. It stopped there. The damage was huge. Roughly $12.6 trillion in household wealth had simply disappeared between mid-2007 and the third quarter of 2009.

What caused the credit and financial crisis and ensuing recession? There are dozens of books and hundreds of articles that dissect it all, and I'll leave it to others to describe the gory details. Hank Paulson wrote a wonderful postmortem that I recommend, *On the Brink*, from the perspective of those who were managing the crisis on a daily basis.

There are a lot of mechanical explanations for what drove the crisis, involving esoteric concepts like "liquidity crunches," "derivatives," and "counterparty issues." To me, the simple answer is that too many people in financial services forgot that it's not just money we deal with . . . its *people's* money. It needs to be treated that way. Leverage created inappropriate levels of risk. And too many people with good intentions pushed easy credit and encouraged borrowing, whether it was wise or not. Too many consumers took up the opportunity and overextended themselves. I have always said to the Schwab bankers, "Only lend money to people who can pay it back." Sounds simple, but what the debacle showed is how people who were lending were focusing too much on making money on the process: the application and credit check fees, the reselling of mortgages (banks rarely kept the loans on their books), the bundling of those mortgages for resale in increasingly complex products. There wasn't enough focus on each individual loan—can the borrower pay it back? The primary function of the credit markets and financial services industry in general shouldn't be to drive profits and revenues higher at all costs or engineer our country's way into prosperity, but to support reasonable growth and manage risk carefully to maintain public trust and confidence. Without trust and confidence, the system fails.

THROUGHOUT THE CRISIS, SCHWAB was in fine shape. Not just fine, doing well. In October 2008, for example, at the height of the crisis, we opened 30,000 accounts, up 88% over the year before. Our branches logged five million client interactions that year, a number I couldn't have fathomed when I started Schwab. All that we had done to get through our reorganization in 2004 through 2006 put us in a solid position to ride out the storm. We weren't the young inexperienced firm we were in 1987 during that market downturn.

But all that success didn't make the situation feel much better to me. Despite all the government was doing to stop the financial crisis, and all we were doing for our clients, investors were panicked. Our clients were no exception. The branches and telephone service centers were flooded with questions about what to do—or worse, receiving panicked "sell-it-all" orders.

"Should I get out of the market?" That was the common refrain.

I'd seen this play out before and felt I needed to speak out and do what I could to calm nerves. The natural inclination as an investor is to run when the stock market plunges. I knew that was the wrong thing to do. History was proof of that. I asked the marketing team to get me in a studio as soon as possible. We flew out to New York, and on a cold day in October 2008 we spent it in a loft on 14th Street repurposed as a film studio to tape a set of video messages from me. With bright lights and sound technicians and all the other production people cramping around me, the director had me read take after take of scripted remarks.

It just wasn't working. It didn't feel genuine. I was stiff, uncomfortable. I wanted to talk to my clients in the clearest and most sincere way, not through stilted, careful, perfect lines. After dozens of awkward takes I stopped the production, tossed the script, and had my communications person simply ask me some questions, which I answered from the heart.

"The most natural instinct is to run for the door. To sell. Sell everything," I said. "You've got to fight that emotion because you want to be able to hang on for the recovery. Which has happened every time we have had an experience like this in my career . . . and that goes back now some 40 years . . . nine different cracks in the market like this. Smart investing is about taking it year by year by year. It is a little bit of a nightmare, but we handle those by living through them and looking forward to a better day."

How does it feel? What do you do?

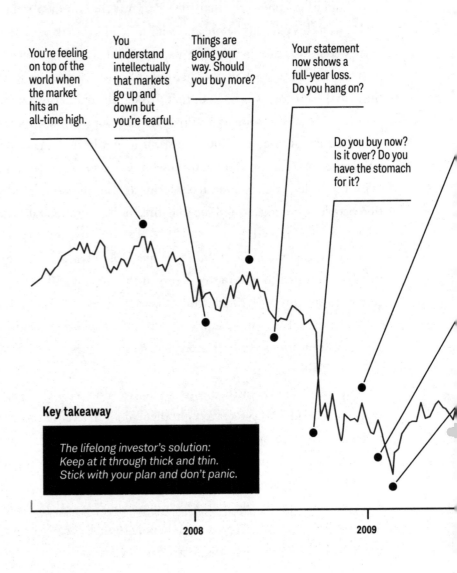

You're feeling on top of the world when the market hits an all-time high.

You understand intellectually that markets go up and down but you're fearful.

Things are going your way. Should you buy more?

Your statement now shows a full-year loss. Do you hang on?

Do you buy now? Is it over? Do you have the stomach for it?

Key takeaway

The lifelong investor's solution:
Keep at it through thick and thin.
Stick with your plan and don't panic.

2008

2009

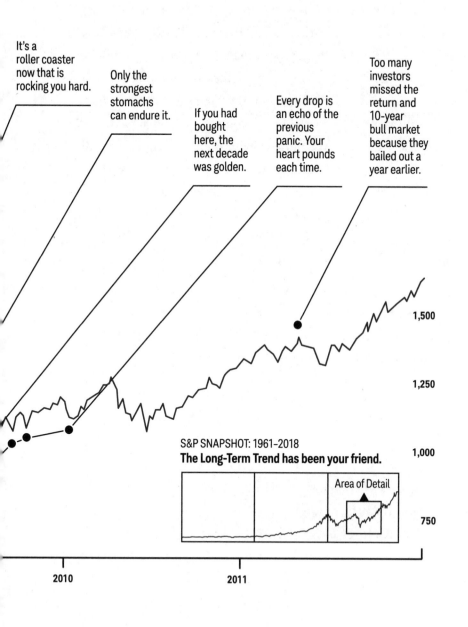

It's a roller coaster now that is rocking you hard.

Only the strongest stomachs can endure it.

If you had bought here, the next decade was golden.

Every drop is an echo of the previous panic. Your heart pounds each time.

Too many investors missed the return and 10-year bull market because they bailed out a year earlier.

1,500

1,250

S&P SNAPSHOT: 1961–2018
The Long-Term Trend has been your friend.

1,000

Area of Detail

750

2010

2011

Did I get the timing right with my advice? Not exactly. You never do. And that's exactly the point. The market bounced around for a few months after we started running the TV spots in January 2009 and then took that final dive to the bottom on March 9. But timing the market is impossible. As the saying goes, it's not timing the market that counts, but time *in* the market. By the end of 2010, the Dow Jones was back to where it had been before its precipitous slide on September 29, 2008. Had you invested in the Dow Jones Industrials, the S&P 500, or even more broadly into the Schwab 1000 Index (the largest 1,000 companies in the US, accounting for 90% of the US market) on the day we shot those television clips, despite the additional downward move of the stock market for five months, within a year you would have been up nearly 25%. Unfortunately, too many people jumped out of the market during that painful 18-month bear market—and then they missed the turn afterward. Like other turns before, it came unannounced and moved fast.

||||||||||||||||||||||||||||||||||||||||||||||||||||||||||||||||||||||||||||||||||||||||||||||||||||

To be a successful investor, you've got to be an optimist. You have to believe in the innovations that come from the human mind and the human spirit.

||||||||||||||||||||||||||||||||||||||||||||||||||||||||||||||||||||||||||||||||||||||||||||||||||||

Investing is all about being a part of companies that create new value. And that will continue to be true, but we go through these undulations in the process of discovery. "The bottom line," I said, "is that you've got to be somewhat optimistic and know that the future will be better than the past."

I believed it then, I believed it when I started Schwab against so many odds, and I still believe it today. To be a successful investor, *you have to be optimistic.*

30

READY

As I thought about what I wanted to say about our decision to appoint Walt Bettinger CEO in July 2008, I knew one of the most important things you do in your tenure as a CEO is pass the baton to the next CEO. It's your opportunity to put the company on the right footing for another generation and to ensure your values endure. It's especially true when you are the founder of the business and you believe deeply in what you've built and its purpose. A business like ours comes down to two things: a big idea that makes a difference in people's lives, and people who believe in it and will see it through to fruition day after day despite what may get in the way. You have to get both right.

A little over three years back as CEO, I was ready to make that handoff and I had identified someone I felt was right for the job. It was my second go at it, and I had been planning for it and thinking about it for some time. I've joked to people that Schwab is so much a part of me it's like my baby. Handing off that responsibility to someone else was a big step. You don't make a choice like this lightly, and you hope that it's a choice that will daisy-chain into the future: a leader who shares your values and who will find future leaders in the same mold.

I had returned to the CEO position in 2004 when the board and I felt there wasn't anybody ready for the CEO position after we let Dave go. But I knew it wouldn't be forever and certainly didn't want it to be. Being chief executive is a huge job, and in 2004 it was made bigger by all that we needed to do and the urgency to do it quickly. Huge changes had needed to be made, and I think they were changes that only I could have asked for—as the founder. When I came back in 2004, I told people I thought it was a two-year transition. But the time had flown by as we initiated change after change. And here it was 2008.

The board was on me from the get-go about succession planning. Walt had been on my radar for some time. Back in late 2005, I had called him and told him that I had made the decision to ask Bill Atwell to step down as the head of the individual investor business. I was taken by surprise when Walt thought that meant he should step down as well, assuming that if I was unhappy with Bill's progress, I was unhappy with him, since he reported to Bill. I cleared that up quickly, letting him know I wanted him to take over retail.

Walt had stepped into that role in 2005, facing not just the environmental business challenges but also organizational challenges, a lack of complete agreement on the strategy and how to put it into action, and a lot of senior executives with large staffs and their own views on what should and shouldn't be done. Just as I had when I took on the CEO role again, he realized that he needed to be clear and concise about the strategy going forward and he quickly laid it all out. The first thing he did was change the name of the organization from the Individual Investor Enterprise to Investor Services, because, as he said, "we are in the business of serving people." And that gave him an umbrella idea over everything. The new name signaled what we're all about.

Second, he needed something to band together and galvanize the teams under him. He said, "Here's our strategy, *Through Clients' Eyes*," which was shorthand for offering products and services that we believed were aligned with our clients' best interests and made their investing experience as good as possible. It also meant avoiding business practices that could put us in conflict with our clients. The organization had been arguing for a year on what their strategy was. Within a day or two after taking over retail, Walt took that debate off the table. Coupled with the strategy was a set of guiding principles that became a way to filter choices and make decisions. Things like, "Every client interaction changes our company's future—either to the positive or the negative; Clients value relationships—with people and organizations that they have confidence in and trust will act in their best interests; Price matters—clients expect great value from us." Everyone in the organization was able to litmus test everything Walt and the leadership team were doing in terms of the guiding principles. Clear. Concise. Direct.

As Walt expanded his role and executed on his plans, we met weekly so that I could provide any guidance I could on the challenges he faced. In February 2007, I promoted him to be president and chief operating officer. It was a partnership that worked and was growing stronger.

YOU COULD ARGUE THAT 2008 wasn't the best time to put a new CEO in place. The financial system was in a developing crisis and the economy was smack-dab in the middle of a major recession. But for the preceding two years I had placed all my personal bets that Walt would emerge as my successor CEO. It takes a long time to get comfortable and form a relationship of this type, but we'd been at it for some time. I had seen him at work for 15 years. I knew him well, and he knew me well. His temperament was akin to mine. He was not a flamboyant guy. When called upon, he did his stuff. Which I was attracted to. It was similar to my personality. I have a public persona, but it didn't come naturally to me. I'm not comfortable being out there as a song-and-dance guy. I speak about what I know. And that's about it.

We had a lot of mutual respect. He was a young entrepreneur when we first met. I liked that about him. His track record was very important: He had started a company from nothing, much like I had. I had seen what he had done in the 401(k) space all the way up to today, with his unique vision for an index-based model and low costs. He had shown similar judgment and creative thinking while heading the branches and as head of retail and then COO. His ideas about the importance of moving from being transactional to having deeper personal relationships with clients was a key part of our transformation to the firm we are today. His responsibilities had grown rapidly as I gave him more, and he used me as a sounding board when he needed it. The respect he had for me and how I liked to be involved was important in making it work. He understood, and I believe valued, that I wasn't going anywhere anytime soon. We met regularly or used email to keep in touch on what was going on. That continues today. Great open communications. I offered my advice, but that's all it was. I knew he could handle the complexities of being the CEO and he had the right temperament, the right judgment. He had a sense of humility and didn't take credit for things where credit was shared or where it was something out of our control. I knew he had respect for who we are and what we stand for, but he wasn't boxed in by the past. He was very willing and able to make changes. At the same time, the changes he suggested were always in support of our unique character, not change for change's sake. He was hardworking, thoughtful, fair, confident but considered, approachable. A good communicator. He respected his management team and gave them visibility in meetings with me to give them their due. His first motivation wasn't about himself. He'd done well financially, but I didn't sense he was driven by money: that wasn't his first instinct and that was clear in all the discussions leading up to his becoming CEO. He was respectful of my role and my practical value as founder and namesake and willing to use that to the company's advantage, and with no sense of jealousy about it. We shared a pragmatic view of it, and understood the marketplace today wants to see continuity.

Most important, I could see his values matched mine and he had a deep commitment to our mission. He thought about the client first when faced with business decisions. It came naturally and that mattered very much to me. For example, I had shared with Walt early on my belief that the most important thing for him to learn deeply and completely is how we manage the considerable amount of client cash we hold. It is the bedrock of our business, because at the end of the day we are the custodians of our clients' money, and their financial security. Their trust and confidence that we take as an absolute responsibility should never be broken. That commitment to the balance sheet brought us through the crisis unscathed and without the need for TARP. He absorbed those perspectives and made them his own. "OPM," he often says. "It's other people's money."

ON JULY 22, 2008, we announced Walt's appointment to be president and CEO of The Charles Schwab Corporation, effective October 1 that year. "It couldn't have been a worse time to become CEO," Walt has said with a smile many times over in the years since. And it wasn't the financial crisis that would be a problem. Thanks to tireless and brave efforts by Hank Paulson and hundreds of others, the crisis was largely contained by the end of 2008 and early 2009. Technically, the recession was over by July 2009. But in its aftermath we were heading into the perfect storm for a firm like ours: interest rates were crushed, trading slowed to a trickle, investor optimism turned to long-term fear and disengagement—all of which meant we were about to live through one of our greatest revenue challenges yet. Fortunately, Walt and his team were ready, I was ready, Schwab was ready.

31

COILED SPRING

On June 25, 2010, I received a memo from Walt that outlined his thinking on the company's strategy. The stock market had bounced back nicely for a period after the financial crisis, but individual investors were still shell-shocked. Even small drops rattled people. In early May, we had experienced a significant drop. The market recovered right away, but it was yet another blow to the average investor's confidence. More than a year into the economic recovery and they were still walking on eggshells, sitting on cash more than normal, not investing, waiting for the next shoe to drop.

The federal government wasn't helping the mood. Back in the midst of the credit crisis and recession, the Federal Reserve had embarked on its experiment with historically low interest rates in order to kick-start the economy (by now nicknamed "ZIRP," *zero interest rate policy*). Every six weeks, with each regularly scheduled meeting that went by where they kept the rates at zero, they were signaling the economy was still in its sickbed. There was no end in sight as far as they could see. In fact, as it turned out, they stuck with that course far longer than anyone anticipated. Rates weren't raised again until the end of 2015, and then only a quarter point. It's been a very gradual process up since then. As of 2019, rates still aren't at historically normal levels, which are closer to 5%. The Fed had boxed themselves in: they worried if they raised rates they would stall the recovery and possibly slip back into another recession. Sticking with low rates as they were doing might help the banks recover and help the economy continue to mend, but at what cost? It was a signal that the economy was still unhealthy, damping businesses' inclination to invest.

And at near 0% interest on a bank savings account, if you were in retirement and relying on interest payments for income to live on, you were suffering. I thought the Fed had made the right move lowering rates during the crisis, but then should have returned to normal as soon as possible. Otherwise, the normal asset pricing mechanism of the market was missing. Markets tend to seek a natural equilibrium of prices that balance the return an asset can provide, versus its risk of losses. Essentially all assets are constantly being compared to one another. By lowering interest rates, the Fed was upsetting that natural balancing system. I thought it was the wrong path forward. It was demoralizing for everyone to feel like we were still on life support, and for savers who had done the right thing all their lives by putting money away to earn interest in retirement, it was debilitating. But the Fed stuck with it.

AFTER A SOLID RISE following the market bottom in 2009, by mid-2010 Schwab stock had slipped back down to financial crisis levels. It was the worst environment for a business like ours: every form of revenue was impacted. Clients weren't trading and in fact had moved money out of the markets in large numbers from mutual funds or stocks into money markets and cash. Interest rate spreads normally made up an important part of our revenue, as we could manage the cash in our clients' accounts very conservatively (purchasing very short-term government debt, for example) and earn some interest.

But interest rate spreads available to us were constrained by ZIRP; we were waiving our normal management fees on money funds to ensure clients were paid even a nominal 0.01% return on their money, and as a result the stock market was discounting our prospects.

||||||||||||||||||||||||||||||||||||||||||||||||||||||||||||||||||||||||||||||||||||||||||||||||||||||||

You don't manage a company according to its stock price, but you don't ignore it either.

||||||||||||||||||||||||||||||||||||||||||||||||||||||||||||||||||||||||||||||||||||||||||||||||||||||||

Walt's June memo was designed to answer the question he thought could be on people's minds. *Should we move in a new direction?* He and I sat down for our regular weekly status meeting in my office to discuss the memo. Point number one in the memo was, *We must not panic and overreact to the current economic environment and decline in our stock price.*

"Looking forward and seeing nothing but ultralow interest rates ahead, it would be easy to panic and begin changing almost every part of our business," he said as we talked it through. "But we don't want to take the risk of trying to pull a rabbit out of a hat. We should stay the course."

He was absolutely right. We'd made that mistake before in the early 2000s. Now, everything we had done to repair ourselves after 2004 put us in shape to survive the financial crisis and the slow grind that was following it. And, in fact, by the measures we really cared about most—client satisfaction, new assets, new accounts, and new clients—we were doing very well. During the worst of the financial crisis and its immediate aftermath from 2008 through 2011, for example, clients invested more than $300 billion in net new assets with Schwab—more than the comparable amounts reported by our publicly traded competitors combined. We didn't need to make big changes; we needed to have the resolve to stay the course, keep our expenses in check, invest when we could in improvements to the client experience, and not allow ourselves to get distracted. In many ways, these are often the harder choices to make. It takes great patience and confidence. There is always the enterprising reporter, assertive Wall Street analyst, or short-term-oriented activist stockholder willing to make the case that you're not doing enough.

Walt and his team also faced the task of keeping employees focused. It was probably the biggest issue. Some—especially those who hadn't been around when the internet bubble burst and seen what it had looked like then as we got off our strategy—were voicing concerns about the strategy. "Isn't it time to do something different?" Walt was hearing. His memo was for them as much as anyone.

Walt's office has a view out to Treasure Island, halfway across the Bay Bridge. Given our trademark fog, Treasure Island was often shrouded in a mist that made it impossible to see. During presentations to employees, Walt took to using the fog as a metaphor for our situation: "Out on Treasure Island they're busy redeveloping it into a beautiful place to live and work, with great views back to the city. You just can't see that progress right now, as the island is shrouded in fog. At Schwab, too, so much is being done, but it's hard to see it in the fog of these extraordinarily low interest rates and stalled equity markets. But one day soon, the fog is going to lift and all that work is going to be revealed. We just have to be confident and patient and remind all our colleagues what has been accomplished and will pay off soon."

We had been asked on occasion prior to the financial crisis why we weren't taking more risk with the kind of financial investments we made with our cash balances, something many firms were doing. For example, why not add riskier investments to the mix? "It's a great way to boost your financial returns," we were told. But we'd never gone that route; we'd always been conservative with the balance sheet. It proved to be the right thing then, and even though we were getting questions again about taking on greater risk, there was no reason to think it wasn't the right approach now. Months earlier, *Bloomberg/BusinessWeek Magazine* had come to our offices to do a feature on the company, "Can Schwab Seize the Day?" Walt reminded me that the reporter had asked why we weren't taking some big bets through acquisitions while competitors were weakened. For example, E*Trade was struggling and rumored to be on the block. We had told the magazine we had no interest in taking on the balance sheet challenges that came with it. We didn't know, we didn't like, and we didn't want troubled assets. Stability mattered hugely to our clients, and the wave of new prospects coming to Schwab—one million in 2009, 99,000 in December of 2010 alone, our strongest month in eight years—was testament that we dare not mess it up. Clients want stability. They especially did after the financial crisis. Schwab had become their safe harbor in the storm.

As founder, chairman, and a significant stockholder, I was in a unique position to be able to support the leadership team and give them the room and permission to do the right thing. It could have been a very different situation for Walt and his team had it been someone else in that seat. It's very hard to take the long-term view; it's made easier when those watching have some confidence your instincts are probably right. Fortunately, both the board and our largest investors were 100% behind us and encouraging us to stay the course. As it turned out, those investors ended up doing quite well with that show of support.

We were very clear about the strategy. We stuck with the name Walt had given it back in 2005, *Through Clients' Eyes*; it was the essence of who we were and still are today. While the results weren't showing up in revenues and earnings growth yet, and our stock price was stuck, the strategy was right and it was helping us build momentum. I was confident we could wait. We described it as *a coiled spring*; we knew it would uncoil once those rates started to change and as investor confidence started to rise. Ever since the financial crisis, we continued to bring in new clients and new assets at a steady and growing clip, putting more energy into that spring. We were intent on not making the same mistake we had from 2000 to 2004, where we got distracted by far-afield opportunities and let expenses get the better of us. So we had reduced our head count the previous year, particularly at the top of the management team, to be sure lower revenue growth didn't mean we couldn't invest in the business. The cuts helped us fund investments to the tune of about $500 million, most of it improvements for clients: better service, lower costs, and new products—without our total expenses getting out of whack. It would have been an impressive list of new initiatives if it had been in a healthy business environment; we were getting it done in the face of serious headwinds.

In the eight years from 2009 to 2017, we reduced equity trade commissions to a flat $8.95 and then again to $4.95 regardless of the number of shares someone traded. ($4.95! What a victory for individual investors. I don't think I could have dreamed it in 1975 when even at the 75% discount I offered compared to the standard price on Wall Street, a trade was still close to 20 times that.) We created new low-cost exchange traded funds that traded without commissions. Other companies have now followed suit. We slashed fees on our mutual funds to signal to investors that we were still a leader in low-cost investing. We supplemented our high-yield checking account with a savings account that also offered higher rates than those of the big banks; added services that handled the investment management decisions for our clients; built a new state-of-the-art technology platform for investors who traded actively; launched a new network of independent branches in a franchise model; engaged with millions of clients in financial planning and investment strategy discussions; offered the industry's first no-questions-asked satisfaction guarantee; and launched automated "robo" investment services that apply the power of artificial intelligence to portfolio management.

We'd learned the lesson before and we were going to double down on it now: stay focused on principles that work over time.

||||||||||||||||||||||||||||||||||||||||||||||||||||||||||||||||||||||||||||||||||||||||||||

**Don't panic and overreact to the economic environment
or the stock price; stay focused on what works.**

||||||||||||||||||||||||||||||||||||||||||||||||||||||||||||||||||||||||||||||||||||||||||||

Keep costs low and invest in a better client experience. Find ways to challenge the status quo to benefit investors: clients will choose you over your competitors, the business will grow, stockholders will eventually benefit . . . and around and around it goes.

JUST AS WE KNEW it would in 2010 when Walt and I met that day to discuss our path forward, the tide did turn. Investor confidence began to slowly rise later that year and continued rising over time. With it came a renewed level of engagement in investing.

The long dry spell of zero interest rates also passed and savers began capturing income again from their savings, and Schwab was able to earn tiny amounts on millions of accounts that together combined to create revenue for growth and investment back into new services. Today, client accounts, assets, revenues, and profits are all at record levels; our stock price has recovered; and we have a deep bench of strong and energetic executives to take us into the future. We are gaining share of the investable wealth pie in the US. What excites me most, we are using that momentum to build new things for our clients. That's the thrill of what we do.

We're a different firm from when I started out, but also not so different. The dream of an integrated financial experience for individuals, from banking to brokerage to financial planning and personalized investment advice and everything in between, is a reality, and we're integrating the latest technologies and amazing computing power to make it as easy and effective as possible. In many ways, 2004 to the present was the final piece of our development, by moving from being exclusively a transaction specialist to now being able to provide personal relationships. And now because of our scale, we can do it while keeping our expenses incredibly low. This puts us in a fabulous competitive position that I don't think other players can match.

32

CHUCK'S SECRET SAUCE

January 12, 2016, a cold New York winter evening. I was at the annual fund-raiser for the Museum of American Finance to accept a lifetime achievement award for innovation. The museum sits at 68 Wall Street in the old historic center of New York, just two blocks from where the New York Stock & Exchange was established in 1817 under a buttonwood tree.

I was there in the heart of Wall Street, about to take the stage to accept the museum's inaugural lifetime achievement award for financial services innovation before an audience of hundreds of financiers, bankers, money managers, brokers—some of whom were from the very businesses I had spent the last 40 years trying so hard to compete with and disrupt. Businesses that had tried on more than one occasion to stop me. Many of our innovations at Schwab had come at great cost to our competitors and the ways of doing business that existed when I started out. There were times when what we were trying to do made us a pariah in the industry.

"Let people trade on their own? What do they know?"

"Lower commissions? That's unethical!"

"A ground-floor branch in the building where our offices are perched at the top? Stay away!"

"Share our mutual fund management fee with you? Why do that when investors can come to us directly?"

"Online trading? That's like putting a loaded gun in the hands of a child!"

"No-fee IRAs? That'll put the industry out of business!"

"$4.95 trade commissions? You're starting a price war!"

"Free access to any bank's ATM machines? That's not fair!"

We'd heard it all.

I'M RELUCTANT TO ACCEPT awards and prefer not to draw the attention if I can avoid it. It just feels a bit bombastic and uncomfortable. I'd prefer to get on with building things. But this recognition by the museum for innovation was different, and I had accepted. It was meaningful to me and to all my colleagues at Schwab—past, present . . . and future, I hope. It got right to the heart of who we are and have always tried to be.

It was a great turnout. Lots of people who played important roles in the country's financial industry were there: former Federal Reserve Board chairman Paul Volcker; Treasury secretaries Timothy Geithner and Robert Rubin; financiers and bankers like Bob Willumstad of Citigroup and then AIG; Dan Lufkin, cofounder of the Wall Street firm Donaldson, Lufkin & Jenrette; my friends Ameritrade founder Joe Ricketts and mutual fund giant Ron Baron.

My wife, Helen, and my children, Carrie, Virginia, Katie, and Mike, were there with members of the Schwab board to support me, including Chris Dodds, who retired from Schwab after helping to pull off our wonderful second act starting in 2004 and now sits on our board. There were friends there in spirit as well, I'm sure: Uncle Bill had passed away in the late 1970s, Hugo Quackenbush in 2007, Larry Stupski in 2013. Many employees had moved on to other opportunities or simply retired. I thought of them and all the others on the team who had made a mark on the way Americans invest today.

When I started Schwab, I could not have imagined this moment. We were a tiny upstart on the opposite coast that built itself as an outsider and attracted clients who were tired of the traditional Wall Street ways. Yes, we had enormous hopes and dreams, but they were modest in the grand scheme of the giant financial services industry. We had designed our business to stand apart from the establishment, never with the idea we would someday be accepting recognition here at its very heart. And truthfully, you don't have the luxury to think too far out ahead when you're starting a business. The challenges are there right in front of you, day to day.

My friend George Roberts, himself a master of innovation in finance and an important contributor to Schwab's history, introduced me. Then I took the stage. I talked about how America's financial history is full of developments unique to the world, all of which helped make this country a great economic and democratic model. And about how absolutely important investing is for a vibrant and open economy like ours.

I described how all of us at Schwab have been proud that we had a hand in changing how the individual investor looked at investing and became involved in such large numbers—building wealth for their future. That was always our goal. And I acknowledged that we weren't alone in this innovation game . . . many others played a role in this success story.

I described how Schwab had gone from a tiny start-up to the world's largest publicly traded investment services firm in just 40 years. I acknowledged the luck involved . . . there was plenty of that! But in the end, I said, it was really one thing that brought us success: a zealous team of people on a mission that I fondly refer to as "Chuck's secret sauce," all of them in lockstep pursuing a simple innovation, *total empathy for our clients*: make it better, easier, more successful for the investor.

I called it the *mother lode* of our innovations, more important than any single technology or new product. It was building a company from a basic belief: view your decisions through your clients' eyes.

|||||||||||||||||||||||||||||||||||||||||||||||||||||||||||||||||||||||||||||||||||||||||||||||||||

> **The secret sauce was building a company from a very simple and basic belief: that you view your decisions through the lens of your clients' needs and goals. What would they think; what would make their lives better, easier, more productive; what would they believe is the right thing to do? If you do that, then everything else will follow.**

|||||||||||||||||||||||||||||||||||||||||||||||||||||||||||||||||||||||||||||||||||||||||||||||||||

New ideas, better ways to serve, trust, growth, financial success, an attractive brand, an enduring positive reputation. All can follow from a devotion to that basic client-focused proposition. Build it as if you're building it for yourself and would recommend it to your mother.

IT WAS A GOOD night. The museum exceeded their fund-raising target and the money they raised went to good use creating educational programs that help schoolchildren and other visitors understand the role and evolution of finance in the American social fabric.

As I left the museum that night, I thought more about the Schwab story and about innovation. Is Schwab what it is today because we decided to break the rules and turn things on their head? Many people think of us that way. *Feisty, upstart, innovator, challenger.* I've heard those words a lot over the years. Was it all just a question of disruption? Not really. Though we really did turn things upside down at times and created changes that will endure. We never innovated for innovation's sake. We had a different goal and purpose in mind. My story started with a simple dream: to be independent, to build a business, a dream that so many American entrepreneurs share. But it was a dream that evolved into a belief that the old rules could and *should* be changed. Our innovations, our success, came from that sense of purpose. It's a simple enough formula. Putting it into practice wasn't always easy, though there is something magical and endlessly fun about banding together with people to do something no single person could ever accomplish. And the work, the innovation, is never done. There's always another new idea, another convention to challenge, a million ways to make investing better. We just need to do it.

Personal Reflections

I set out to write about Charles Schwab, *the company*, and how the events I experienced and the decisions we made over these last decades shaped Schwab and in turn shaped the world of investing.

Looking back, I am reminded there is another side of the Schwab story I've said less about. And that is how those years have shaped me, Charles Schwab, *the person*. And, of course, they have, in countless ways big and small.

That was not the point of this book, but for anyone aspiring to the life of an entrepreneur or a business leader, know that your journey will impact you deeply. Here are just a few of the impacts these years have had on me, and what I think I've learned from them.

Family—Family is life's cornerstone. It gives you purpose and strength.

In 1972, just before the company really got its start, Helen O'Neill and I got married. Shortly after that I told her what I was planning to do with my little brokerage business—change the name from First Commander to Charles Schwab & Co. Inc., and change its purpose to discount brokerage. Her support of my crazy idea was seminal. Having a partner who supports your dreams and goals through all the ups and downs of building a business, a family, and life together helps make the seemingly impossible possible. Helen gave me undivided support through the years. We scrimped, we mortgaged our house early on to support the business, and we put everything we had into it. I worked every night after dinner and most weekends, we raised our two children together, and we knit together a larger family that included my three older children.

In those early years, with me traveling, opening offices, doing public relations city to city to city (I never missed an opportunity to go on television or radio shows to explain discount brokerage and the benefits for individual investors), all those things I did to build a business soaked up time and attention. A strong supporting family is the most important ingredient for a man to succeed, and I can't thank Helen enough for partnering with me on this trip.

Through the ups and downs of building a business, family can keep you motivated and focused on the future. My five children are all unique in their variety of interests, individual character, and sense of values, and they all express this in different ways. Only one, Carrie, works for the company. And my children have given me the best bonus—thirteen grandchildren. They, too, are all wonderfully different, which is exciting to see and to be around. To see the incredible creativity in each one of them has been a profound experience. They are a full delight and we visit often with them.

People—You don't do anything of significance in business alone.

I learned early on that I had my limits. It was humbling at first, but it taught me that I had to find people who brought skills I didn't have, and that has made all the difference. I discovered early the power of delegation and teamwork and what I call "personal leverage," multiplying the impact of ideas into large waves beyond what you could ever dream of doing on your own.

Business is all about people and you need to find those who share your vision and values, who will bring their own passion and strengths to the task. And you need that at every level of the organization, from the mailroom up to the boardroom. I've been unbelievably fortunate in that regard over the last 40 years.

Wealth and Philanthropy—Give back and connect your giving to your life's passions.

Having wealth is a lot better than not. I know because I started without. That wasn't a bad thing; young people need an incentive to develop and strive. Inherited wealth can sometimes hamper that.

Once you have it, you need to think about what you can do with it and how you can give back to the community that helped you get there. I believe those of us who have had great success have an obligation to the system to give back a substantial portion to philanthropic purposes or other good deeds.

For me, connecting philanthropy to the things that impacted my life and success has made the process rewarding and engaging:

> My wife, Helen, and I have invested heavily in research and programs to serve children with learning difficulties, dyslexia in particular. In the 1990s, our first concerted philanthropic effort was to create the Parents Education Resource Center, an operating foundation that was devoted to helping parents who had children with dyslexia. We operated the Center for over 10 years, and our learning specialists saw thousands of parents and their children. Dyslexia has gone from the complete mystery it was in my youth to a well-understood and

researched medical diagnosis, and now with a much better understanding of how to remediate kids with this handicap. Eventually we gifted all the tools and resources we developed to other organizations. We look back now and are proud of the role we played in helping to change the way families can navigate through the challenges of dyslexia.

Education played such a pivotal role in my life, and so I give happily to schools, especially Stanford, which helped me so much to come into my own and build strengths and capabilities that have served me my whole adult life. Because I know how important and life-affecting education can be, we also give to schools that serve people from less-fortunate backgrounds—for example, the KIPP charter schools, free college-preparatory public charter schools focusing on educationally underserved communities.

Good medical care is a linchpin to anyone's successful journey in life, and so I have given time and money there. I was fortunate years ago to be on the board of the St. Francis Hospital in San Francisco, and it was such an eye-opener to the challenge that hospitals face with funding and how crucial individual philanthropy is to their mission of serving everyone in the community, even those who cannot pay.

From the time I was young I have been a visual learner. I saw how art opens completely new ways of thinking about the world. Thoughtful artists think about the big issues in life and address them through their art. That same tendency led me to think differently in business and not be constrained by tradition. Helen is passionate about art as well, and she and I started collecting art as soon as we were able, first with prints or pieces by artists not yet commanding the big prices, and we grew from there. Investing in the arts became a passion. I went onto the board of the San Francisco Museum of Modern Art and became its chairman for 10 years. What a thrill it has been to work with Neal Benezra, the museum's director, to help establish SFMOMA as the premier modern art museum in America. Together with the San Francisco community, we raised hundreds of millions of dollars, built a new museum, and established the home for Don and Doris Fisher's (founders of the GAP clothing stores) incredible collection of modern art.

Government policy in the US, different from other parts of the world, has created a lot of financial incentive to give. So many social needs are served by philanthropy as a result. Charitable giving is an enormous resource in the US today, and I believe people who are wealthy are obliged to give back.

Health—Make health a priority, individually and for your organization.

I never thought much about health until I met a cardiologist who had developed a wellness program for corporations. It was the mid-1980s and new research was zeroing in on cholesterol as a major culprit in heart attacks and strokes.

His idea was that the stress and busy lifestyle in business put employees at higher risk, and that a company could control that risk with wellness programs for employees. I thought it made sense for the company. I doubted it applied to me.

I did the tests along with other executives. The results were a surprise. The cardiologist couldn't believe that with all the stress and my high cholesterol I was still okay. He tested some more and discovered blockage that required an angiogram to fix. Just in time, he said.

Later, Larry Stupski, my second in command, had his heart attack. Over the years I've seen many able businesspeople set back by health problems.

Today, we pay employees to take screenings and pay them to take healthy steps. We promote health activities and healthy food at our cafeterias. Employees are your most important resource. Helping them take care of their health is simply good for business. Taking care of your own is as well.

Personal Passions—Find passions that fuel different parts of your soul.

My father, a lawyer, owned a couple-hundred-acre rice farm in the Sacramento Valley as an investment when I was young. When I was old enough, he taught me to shoot and got me a .410 gauge shotgun of my own, and I would hunt there during the fall bird season while the fields were fallow. We always ate what we hunted; it wasn't just for sport. I go now every fall, and each time it reminds me of, and reconnects me to, my Sacramento Valley roots and friends.

I've also grown to love fly fishing and have done it all over the world. There is nothing like the sense of quiet and relaxation you get with a day in the fields or on the river. My interest in hunting and fishing sparked a love of nature and set the stage for my participation in the National Parks Foundation Board in my 50s when President George H. W. Bush appointed me. In life, you find that one thing leads to another.

And then there is golf. I have talked here in these pages about how it played such an important role as I was growing up: it gave me confidence, created new friendships, strengthened my social skills, and heightened my competitiveness, and I'm convinced it got me into Stanford, which triggered so many good things for me. Golf has been important to me now for nearly 70 years. It's a sport of endless challenges and camaraderie that you can enjoy throughout life. My tennis playing has waned; I ski less than in years past . . . but golf is always at the center of my life. It's been so important to me that I do all I can to broaden its reach through the First Tee organization, a group that uses golf to instill strong values in young people. And I've had a hand in building two golf courses.

All these activities have enriched my life and refreshed my spirit regularly when I needed it. Without them I don't think I could have been as enthusiastic an entrepreneur as I have been.

Politics—Get engaged, be a participant, shape the future.

I love what the Constitution stands for. It has been the backbone of America's greatness. To me, its most critical feature is the focus it puts on personal freedom because it unleashes personal passion and the desire to fulfill things for yourself and your community.

I have been fortunate to be able to travel all around the world. During the late '80s, *Time* sent a group of CEOs on trips across the globe to visit with controversial leaders of other countries and share perspectives across borders. We visited Havana, Moscow, Bangalore, and Hong Kong, among many others. That experience and my travels since convinced me there is no place that unleashes personal freedom better than here in the US. The foundation of that is our Constitution. My goal by engaging in politics is to support that source of personal and economic freedom and all the results that come from it. The opposite, totalitarianism and socialism, are simply soul crushing.

Being engaged in something so important to our future is incredibly rewarding. We're in a tough time of political disagreement today, but I know we'll iron many of our differences out and find common cause. In our heart, we all share a common desire to improve our country and our lives.

Business—Embrace the human spirit of curiosity and creativity.

Business is a creative process. You move forward into the unknowable future, try new things, make discoveries along the way, and repeat. It's all about learning and growth. It is why I love it and the free market of ideas that enables it and makes so many great new things possible. I like to say business is organic, like life itself, ever changing. It is the human spirit of curiosity and creativity brought to life, and why I am ever optimistic about the future.

—Charles R. "Chuck" Schwab

ACKNOWLEDGMENTS

Over the 45 years of this company's history, we have employed more than 125,000 people, each of you helping turn new ideas and dreams into reality and making investing better in the process. I want to thank every one of you for your passion and commitment to our clients.

To Helen, without you none of this wonderful story could have been as good. It is your story as much as mine.

I want to express my special thanks to Greg Gable. For more than 20 years he has helped me with my public voice—in writing, with speeches, for media appearances, and in recent years as my chief of staff. He has helped me take my stories of our journey as a company and collect them into a factual and readable history. Thanks, Greg.

To my assistant for many years at Schwab, Miki Grandin, thank you for your attention to detail, for keeping me on track, and for your energy and positive spirit.

Finally, thank you to the millions of clients who have trusted Schwab with their dreams and hopes for the future. Some of you have been with me since the beginning. Having your trust and confidence is an honor.

INDEX

ABOUT THE AUTHOR

Charles ("Chuck") R. Schwab started the San Francisco–based Charles Schwab Corporation in 1971 as a traditional brokerage company, and in 1974 became a pioneer in the discount brokerage business.

Mr. Schwab took an early lead, offering a combination of low prices with fast, efficient order executions, and soon became the nation's largest discount broker. Today, the company is the nation's largest publicly traded investment services firm with over three trillion dollars in client assets. Often credited with "democratizing" investment, Chuck Schwab has driven countless innovations in the investment services industry designed to help individuals make the most of saving and investing, including 24/7 access to services, the one-stop mutual fund supermarket providing access to thousands of no-load, no transaction fee mutual funds, custodial services for independent registered investment advisers, online trading, integrated banking and brokerage services, and many others. Today, the company has expanded from its roots as a discount brokerage and provides a full-service investing and banking experiences to millions of clients domestically and abroad.

Mr. Schwab has been chairman of The Charles Schwab Corporation since its inception and has served as CEO for most of its history until October 2008. He is also chairman of Charles Schwab Bank.

In addition to his professional commitments, Mr. Schwab takes an active interest in a variety of nonprofit activities. Along with his wife, Helen, he supports organizations working in education, poverty prevention, human services, and health. Mr. Schwab also served for 10 years as chairman of the San Francisco Museum of Modern Art.

On January 22, 2008, President George W. Bush named Mr. Schwab chairman of the President's Advisory Council on Financial Literacy, a groundbreaking initiative that advised the president and the secretary of the Treasury on ways to promote and enhance financial literacy.

He is the author of several bestselling investment books, including *How to Be Your Own Stockbroker*; *Charles Schwab's Guide to Financial Independence*; *It Pays to Talk*, written with his daughter, Carrie Schwab Pomerantz; and *You're Fifty—Now What?*

Mr. Schwab was born in Sacramento, California. He is a graduate of Stanford University, earning a bachelor of arts degree in economics and a master of business administration degree from Stanford Graduate School of Business.